DILEMMAS OF
INTERNATIONAL TRADE

DILEMMAS IN WORLD POLITICS

Series Editor
George A. Lopez, University of Notre Dame

Dilemmas in World Politics offers teachers and students in international relations a series of quality books on critical issues, trends, and regions in international politics. Each text examines a "real world" dilemma and is structured to cover the historical, theoretical, practical, and projected dimensions of its subject.

BOOKS IN THIS SERIES

DILEMMAS OF INTERNATIONAL TRADE

■ ■ ■

SECOND EDITION

Bruce E. Moon

LEHIGH UNIVERSITY

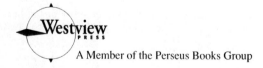

A Member of the Perseus Books Group

Dilemmas in World Politics

Copyright © 2000 by Westview Press, A Member of the Perseus Books Group

Published in 2000 in the United States of America by Westview Press, 5500 Central Avenue, Boulder, Colorado 80301-2877, and in the United Kingdom by Westview Press, 12 Hid's Copse Road, Cumnor Hill, Oxford OX2 9JJ

Visit us on the World Wide Web at www.westviewpress.com

Library of Congress Cataloging-in-Publication Data

Moon, Bruce Edward, 1950–
  Dilemmas of international trade / Bruce E. Moon—2nd ed.
    p. cm. — (Dilemmas in world politics)
Includes bibliographical references and index.
ISBN 0-8133-6768-9
  1. International trade. I. Title. II. Series.

HF1379. M66 2000
382—dc21   00-040832

The paper used in this publication meets the requirements of the American National Standard for Permanence of Paper for Printed Library Materials Z39.48-1984.

□ □ □

Contents

□   □   □

Illustrations

Tables

Figure

Cartoons

Boxes

□　□　□

Acknowledgments

It is impossible to acknowledge adequately all those who have contributed to this volume, and I shall not attempt to do so. However, special mention must be made of the contributions of my students at Lehigh University, who have read and commented upon several drafts of this work. Their indispensable efforts are gratefully acknowledged.

I owe more to my family, especially my wife, Beverly, than I can possibly express. She has provided support and patience far beyond what anyone has a right to ask.

Bruce E. Moon

□ □ □

Acronyms

APEC	Asia Pacific Economic Cooperation
CAP	Common Agricultural Policy
CGE	computable general equilibrium
CUSTA	Canada–United States Trade Agreement
DM	Deutsche mark
DSB	Dispute Settlement Body
EC	European Community
ECB	European Central Bank
ECSC	European Coal and Steel Community
ECU	European currency unit
EEC	European Economic Community
EMS	European Monetary System
ERM	Exchange Rate Mechanism
ESC	Economic and Social Committee
EU	European Union
EURATOM	European Atomic Energy Community
FDI	foreign direct investment
FTAA	Free Trade Area of the Americas
FTC	Federal Trade Commission
GATS	General Agreement on Trade in Services
GATT	General Agreement on Tariffs and Trade
GDP	gross domestic product
GNP	gross national product
H-O	Heckscher-Ohlin (theory)
IBRD	International Bank for Reconstruction and Development (World Bank)
IMF	International Monetary Fund
ISI	import-substituting industrialization
ITO	International Trade Organization
LAN	Local Area Network
LDCs	less developed countries
MFA	Multi-Fiber Agreement
MFN	most favored nation

MITI	Ministry of International Trade and Industry (Japan)
MNCs	multinational corporations
MOF	Ministry of Finance (Japan)
MPs	members of Parliament
NAFTA	North American Free Trade Agreement
NICs	newly industrializing countries
NTBs	nontariff barriers
OECD	Organization for Economic Cooperation and Development
PRC	People's Republic of China
PRI	Mexican Partido Revolucionario Institucional
SII	structural impediment initiative
SPS	Sanitary and Phytosanitary Measures Agreement
TAA	Trade Adjustment Assistance program
TRIM	trade-related investment measures
TRIP	trade-related aspects of intellectual property
TPRM	Trade Policy Review Mechanism
UNCTAD	United Nations Conference on Trade and Development
UNDP	United Nations Development Programme
USTR	United States Trade Representative
VAT	value-added tax
VIE	voluntary import expansion
VERs	voluntary export restraints
VRAs	voluntary restraint agreements
WTO	World Trade Organization

ONE

□ □ □

Trade and Trade Issues

This book has two missions. The first is to explain the fundamental dilemmas that surround international trade and trade policy issues. How we respond to these trade dilemmas will not only shape our economy but also determine the kind of society in which we will live. Too often, trade is treated purely as an economic phenomenon that is—or ought to be—divorced from politics. In fact, because the political and the economic components of international trade are intertwined, neither can be understood without the other. I examine the dilemmas of trade in the context of several contemporary controversies, especially the Japanese-U.S. trade relationship, the Asian financial crisis, the **European Union** (EU), the **North American Free Trade Agreement** (NAFTA), and the **World Trade Organization** (WTO).

The second mission is to introduce the basic principles of international political economy by examining how politics and economics interact to shape trade policies. To provide historical and theoretical perspective, I discuss nineteenth-century British trade policy and the evolution of the international economic system from the **Bretton Woods** institutions of the post–World War II era to the "Battle of Seattle" over the contemporary WTO. To demonstrate the enduring relevance of these basic principles and fundamental dilemmas, I also discuss their role in shaping recent proposals to revise the architecture of global economic institutions and to rethink the trade policy advice given to developing nations.

THE THEMES OF THE BOOK

Whenever people purchase products made abroad, they unknowingly act in accord with one set of interests, values, and theories concerning international trade but in discord with another set. The decision by a firm to market its goods abroad also carries implications beyond its immediate

1

intentions. This book demonstrates that the consequences of these individual choices pose fundamental policy dilemmas for governments as well as for the people directly involved. States seek many outcomes from trade—full employment and improved living standards for its citizens, long-term growth and stability for its economy, and power, security, and friendly external relations for the state itself—yet discover that these desirable outcomes are frequently incompatible. The resulting dilemmas can be seen with clarity only when the standard economic theories of international trade are understood to be partial and incomplete. They must be augmented with treatments rooted in the perspective of international **political economy**.

Since the nineteenth century, **economic liberalism** has been the dominant theoretical perspective on international trade. **Liberal** economic theorists maintain that free markets establish prices that result in the most **efficient allocation of factors of production,** such as land, labor, and **capital**. Thus, from the time of Adam Smith (1723–1790), they have concluded that **free trade** is the surest path to economic prosperity and growth. Both the global economy as a whole and each nation within it are said to be better off when unencumbered trade permits each consumer to buy the most desirable products and each **entrepreneur** to invest resources in the most productive way. Consequently, they have urged that governments refrain from interfering with private entrepreneurs and free markets in international trade. Yet in the intervening two centuries, virtually no national government has followed this advice.

This book probes the reason for this curious disparity between accepted economic theory and established political practice, rejecting the interpretation proffered by some economists that the discrepancy results from irrational or corrupt policy. Instead, the book's political economy perspective acknowledges that governments seek to influence trade because markets generate multiple consequences, many of which exceed the boundaries of economic theory yet touch the fundamental responsibilities of government. For example, just as trade affects the prices of individual products, global markets influence which individuals and nations

---

The Meaning of Economic Liberalism

The term "economic liberalism" is not to be confused with the ambiguous way that the term "liberal" is applied in U.S. politics. Economic liberalism is wary of government interference with the market, whereas those called liberals often advocate it.

accumulate wealth and political power. They determine who will be employed and at what wage. They determine what natural resources will be used and at what environmental cost. They shape opportunities and constraints in foreign policy. They even affect the viability of domestic policies, the sustainability of economic growth, and the integrity of a nation's culture and institutions. Because trade affects such a broad range of social outcomes, conflict among alternative goals and values is inevitable. Because these social outcomes affect various individuals and groups differently, these conflicts are inevitably politicized. As a result, governments, which seek to balance all the interests and values of society, confront dilemmas that require painful choices.

In this book I describe the dilemmas resulting from the distributional consequences of trade, the competing values affected by trade, and the impact of trade on the concerns of the state. I also explain how various governments (and individuals) respond to these dilemmas and why.

THE IMPORTANCE OF TRADE

Most economists and policymakers believe that trade provides substantial benefits for individual nations and the global economy as a whole. Exports enable corporations to earn higher profits, employ more workers, and generate greater tax receipts for governments than if they were restricted to selling in a single national market. Exports also bring in revenue in the form of foreign currencies that can be used to purchase imports. The very fact that individuals choose imported products implies either that similar goods cannot be produced domestically or that imports are of higher quality or lower price than domestic alternatives. In either case, import expansion implies an increase in welfare for consumers.

Considerable evidence supports the view that trade improves productivity, consumption, and therefore welfare. The growth of the global economy has been most rapid during periods of trade expansion, especially during the quarter century after World War II, and has slowed when trade levels have fallen, especially during the **Great Depression** of the 1920s and 1930s. Periods of national growth have also coincided with trade expansion, most notably in Germany, Japan, and Korea. There is some uncertainty about whether trade leads to growth or growth leads to trade, but there is little doubt that most governments believe that trade expansion improves living standards.

Table 1.1, which shows the importance of exports in selected nations in 1960, 1980, and 1997, demonstrates that trade has grown substantially, becoming an important element in the economies of all nations. Because global trade has grown nearly twice as rapidly as total global production

TABLE 1.1   Exports as a Percentage of Gross National Product

Nation	1960	1980	1997
United States	5.2	10.2	11.6
Canada	17.0	28.2	39.6
Mexico	8.6	10.7	30.2
United Kingdom	20.9	27.3	29.5
France	14.5	21.5	24.0
Sweden	22.7	29.5	40.0
Belgium	38.2	57.0	68.5
Ireland	30.6	47.6	76.4
Japan	10.7	13.7	9.9
China	4.6	6.3	23.0
Hong Kong	84.4	89.9	131.6
Korea	3.3	33.9	38.1
Thailand	15.7	24.1	47.0
Malaysia	51.4	57.5	94.3
Indonesia	15.6	34.2	28.0
Philippines	10.6	23.6	49.0
Argentina	7.6	5.1	9.0
Brazil	6.8	9.1	7.6
Jamaica	33.2	51.1	51.0
Republic of Congo	20.5	60.0	76.9
Nigeria	9.2	29.4	40.9

SOURCE: World Bank, *World Development Indicators 1999* CD-ROM.

since 1950, about a quarter of all goods and services produced globally are now traded among nations. Technological advances in transportation and communication can account for much of this growth, with freight costs having declined by two-thirds since the mid-1980s. However, driven by the liberal theory described in Chapter 2 and the political dynamics portrayed in Chapter 3, governments have adopted policies and created international institutions that have played an even greater role in facilitating trade expansion. Chapter 4 shows that the Bretton Woods system initiated after World War II has been especially significant in expanding trade and that the recent addition of the WTO promises even greater integration among national economies. The vast economic restructuring entailed by this **globalization** has had a far-reaching impact on many aspects of economic, social, and political life, making it evident why trade issues have become so politically explosive in recent years.

Table 1.1 also reveals considerable variation in the importance of trade across nations and suggests some patterns within that variation. Larger nations, which have sizable domestic markets of their own, tend to rely less on trade than smaller nations. For example, Japan, with exports constituting less than 10 percent of its **gross national product** (GNP), is much less dependent on trade than any European nation, despite its reputation as a great trading nation. The sheer size of Japan's economy, second only to that of the United States, enables it to meet most of its own needs and to consume most of its own production. Smaller nations, such as Belgium and Jamaica, must engage in greater levels of trade because they can neither supply goods to meet all their own needs nor provide a market sizable enough for many industries to produce in the large volumes required to be efficient. For the same reasons, trade constitutes a larger share of GNP in most poor countries than in more developed ones. In recent years the export volumes of nearly fifty nations have approached or exceeded half their total economic output, and they have relied upon imports for a comparable share of their total consumption. Because any major reduction in trade would require a vast economic restructuring that would entail huge welfare losses, such heavy dependence guarantees that trade-related issues will dominate the political agenda.

Even if we allow for differences in size and wealth, however, trade has been much more significant for some countries than others. East Asian nations, for example, maintain trade levels more than double those of comparable Latin American economies. The variations in government policy largely responsible are sketched below, and the explanation for these disparate choices is the focal point of much of the book. Chapter 5 illustrates these variations by contrasting the policies of Japan and the United States. Chapter 6 emphasizes regional organizations, beginning with the European Union, which facilitates trade within Europe, and concluding with the North American Free Trade Agreement (NAFTA), designed to allow a similar growth of trade among the United States, Canada, and Mexico. Together with the advent of an East Asian group centered around Japan, these developments may foreshadow a world of **trade blocs** in which free trade prevails within each bloc but trade between blocs is restricted.

The growing importance of global trade and its accompanying dilemmas are exemplified by the experience of the newly industrializing countries (NICs) of East Asia, detailed in Chapter 7, especially Korea, Thailand, Malaysia, Indonesia, and Philippines. The United States and Japan, each in its own way, have been influential in driving the policy approach of these NICs, which have made international trade the centerpiece of their economic development strategy. As Table 1.1 reveals, there is considerable irony in this role, since the United States and Japan are less reliant on exports than all but a handful of other countries (at about 10 percent of GNP), whereas these NICs are massively dependent (between 28 percent and 94 percent). Though U.S. trade reliance has increased dramatically, it has still not reached the level that was common in Europe decades ago, which helps to explain why the trade issues that have occupied Europe for many years have entered the policy agenda in the United States only quite recently. Although the United States has long been the world's strongest advocate of the liberal theory that encourages trade, it has less experience than most with the dilemmas posed by relying upon it.

CONCERNS ABOUT THE TRADE BALANCE

Whereas nearly all nations have sought trade expansion for its economic benefits, they have generally tried to avoid an excess of imports over exports, which is known as a deficit in the **balance of trade**. Trade deficits are controversial and difficult to analyze, because they generate complex and unpredictable consequences, many of which become visible only in the long term. The immediate concern is that the consumption of imports permits foreigners to enjoy employment and profits from production that might otherwise benefit citizens of the home country. For example, as suggested by the cartoon, the high levels of unemployment and attendant social problems suffered in Detroit since the mid-1970s have been ascribed partially to annual sales of nearly 2 million Japanese cars in the United States. This would be of little concern if these imports were balanced by exports that produce comparable levels of employment and profits from U.S. products sold abroad, but during a **trade deficit** they are not.

Table 1.2 demonstrates that the United States has run a persistent balance-of-trade deficit since the 1970s, with the annual deficits assuming huge proportions since the middle of the 1980s. To put in perspective these vast sums, the record $347.1 billion deficit for 1999 approached $1 billion *per day*, which means that imports exceeded exports by more than $1,200 per American, over 4 percent of the U.S. GNP. At the estimated rate of 20,000 jobs lost for every $1 billion in trade deficit, this corresponds to nearly 7 million jobs lost to the deficit. With the U.S. unemployment rate at an historic low in 2000, it is easy to be complacent about this effect, but the longer-term repercussions, though uncertain, are unlikely to be so benign.

The long-term danger of trade deficits stem from the capital flows associated with them. Consider that since the last U.S. trade surplus in 1975, much more money has flowed *out* of the U.S. economy in the form of dollars to pay for imports than flowed back *into* the economy through payments for U.S. goods purchased by foreigners. In fact, these annual deficits cumulate to more than $2 trillion, more than a quarter of annual U.S. GNP. The obvious question is, What are foreigners *doing* with those dollars? The answers point to the dangers inherent in trade deficits.

STICKER SHOCK

IMPORT
MADE IN JAPAN

4-DOOR SEDAN	14,000
DEALER PREP	600
SHIPPING	400
HIDDEN COSTS	
GOVERNMENT PAYMENTS	
TO US UNEMPLOYED	32,571
LOST REAL ESTATE	
COMMUNITY TAXES	11,374
WELFARE PAYMENTS	15,304
FACTORIES CLOSED	12,712
SCHOOLS CLOSED	7,401
DECLINE IN US R&D	5,171
TRUE COST	**99,533**

DANZIGER
The Christian Science Monitor

Hidden Costs. Danziger © *The Christian Science Monitor*

Some are investing these dollars in the United States to generate future income. For example, the U.S. federal government **budget deficit**—in the magnitude of $200 billion annually from the early 1980s to the mid-1990s—was financed partially by the selling of **Treasury bonds** to foreigners, especially Japanese investors. When the government sells Treasury bonds, it borrows money and agrees to pay interest on the debt. Thus, some of the money sent abroad by U.S. consumers to pay for imports has been borrowed back by the U.S. government at interest rates that will keep the United States paying for this balance-of-trade deficit for years to come.

Some of the dollars piling up abroad have also returned to the United States in the form of investments in new plant and equipment—funded by the profits of Japanese auto firms—such as the Honda plant in Marysville, Ohio. New auto plants produce U.S. jobs, of course, but the profits are earned by Japanese corporations, which will presumably return them to Japan one day. Such **repatriation** of profits again implies that paying for trade deficits can be postponed, but the burdens of such a deficit must eventually be faced.

Finally, some foreigners have been content to accumulate dollars, using them much as they do their own currency—as a convenient storehouse of

TABLE 1.2   U.S. Balance of Trade, 1975–1999 ($ billion)

	Exports ($ billion)	Imports ($ billion)	Trade Balance ($ billion)	Trade Balance (% of GNP)
1975	107.09	98.18	8.91	0.56%
1976	114.74	124.23	−9.49	−0.54%
1977	120.81	151.91	−31.10	−1.58%
1978	142.05	176.00	−33.95	−1.52%
1979	184.47	212.01	−27.54	−1.11%
1980	224.25	249.76	−25.51	−0.94%
1981	237.05	265.07	−28.02	−0.92%
1982	211.17	247.65	−36.48	−1.15%
1983	201.80	268.89	−67.09	−1.97%
1984	219.93	332.41	−112.48	−2.97%
1985	215.91	338.09	−122.18	−3.02%
1986	224.11	368.75	−144.64	−3.39%
1987	250.94	410.18	−159.24	−3.52%
1988	321.09	447.70	−126.61	−2.60%
1989	363.47	478.00	−114.53	−2.18%
1990	390.71	498.95	−108.25	−1.95%
1991	418.58	491.40	−72.82	−1.28%
1992	442.13	536.45	−94.32	−1.56%
1993	458.72	589.44	−130.72	−2.06%
1994	504.45	668.59	−164.14	−2.44%
1995	577.69	749.57	−171.88	−2.44%
1996	613.89	803.32	−189.43	−2.56%
1997	681.27	877.28	−196.01	−2.50%
1998	672.90	921.00	−248.10	−3.04%
1999	683.00	1030.20	−347.10	−4.07%

SOURCE: Based on data for merchandise trade in billions of current U.S. dollars from World Bank, *World Development Indicators 1999* CD-ROM.

value and as a medium of exchange with others willing to accept them. Meanwhile, the United States benefits from their willingness to hold dollars, just as an individual would if he or she could write checks that others would neglect to cash. In the short term, this balance-of-trade deficit means that U.S. citizens are *consuming* more than they are currently *producing*. Thus, they enjoy a higher standard of living than would otherwise be possible.

Economists disagree about whether these developments ought to raise alarm over the longer term.[1] Some emphasize that the above processes are all temporary and that eventually foreigners will demand U.S. goods and assets in exchange for their excess dollars. That demand would require the United States to generate a trade surplus (more exports than imports) to compensate for past trade deficits. Of course, to export more than they import would imply that U.S. residents as a whole would consume less than they produce—and experience the lower standard of living implied by that gap. However, other economists emphasize that the continuing willingness of foreigners to invest in the United States and to accumulate dollars is an indication of their confidence that the U.S. economy will grow fast enough to tolerate these effects without serious damage.

Nevertheless, there are signs from international **currency markets** that the persistent balance-of-trade deficit is eroding that confidence. The demand for dollars by foreigners—to purchase products or investments from the United States—is smaller than the supply of dollars created by Americans purchasing foreign products and investments. As with any other item, when supply exceeds demand, the price falls. As a result, the value of the dollar, equivalent to about 300 Japanese yen when the string of U.S. balance-of-trade deficits began in 1976, declined in 1995 to under 100 yen. The declining purchasing power of the dollar means, for example, that the 1 million-yen cost of a Japanese automobile would translate into a dollar price of about $3,000 at the old exchange rate (300 yen per dollar) but more than $9,000 at the rate prevailing in mid-2000 (about 110 yen per dollar). The higher price that Americans face for foreign products signifies that the process of paying for the trade deficit of the past two decades has already begun.

Of course, the effects of trade deficits are hazardous to forecast because their connection to currency declines are neither automatic nor immediate. Witness that between 1995 and 1999, the United States ran a cumulative trade deficit of more than $800 billion, while Japan accumulated a trade *surplus* of $400 billion—yet during this same period the dollar *increased* in value from about 80 yen to 110 yen. Nonetheless, balance-of-trade deficits tend to lead to such currency declines eventually—sometimes very suddenly and with catastrophic consequences. As Chapter 7 describes in detail, several nations in southeast Asia ran trade deficits greater than 3 percent of their GNP for several years in the mid-1990s with no apparent ill effects. Indeed, they were among the fastest growing nations in the world despite trade deficits that often exceeded 5 percent of GNP and sometimes much more. But when investors eventually lost confidence in the summer of 1997, the fall was dramatic and painful. For example, Indonesia, the fourth most populous country in the world, suffered more than a 70 percent decline in the purchasing power of its currency and a 50 percent decline in its stock market within a few months. The resulting economic chaos included massive bankruptcies, soaring unemployment, plummeting living standards, and social unrest that culminated in a change of government.

Thus we see that trade deficits may permit greater levels of consumption in the short term, but—whether through repayment of loans, repatriation of profits, or the price increases that come from currency declines—they also imply that future consumption will be reduced and standards of living will fall. In short, a trade deficit engineers a shift in welfare from the future to the present.

POLICY ALTERNATIVES

Thus, national governments have traditionally sought to avoid balance-of-trade deficits while expanding the volume of trade. Some nations have given emphasis to one or the other of these twin targets, though most have sought both. Different nations have attempted to achieve these goals in many different ways, but their policy actions fall within four basic approaches. Each is discussed briefly in the following sections, followed by a preliminary exploration of the dilemmas posed by these options and the reasons different governments have chosen among them differently.

The first approach consists of efforts to increase exports by improving the overall international **competitiveness** of a nation's economy. The second uses various subsidies for **export promotion** within a nation's **industrial policy**. The third approach is to reduce imports through **protectionist** trade barriers such as tariffs and quotas. The fourth seeks to enlarge exports by securing international cooperation to remove the trade barriers of other nations and to build regional or global institutions that facilitate trade. The first and fourth are essentially **liberal** approaches that place greater reliance upon the free reign of markets; the other two, which are usually referred to as **mercantilist**, involve government actions to influence or displace the market.

FREE TRADE AND THE SEARCH FOR COMPETITIVENESS

One trade policy approach seeks to increase the international competitiveness of all the nation's firms by solving social problems and eliminating government policies that drive up their costs. (If the factors that burden import-competing or export firms are unique to those sectors, the government may target them directly with a so-called industrial policy, which is discussed in the next section.) Implicit in this strategy is the acceptance of free trade, because protectionism adds to firms' costs at home and encourages protectionism abroad. Furthermore, if competitiveness is achieved, neither protection nor export subsidies are required. The strategy of enhancing international competitiveness is usually motivated by the desire to increase exports, but if successful it will also tend to minimize trade deficits. Domestic firms able to cut costs become more competitive in global markets—thus expanding exports—while they also compete more successfully against foreign producers in their own market, thereby reducing imports.

However, the following brief discussion of factors that affect competitiveness demonstrates the dilemmas that this trade policy approach presents, particularly with respect to the distributional effects of trade and the tension between alternative values. Trade issues cannot be separated from the remainder of the public agenda, because competitiveness problems cannot be solved without sacrificing other values.

First, most U.S. corporations carry the burden of health care coverage for their workers. For example, the U.S. auto industry now spends more for health care than it does for steel. Because U.S. health care costs are the highest in the world—overall, Americans spend about 14 percent of GNP on health care—this burden undermines the competitiveness of all U.S. firms. Those who address this issue cannot avoid contact with some of the toughest issues in U.S. politics: trust in government bureaucracies versus private insurance bureaucracies, breadth of coverage for all citizens versus quality care for some, and the possibility of explicitly rationing health care.

Second, since World War II U.S. expenditures for defense have been many times higher than those of nations with which the United States competes. Ironically, much of that money has been spent directly protecting the very nations against which U.S. competitiveness has slipped, especially Germany, Japan, and Korea. These expenditures erode the competitiveness of U.S. business by requiring higher tax levels, they constrain the funds available to spend on other items that could enhance competitiveness, and they divert a substantial share of U.S. scientific and technological expertise into military innovation and away from commercial areas. The trade-off between competitiveness and defense may be judged differently by different individuals, but it can be ignored by none. Giving up global leadership or national security may be a wise choice, but it is not without costs of its own.

Third, the quality of American education, once the best in the world, has eroded. Although the global division of labor now places a premium on skilled labor, many other countries now have a better-educated citizenry and a better-trained workforce—which may explain why the growth in American economic productivity since the 1960s is among the lowest in the industrial world. Because both the American school day and school year are now among the shortest in the world, fixing education may require a substantial increase in cost, compromises with cherished traditions, and flexibility on the part of parents, teachers, and children. Like defense and health care, this problem acquires more urgency in the context of a competitiveness issue, but there are very good reasons for wanting to improve education that do not involve the balance of trade.

Fourth, the decline of America's infrastructure—decaying roads and bridges and overburdened water, sewer, and mass-transit systems—costs U.S. business daily. Because the provision of infrastructure is largely a function of government, this competitiveness issue is intertwined with questions of taxation, government effectiveness, and citizen trust. Infrastructure problems are unexciting—and thus unpopular as a locus of innovation or spending among politicians—but it is evident that trade competitiveness cannot be sustained without government no matter how vibrant the private sector may be.

Fifth, very high debt levels, including personal credit card debt, corporate debt, and years of federal budget deficits, require that savings be used to fund past consumption rather than to invest in the future. Furthermore, because the American personal savings rate is the lowest in the industrial world, U.S. interest rates must be kept higher in order to induce foreigners to supply the investment funds from their savings that Americans do not provide. But these higher interest rates—what economists would call the higher cost of capital—become an additional expense for American businesses that must borrow money for expansion. This problem illustrates exactly how close to home competitiveness issues can come: The family budget is a matter of national security!

Sixth, other social problems, including crime and drugs, contribute in indirect ways to increased costs for U.S. business. Richard Lamm estimates that "American business spent $51 billion in 1986 for private anti-crime measures such as alarms, iron bars, video cameras, and security guards."[2] U.S. tax dollars support nearly two million inmates, with the U.S. incarceration rate six to ten times higher than in most of Europe and seventeen times greater than in Japan. Even ecological problems affect business, because the deteriorating environment diminishes the health and productivity of workers, forces higher costs for health care, and complicates the choice of business location.

Finally, some have blamed corporations themselves for fixating on the short term and ignoring long-term competitiveness. Expenditures on research and development occupy a much smaller portion of corporate spending in the United States than in Japan or Germany, for example, and the pay of top corporate executives is much higher in America than in its chief competitors.

Some proposed solutions to the competitiveness problem violate the definition of competitiveness laid out in a report from the President's Commission, "the degree to which a nation, under free and fair market conditions, produces goods and services that meet the test of international markets *while simultaneously maintaining and expanding the real incomes of its citizens.*"[3] The last clause of this definition disqualifies from consideration such proposals as the abolition of the minimum wage, Social Security, workplace safety regulation, pensions, sick leave, workman's compensation, unions, vacations, holidays, and so on.[4] This list exemplifies the dangers of affording competitiveness concerns too high a priority on the national agenda: Cutting wages and benefits for workers would surely make U.S. corporations more profitable and better able to compete, but the attempt would be self-defeating from the standpoint of national welfare. National policy should seek to make corporations more competitive in order to improve the lives of its citizens, not compromise citizen welfare in order to improve competitiveness. The United States has been able to avoid the most damaging of these compromises, but the many developing countries whose firms compete principally on the basis of cheap labor have not been so fortunate. For them, this trade-off between alternative values poses an especially painful policy dilemma.

EXPORT PROMOTION AND INDUSTRIAL POLICY

The second method employed to maintain a desirable volume and balance of trade utilizes export promotion, usually in conjunction with what is called an industrial policy. By industrial policy is meant a set of government actions designed to encourage the growth of particular industries, usually those believed to be especially important for the future of the economy. Most nations with aggressive industrial policies—Japan is the most frequently cited example—target the export sector because of the growth prospects offered by the global economy, though industrial policy often has other targets as well.

Export promotion is accomplished through a variety of techniques. The simplest is a direct export **subsidy** or bounty, a government payment for each good exported from the target industry. The result is that a domestic firm has the incentive to export goods, even though it may not have a cost advantage in comparison with competing firms in other nations.

Such a policy has at least three aims. First, increased production in the chosen industry will likely lead to employment growth, perhaps enough for the government to enjoy the political benefits of having reduced the unemployment rate. Second, these firms will gain a greater share of foreign markets, which might give them greater leverage to increase prices (and profits) in the future. Third, increasing exports will improve the balance of trade, thus avoiding the problems inherent in trade deficits discussed earlier.

This policy also yields distributional effects—and the political controversies they engender—because its impact on prices benefits some people and harms others. For example, the domestic consumer will see the price of subsidized goods rise by the amount of the subsidy, since otherwise firms would prefer to export the product in order to earn the bonus. Furthermore, the revenue to pay for that bounty must be raised through taxes. The domestic consumer would thus appear to be a double loser while the exporting firm gains, but there may also be distributional effects that become apparent only over time. For example, the sacrifices of the current generation may benefit future consumers if this subsidy eventually transforms an **infant industry** into a powerful enterprise that can repay the subsidies through cheaper prices, greater employment, or higher tax payments.

Another form of industrial policy is simply to provide subsidies to particular firms or industries that appear to have long-term export potential, whether or not they are presently exporting. Such subsidies might be direct cash payments, special tax advantages, help in attracting investment, or relief from regulations that might otherwise constrain the industry. Many newly industrializing nations have found that their existing firms have very limited trade prospects despite government subsidies, so their industrial policy has focused on persuading multinational corporations to establish new firms. They offer an array of benefits in the hope of luring foreign investment that would expand the economy's export potential as well as employ otherwise idle workers. Industrial policies that invite foreign investment through these special benefits are often combined with a more general competitiveness approach designed to allow firms to cut costs by minimizing taxes, limiting regulation, and holding down wage rates.

Many forms of export subsidies are now prohibited by the **General Agreement on Tariffs and Trade** (GATT), an international treaty that forms the basis for much of the international law that governs trade matters. Not all are prohibited, however, and the exact limits are both highly technical and much disputed. Furthermore, subsidies are not always easy to see. The United States, which explicitly rejects industrial policy, nonetheless engages in behavior that yields the same outcome. For example, U.S. military expenditures often have spillover effects into civilian production, especially for export. The Boeing B-52 bomber introduced many elements that led to the highly successful Boeing 707 passenger jet. U.S. agriculture has benefited from the activities of the Agricultural Extension Service and other subsidies of agricultural research. Grants to universities for research yield benefits for industry. Some nations promote their exports by lending the sale price to importing nations; in the United States, these export credit subsidies are handled by the Export-Import Bank.

Such industrial policies are controversial, both in the nations that enact them and in those with whom they trade. Liberal theorists contend that they don't really work or that their costs usually outweigh their benefits, a position generally accepted in the United States, especially by the Republican Party. Moreover, export promotion policies attract the opposition of other nations because such policies place their firms at a severe competitive disadvantage. The U.S. steel industry has been particularly outspoken in its denunciation of steel imported from foreign companies that are heavily subsidized by their governments. They contend that American jobs and American profits are being undercut by this unfair competition. They call for the U.S. government to guarantee "fair trade," either by prohibiting the importation of such subsidized goods or by levying heavy taxes on them (so-called **countervailing duties**). Export promotion as a form of industrial policy has interesting distributional implications, however. For example, it benefits the consumers of countries into which subsidized products are imported, at least in the short term.

FORMS OF IMPORT RESTRICTIONS

The third approach to trade policy is protectionism, which seeks to achieve a favorable trade balance by limiting imports. Protectionism has been very common historically; indeed, all nations engage in at least some protectionist measures. In the 1950s and 1960s, protectionism was the dominant approach throughout Latin America, where states sought to develop their economies through a strategy known as **import-substitution industrialization** (ISI). They insulated domestic firms in certain sectors from foreign competition, hoping to replace imports with domestically produced products, thereby both improving the trade balance and building domestic industrial capacity. Nations that give priority to avoiding trade deficits frequently combine import restrictions with industrial policy designed to expand exports. The origins of both in the mercantilism of early England is the subject of an extensive case study in Chapter 2.

There are many forms of import restrictions, all of which are designed to limit purchases of goods from abroad. Domestic import-competing industries, protected from foreign competition, can then capture a larger share of the market. The simplest of these mechanisms is the **quota**, a government restriction that places a fixed limit on the quantity or value of goods that can be imported. This limitation is usually accomplished by requiring that importers obtain import licenses that are strictly rationed by governments. The usual effect of a quota is to raise the domestic price of the commodity by restricting the number of lower-priced products that can be imported. A quota allows domestic producers to gain a larger market share, but this artificial restriction of supply also enables both domestic and foreign producers to charge higher prices to consumers. Prohibitions are a special case—namely, they set a quota at zero. This form of trade barrier is relatively infrequent today, but it was common in an earlier age. In fact prohibitions were the major source of protection in early England.

The most widely used trade barriers are tariffs (or import duties), which are taxes applied to imports. Most are ad valorem, calculated as a percentage of the value of the good imported. All nations use tariffs to one degree or another, though not entirely for protectionist purposes. Historically, tariffs have been a significant source of government revenue, especially in poor countries that find it difficult to maintain effective income tax systems. In 1980, for example, tariffs provided more government revenue than either income taxes or sales taxes in about forty nations. Most countries maintain elaborate tariff schedules which specify different tax rates for different products, allowing each rate to be set at a level that provides the desired degree of protection for each particular industry. This wide variation in rates across hundreds or even thousands of product categories makes it difficult to generalize about the exact level of tariff protection in any given country.

Still, it is clear that tariff rates, like the level of trade they are designed to control, vary widely across nations. The highest rates are found among less developed nations whose firms are especially threatened by foreign competition. The average tariff rate is around 30 percent in India, Nigeria, and Tunisia—depending upon how the average is computed—and between 10 and 20 percent in most other developing nations. U.S. tariffs average about 4 percent, roughly the same as most developed nations. All of these figures understate the actual protective effect of tariffs, however, because rates can be many times higher than the average for products where a nation's firms actually face foreign competition, whereas they are usually low or zero in categories where no domestic industry exists to protect.

Tariffs have also varied enormously across time, with average tariff levels throughout the world having declined steeply from their peak in the 1930s. In the United States the average tariff rate reached a modern high of 59 percent in 1932 under the Smoot-Hawley Act, a remarkably irresponsible tariff law widely credited with triggering a spiral of restrictions by other nations that helped plunge the global economy into the Great Depression of the 1930s. The average tariff level had previously reached 70 percent in 1813 and about 60 percent in the "tariff of abominations" of 1828, but it remained between 40 percent and 50 percent from the Civil War until the turn of the century. It was reduced to 25 percent after World War II and declined to about 5 percent after the Tokyo Round of GATT negotiations concluded in 1979. Average ad valorem import duties reached their high in Britain in the 1820s at more than 50 percent, retreating to about 5 percent at the height of the British free trade era in 1880 before spiking again in the 1930s at about 50 percent.

Probably the most controversial remaining tariffs are the duties imposed by the EU in the context of the **Common Agricultural Policy** (CAP). These tariffs sustain higher food prices in Europe than would prevail if cheaper North American grains were admitted without barrier. Because the higher prices of European producers leave them unable to compete on global markets, the revenue derived from the tariffs is used to subsidize exports. Both elements of the CAP have infuriated the United States in recent years: its restrictions on American exports to Europe and the advantage its subsidies provide to European agricultural producers wherever they compete with American exporters.

Although tariffs have declined, a variety of **nontariff barriers** (NTBs) have arisen since the early 1980s. An early version was the 1969 **voluntary restraint agreement** (VRA) with Japan and the **European Community,** which was designed to reduce steel imports into the United States. Over the next twenty-five years, **voluntary export restraints** (VERs) became common. The most famous case of a VER is that in which Japanese automakers in 1981 "voluntarily" agreed to limit exports to the United States.[5] (Had Japan refused, a quota that would have been more damaging to Japanese automakers would have been imposed in place of the VER.) The Federal Trade Commission (FTC) has estimated the cost to U.S. consumers at about $1 billion per year in the form of higher prices for autos. Not only did the restricted supply of Japanese autos cause their prices to rise because of the artificial shortage but it also enabled U.S. manufacturers to maintain higher prices in the absence of this competition. A VER is essentially a quota system that is managed by the exporter rather than by the importing nation.

Other protectionist measures include local content regulations that restrict imports by imposing a burden on purchasers of intermediate goods to make sure that imports do not exceed a prescribed fraction of their total purchases. Another form is government procurement policies, which often favor domestic firms. For example, the EU requires that government contracts be open to all bidders, but they permit governments to give a 3 percent "preference margin" to European firms or to exclude entirely any product produced largely outside of Europe.[6]

Other regulations, such as product-safety standards, can have a protectionist effect even though their motivation may be open to interpretation. The European Union, for example, bans the importation of beef treated with hormones, citing cancer risks. The United States, where most cattle receive hormone treatments to stimulate growth, successfully challenged the EU ban in the WTO as a disguised form of protection against U.S. products.

The GATT has sought to sharply limit all **nontariff barriers** (NTBs) by converting them to tariffs, which are more visible and easier to reduce through international negotiations. For example, quotas are now permissible only in quite specific circumstances, and so-called gray-area measures such as VERs are to be eliminated entirely. But imports can be restricted by so many different means—even increases in income taxes or interest rates tend to reduce imports—that a nation seeking protectionism can always find numerous policy tools to accomplish it.

INTERNATIONAL COOPERATION TO STIMULATE TRADE

A fourth approach to trade policy emphasizes creating conditions abroad that are favorable to trade expansion. This strategy, which lies as much in the realm of foreign policy as trade policy, involves securing the cooperation of other nations. The most common form, an explicit reaction against protectionism, involves direct negotiations to lower the trade barriers imposed by others. All nations—including those which practice protectionism themselves—utilize this technique to improve their export prospects, though of course they do so with varying degrees of success. Usually nations try to induce others to lower trade barriers by agreeing to lower their own in return.

A more expansive version of this approach consists of diplomatic efforts to create and maintain regional or global institutions that facilitate trade. The simplest of these institutions provide a forum for nations to negotiate limitations on trade barriers, but others go far beyond that. The most extensive and most successful effort to achieve free trade at the regional level is the European Union. Conventional trade barriers among its nations have virtually disappeared, but to fully exploit the benefits of free trade and to manage the dislocations it produces the EU has found it necessary to build a much more comprehensive set of regional institutions. Most importantly, it has found that stable trade patterns cannot emerge without a stable monetary system that facilitates the financial transactions necessary for trade to occur. For example, in order to eliminate the trade disruption inherent in fluctuating currency values, the currencies of individual nations are being phased out in favor of the **Euro**.

High levels of trade bring an increasing **interdependence** among nations, so that individual states are no longer able to solve economic, environmental or social problems without considering the effects created by the policy actions of others. In fact, many traditional activities of the nation-state have been absorbed by the legislative, executive, and judicial branches of the EU. Monetary and fiscal policies are now coordinated at the regional level, with more standardized tax rates and regulations. The EU illustrates that trade expansion requires more than merely eliminating barriers; it must also have facilitating arrangements in monetary affairs and some provision to cope with the resulting interdependence. Various other regions have experimented with a much more limited version of encouraging regional trade, most notably NAFTA, which is designed to expand trade among the United States, Canada, and Mexico.

The outstanding example of a similar strategy at the global level is the **Bretton Woods** trade and monetary regime, created under the leadership of the United States at the end of World War II. The Bretton Woods regime, centered around the institutions of the **General Agreement on Tariffs and Trade** (GATT) and the **International Monetary Fund** (IMF), has governed international trade and finance for more than fifty years, though it has evolved and changed markedly in that time. Before being superseded by the World Trade Organization (WTO) in 1995, the GATT provided a setting for nations to negotiate reductions in tariffs and other barriers to trade, while also helping to resolve trade disputes. The WTO has continued to broaden the range of national policies deemed to constitute unfair impediments to trade and thus to be subject to international negotiations designed to increase trade opportunities. Increasingly, the resultant restrictions on the policies of nations have aroused opposition, because they pose the dilemma of exchanging the gains of trade for some loss of **national autonomy.**

Recent experience in Latin America and Asia has also demonstrated that trade expansion requires steps beyond the mere dismantling of overt trade barriers. Trade of goods cannot occur unless foreign currencies can be exchanged as well. Furthermore, trade expansion is not necessarily accompanied by a balance between the imports and exports of individual nations. Such imbalances can destabilize currencies, wreck national economies, and eventually disrupt trade, unless some institutional mechanism exists to contain the deleterious effects of extreme interdependence. After all, when all nations come to rely heavily upon trade, a financial disaster anywhere in the system threatens stability everywhere. Historically, the major responsibility for building institutions to cope with these problems has fallen to those nations with the political power to exert global leadership. The United States originally sponsored the IMF to expand trade by guaranteeing stability in monetary affairs and providing mechanisms to finance imports and adjust trade imbalances. In the light of the recent Asian experience, where the trade imbalances inherent in open trading systems shook the growth prospects of nations half a planet away, the entire architecture of global economic affairs has been brought into question.

THE DILEMMAS OF INTERNATIONAL TRADE

All nations seek to expand trade and avoid trade deficits, but they have chosen among these four trade strategies in very different ways. That is because, as the foregoing discussion suggests, no single trade policy is objectively and unequivocally "best." Instead, each option offers its own set of advantages and liabilities, which each nation weighs from its own perspective. The complexity of these considerations can be reduced somewhat by organizing the choices in terms of three sets of dilemmas that must be confronted. Each is elaborated in the following sections; together they constitute the focus of our discussion of trade policy and its consequences throughout the remainder of the book.

The first, the **distributional dilemma,** stems from the unfortunate fact that no trade policy benefits everyone. Instead, each rewards some individuals and groups but harms others, affecting the domestic distribution of income, wealth, and political power in the process. Thus, in addition to seeking an optimal level and balance of trade, governments must also weigh which groups it wishes to help, which it can afford to harm, and how it can make these distributional effects politically palatable to those involved. The second, the **values dilemma** arises because the same economic changes that enable a nation to secure the benefits of trade may imply a compromise of other societal values. Ultimately trade affects the society, polity, and culture as much as it does the economy. Allowing trade levels to be determined solely by the logic of the market—even if we could be confident that maximum economic growth would result—is tantamount to denying the legitimacy of any human motivation other than economic gain. The third, the **state goals dilemma** revolves around the tension between trade and the unique mission of the state to provide security, independence, and peace for the nation. Purely economic theories are not adequate to understand these issues, because state actions are motivated by power and autonomy as much as by growth and efficiency. For example, the high levels of interdependence associated with intensive trade links necessarily limit self-sufficiency. This interdependence may improve economic efficiency and even enhance prospects for international peace, but it also constrains the capacity of the state to act independently of others when required to do so by the national interest.

THE DISTRIBUTIONAL DILEMMA

The distributional dilemma emerges from the propensity of trade to alter the distribution of income and wealth within a nation. Simply put, some individuals and groups gain from trade while others lose. Because any government policy designed to regulate trade yields its own distinctive pattern of winners and losers, trade is inevitably politicized. Standard economic theory tends to de-emphasize these distributional effects in its focus upon the impact of trade on the economy as a whole. Because these distributional consequences have such obvious political implications, however, the state is much more attentive to them than economic theorists are.

The most visible distributional effects are usually sectoral, because trade policy often protects or promotes one industry or sector of the economy at the expense of others. For example, **tariffs** on imported steel protect the domestic steel industry by making foreign-produced steel more expensive, but they also harm domestic automakers who must pay higher prices for the steel they use. As in this case—where car buyers face higher prices—most protectionist barriers to trade benefit some sector of the economy at the expense of consumers. Conversely, the free trade policies advocated by liberal theory usually benefit consumers through lower prices, but as the case of foreign autos and Detroit demonstrates, they also devastate the workers of the corporations that must compete against foreign imports. Further, they also damage the economies of the regions in which those import-competing industries are located.

Just as trade policy redistributes costs and benefits from one sector to another, it also benefits some classes at the expense of others. An especially persistent theme in U.S. trade policy debates has been the fear that trade will benefit the owners of large corporations but erode the employment prospects and wage rates of unskilled workers. For example, the elimination of trade barriers under NAFTA forces some U.S. manufacturing workers into direct competition with Mexican workers who earn a markedly lower wage. Unless U.S. wage rates decline, production may shift to Mexico, and U.S. jobs will be lost. However, if that competition drives down wage rates in the United States, the profits earned by the owners of U.S. business might be maintained at the expense of the standard of living of workers in those industries. The losses from such wage competition will be greatest for workers in high-wage countries employed in industries that can move either their products or their production facilities most easily across national boundaries. Others, particularly more affluent professionals such as doctors, lawyers, and university professors, who face less direct competition from abroad, stand to gain from trade because it lowers prices on the goods they consume.

A final distributional effect of trade policy was illustrated by the observation that trade deficits—an excess of imports over exports—can shift economic welfare across time. Because the imports are enjoyed immediately, whereas the costs of trade deficits are felt later, trade deficits sacrifice the future for the present. In short, trade produces different effects on different sectors, regions, classes, and generations. *Trade opportunities thus pose the distributional dilemma: Whichever trade policy the government chooses, it will harm some group.*

THE VALUES DILEMMA

The values dilemma arises because trade generates many outcomes that citizens evaluate on the basis of ethical principles and social values. Because these fundamental values are frequently incompatible with one another, policies designed to affect trade patterns become an expression of the relative priorities attached to them. The most venerable trade policy debates concern the trade-off between economic benefits and a variety of less tangible interests. Liberal theorists advocate free trade because they believe that it maximizes economic efficiency and therefore material standards of living. Opponents point out that allowing markets to operate freely also allows economic considerations to dominate more important ethical ones.

For example, trading with nations that permit shabby treatment of workers—or even outright human rights abuses—poses a difficult moral dilemma. Should we purchase cheap foreign goods even though they may have been made with child labor—or even slave labor? We may not *intend* to condone those practices, but we cannot escape the fact that our purchases of such goods helps to sustain the system that produced them. Market mechanisms of supply and demand are notoriously poor at coping with such issues, not only because individual consumers can seldom vouch for the production processes of the goods they buy, but also because individual actions can do little to change them. Consequently, trade policy becomes the arena for addressing these value trade-offs, especially in democratic nations where citizens can determine the trade regulations that accord with their own ethical priorities. Trade policy debates invariably become highly charged, because these values, although deeply held, are inherently subjective. Thus, citizens would disagree on the outcomes to be pursued, even if they were certain how trade policy could be used to bring them about.

Cultural considerations are among the many other values that have been cited as justifications for restricting imports. For example, many nations decry the cultural imperialism embodied in U.S. trade. Rock music and Hollywood films not only celebrate ideas that are deeply offensive elsewhere–such as sex, drugs, violence, free expression, and resistance to authority—but also threaten to undermine the cultural industries that sustain national identity. France restricts the hours of TV programming

Values dilemma. Danziger © *The Christian Science Monitor*

offered in English, and Canada restricts the percentage of magazine ads that can advertise U.S. products.

Ecological values have also assumed an increasingly prominent role in trade debates. Some nations have restricted the export of goods whose exploitation threatens their own natural environment, like timber or products derived from endangered species. Because not all nations have done so and because the environment is a planetary resource shared both materially and spiritually without regard to borders, others have attempted to curtail destructive activities by banning the importation of the goods produced by these activities.

Many trade policy issues involve value considerations intertwined with economic interests. The U.S. embargo of trade with Cuba not only protested the absence of democracy in Cuba but also Castro's seizure of property owned by U.S. businesses. Japan banned imported rice not only to protect the financial interests of Japanese farmers but also to sustain venerated Japanese traditions embodied in the image of life in the rural village. Agricultural trade policies elsewhere, most notably in the United States and France, have similarly aimed to protect the family farm for a combination of economic and more abstract reasons.

Some of the most enduring value controversies overlap with issues of distribution and concern the propensity of the distributional effects of trade to generate inequality by undermining the position of workers. For example, the NAFTA debate cited above as an example of the distributional dilemma achieved special salience because of the ethical implications of adopting a policy that would disadvantage unskilled workers, a group already marked by high levels of poverty. Whether one prefers to live in a country with higher growth and greater inequality rather than a more equal but less prosperous one depends not only on whether one anticipates that one would fall within the richer or poorer group but also on highly subjective ethical and aesthetic judgments about the value of equality.

Another reason that trade raises values issues is that it places greater competitive pressure on firms to lower their costs. They, in turn, pressure the state to alter policies that keep them from doing so, including environmental regulations, health and safety requirements, and other restrictions that reflect various legitimate social values. Labor costs are an especially frequent target. Lower wages could be paid if the minimum wage were eliminated and collective bargaining and labor unions were outlawed. The abolition of seniority systems and age-discrimination laws would enable companies to terminate workers when their efficiency declined (or at the whim of a boss). Eliminating pensions, health care, vacations, and holidays would also lower company labor costs. But such actions entail a compromise with very fundamental values about the kind of society in which people want to live. Most people, but not all, prefer that workers have security and a decent standard of living, that income gaps among citizens be moderate, and that the attendant class conflict remain muted enough to sustain social harmony.

If trade competitors do not share these values, however, it may prove difficult for the United States to maintain them—without restricting trade, accepting deficits, or designing state policies to alleviate the most dire consequences, especially the concentration of winners and losers among certain economic sectors, geographic regions, and social classes. Concentrated geographic unemployment, for example, brings a litany of social problems, including inequality, crime, drugs, urban violence, and, potentially, social collapse. Ripple effects cause trade issues to influence many other domains of social concern and public policy, because geographic concentrations often lead to disproportionate effects on particular ethnic groups and sectoral concentrations often lead to disproportionate effects on women or teenagers.

Economists can show that the most efficient approach to many of these problems, in theory, is to earn the benefits of free trade and use the proceeds to compensate the losers. Actually achieving that mix is a good deal more difficult than it sounds, however, so government officials usually prefer to restrict trade instead, even though that also requires that the benefits of trade be sacrificed.

A nation committed to trade also faces pressures from other nations seeking favorable treatment for their firms, which can be expected to object to any policy that raises their costs or restricts their access to markets. Yet nations have many interests that seem to justify trade restrictions; surely the pressures of international trade need not require that we abandon all other values. In the United States, for example, trade restrictions on Chinese imports have been proposed to protest human rights abuses, on tuna imports to protect dolphins, and on exotic hardwoods to protect tropical rain forests. To elevate economic gain to the sole value pursued by trade policy is one option, but it is far from the only one. *Trade policy thus poses the values dilemma: Whichever choice is made, some values must be compromised to achieve others.*

THE STATE GOALS DILEMMA

A third dilemma concerns the effect of trade on the ability of states to meet their goals. Some state goals simply reflect the social values discussed above, but here we concentrate on those that fall within the special purview of the state and its unique mission to embody the nation's autonomy and provide peace and security. These goals apply most directly and obviously to foreign policy, but autonomy and security are elusive and multifaceted concepts, prone to expansive definitions by states.

All states attach the highest priority to preserving the power and autonomy of the state itself, because without the capacity to act effectively and independently no other goals can be achieved. Trade can substantially affect the power and autonomy of the state, both in relation to domestic actors it must control in order to govern meaningfully and with respect to foreign nations with which it must interact to guarantee security. In the most elementary sense, states rely on trade to obtain the revenues they require to function, either directly through import taxes or indirectly through income and sales taxes on the economic activity that trade stimulates. More broadly, however, the state must command the allegiance of its citizens, in part by demonstrating its capacity to manage the economy in a way that provides prosperity while also managing foreign policy in a way that provides peace, security and autonomy.

Although trade is essential to meeting all of these aims, states have an ambivalent attitude toward it. After all, if a nation's trade can enhance the power of its own state, it can also strengthen the state in nations with which it trades. Since states must be acutely aware of relative power when engaged in foreign policy, they cannot be indifferent to the effects of trade on the power and prosperity of others. For this reason, they prefer to trade with allies and to avoid trade with rivals and potential enemies. The profit considerations of private actors often conflict with the power and security considerations of the state, particularly when trade restrictions are used as an instrument of foreign policy. During the Cold War, the United States and its Western European allies sharply limited the products that could be exported to the Soviet Union and Eastern Europe, especially those with either direct or potential military application. Over the strong objections of North American farmers, the list sometimes included wheat as well. The United States has banned all trade with Cuba for decades in an attempt to weaken the Castro regime, and it still restricts some technology exports to any nation.

States are also wary of trade because the interdependence implicit in relying upon foreign actors constrains independent action and threatens autonomy. States fear that the loss of self-reliance will leave them vulnerable to economic disruptions arising out of both impersonal market forces and deliberate threats by other states. The higher the level of trade (and the smaller the nation), the more the state loses control over the economy and relinquishes the capacity to shape the nation's destiny. Because citizen perception of the performance of the government and even the legitimacy of the state itself frequently rests on this very capacity, the risk to political stability can be high. For many developing nations extreme dependence upon trade and the capital flows associated with it subjects the state to irresistible pressures from foreign investors and lenders. As a result, states have been forced into budgetary and regulatory decisions that are more attentive to foreign interests than to domestic constituents, with predictable consequences for either the longevity of the government or the character of the political system.

The international institutions that are necessary to facilitate trade even compromise **national sovereignty,** because membership in them requires a nation to forego some policies that would otherwise be pursued. Protectionism is the most obvious target of prohibitions imposed by such international institutions. However, a wide array of monetary, fiscal, regulatory and social policies have also been ruled inconsistent with the obligations of membership in regional institutions (e.g., the EU and NAFTA) and global ones (e.g., the WTO and IMF). As a result, many nations have avoided such institutions, even though they offer considerable trade benefits. Britain, for example, remains ambivalent about the EU out of concern that the "level playing field" necessary to achieve fair competition under free trade threatens also to level cultural and political differences among nations. Similarly, Canadian fear of the economic dominance of the United States long delayed a free trade agreement, which was proposed as early as 1851. China has resisted full acceptance of the conditions required for its admittance into the WTO.

To minimize dependence, many states restrict trade, especially in sensitive sectors important to the economy (e.g., food, banking, insurance, or steel) or to national defense (e.g., microelectronics, telecommunications, or satellite technology). But states must tread carefully, because these restrictions also limit the benefits of trade, not only to their own economy but to other nations. Strong objections to these restrictions from trade partners can endanger friendly relations and even international peace. It is difficult to generalize about how states will respond to these dilemmas, because although some nations become subordinate and their freedom of action diminishes in the face of trade, others become dominant and expand the scope of their power and influence. All find that they must anticipate the reactions of others much more frequently and tailor their actions accordingly. Whenever trade occurs, tensions inevitably follow. Sometimes—thankfully not often—these escalate into resentment and conflict. The violence of the 1930s and 1940s is an awful historical precedent, which some fear may indicate what lies ahead for U.S. relations with Japan or China.

But theorists of **interdependence** also remind us that trade can force nations to recognize both the need to coexist and the opportunity to "coflourish" through cooperation. The Bretton Woods international economic system created at the end of World War II is an example at the global level. Both the European Union and the North American Free Trade Agreement are examples of these same principles of cooperation pursued at the regional level. Thus the state goals dilemma raises a theoretical question: Under what conditions does trade lead to conflict and when does it generate peaceful cooperation? It also presents a policy challenge: How do we find one path and avoid the other?

Theories that insist upon seeing trade only through the lenses of economic analysis miss these political and social considerations. Thus, the policy advice that emanates from them is, at best, incomplete and, at worst, counterproductive for states, which must balance the benefits of trade against its dangers. *Trade thus poses the state goals dilemma: Any trade policy that strengthens the capacity of the state to achieve its goals in one respect is likely to weaken it in another.*

CHOICES FOR THE INDIVIDUAL

These dilemmas must be confronted in the formulation of trade policy, but they also challenge individual citizens when contemplating any purchase. Economic theory explains consumer behavior as the maximization

Trade dilemma for the individual. Danziger © *The Christian Science Monitor*

of material interests. But a citizen also assumes the role of a moral agent responsible for the chain of outcomes set in motion by the consumer choice. The motivation behind the **Buy America** bumper sticker, for example, is not the logic of best product and lowest cost but an appeal to other ethical considerations.

In fact, every day each individual must—explicitly or implicitly—assume a stance on the dilemmas previously identified. Is it patriotic to purchase domestic products? Should a Japanese consumer buy a foreign car, knowing it means unemployment for a Japanese worker? Does one owe greater obligations to domestic workers and corporations than foreign ones? Should one save money by purchasing an inexpensive foreign product, even though it is cheap because it was made with slave labor or by workers deprived of human rights? Should one choose transportation that requires the importation of foreign oil, knowing it encourages a costly U.S. military presence in the Middle East? Should one lobby the government to restrict the sales of U.S. forestry products abroad because they compromise environmental concerns? Should a French citizen support the end of farm subsidies when ending them would threaten traditional life in the French countryside? Answering these questions inevitably requires normative judgments. However, these judgments must rest upon a keen understanding of the empirical consequences of trade—the main focus for this book.

In particular, trade affects the individual in six different roles, each of which requires him or her to weigh somewhat different values, interests, and perspectives:

1. As a consumer, it is rational to prefer free trade because it makes imports cheaper. (But if the absence of protection drives domestic firms out of business and gives a **monopoly** to foreign firms, future prices could rise.)
2. As a worker, it is usually wise to prefer free trade if one is employed in a sector that exports goods or imports raw materials but to prefer **protectionism** if employed in a firm that competes with imports.
3. As a member of an economic class, it is usually reasonable for a worker to prefer policies that favor labor and for a business owner to prefer policies that favor capital. Since the early 1970s, U.S. labor has generally supported protectionism and U.S. business has supported free trade.
4. As a resident of a community, it is sensible to prefer policies that benefit local industries even if one is not directly involved in that sector. For example, most residents of Detroit prefer protection against auto imports because it contributes to the general prosperity of the region, and residents of agricultural states prefer **export promotion** policies, which increase farm prices.
5. As a citizen of a nation, it is natural to prefer policies that strengthen the nation as a whole. Because it is not always obvious what policies will accomplish that goal, one must analyze the impact of trade on the foreign policy relations between nations as well as the economic gains from trade.
6. Finally, as an individual one must weigh all of these considerations in the context of one's own personal sense of values and obligations. It is not the purpose here to judge whether one's obligation to the interests of the nation should outweigh one's individual interest or to stipulate whether economic interests should dominate more ethereal ethical concerns. It is possible, however, to clarify those consequences of trade and trade policy that individuals should consider when making their own ethical choices.

CONCLUSION: CHOOSING A TRADE POLICY

Obviously, then, part of the purpose of this book is to help individuals make informed decisions. Nevertheless, the central mission of this book is to explain why nations select the policies they do. At the broadest level, that means explaining why they would choose to emphasize either mercantilist or liberal strategies and focus either on the volume or on the balance of trade as the principal policy target. Thus, as a starting point, Chapter 2 describes the historical evolution of both mercantilism and liberalism. It will quickly become obvious that understanding the motivations and the assumptions that underlie these two broad families of approaches requires an appreciation of how they respond to the trade dilemmas discussed earlier.

The cases examined in the remainder of the book suggest that the trade policy choices of governments are partially predictable, because they result from the interaction among prevailing theories of economics and social justice, the state of supply and demand conditions in markets, and the balance of political power among those who represent producers, consumers, and the state. Each of these factors needs a brief introduction here.

Trade policy is affected by both economic theory and ethical doctrines. It is impossible to divorce current attitudes toward international trade from the goals that public policy is expected to achieve or from the social and political values these goals express. The importance accorded to maximizing national economic growth by contemporary trade policy debates is in part a reflection of the set of values that dominate modern Western society. But these ethical theories are not unchallenged, and thus the debates over trade policy contain within them a clash of values. We ask not only, "What trade policy will best achieve our goals?" but also, "What should our goals be?" Remembering the values dilemma—that all debates over trade policy are ultimately debates over alternative values—will help us understand why a nation selects the trade policy that it does. Societies which accentuate the values of stability and community—Japan, for example—or those with a greater commitment to equality—like most of Western Europe—are much less likely to adopt free trade policies than societies where individualistic and material values dominate, such as the United States. As demonstrated by the 1999 Seattle protests against the WTO, groups more interested in ecological values than economic ones resist free trade as well.

Market conditions also affect the desirability of regulating international trade. When falling transportation costs and efficient markets magnify the gains available from trade—among developed countries in the modern era, for example—policies to expand trade usually follow. Nations whose firms cannot successfully compete internationally—most of Africa today—usually opt for protectionism rather than risk the trade deficits likely to follow from liberalizing trade. It is no coincidence that the industrialists of nineteenth-century England agitated for free trade only after the Industrial Revolution had left them with a major advantage against their foreign competitors. Similarly, it is no coincidence that many U.S. trade unions (notably the AFL-CIO) abandoned their free trade position in favor of protectionist sentiments just as U.S. heavy industry began to be seriously challenged by foreign competitors. Of course, in assessing market performance, one must carefully weigh the distributional dilemma of trade—that all debates over trade policy are also ultimately debates over who will win and who will lose.

Whereas prevailing theory and values interact with market conditions to shape attitudes toward trade, it is the balance of political power among various groups that determines how these attitudes are translated into public policy. The dilemmas posed by trade are typically resolved by appeals to theory, to values, and to market conditions, but the theory, values, and conditions cited by proponents of one position are usually very different than those cited by advocates of another. The winning side need not have the best arguments if it has the political power to prevail. Where multinational corporations have greater political power than domestic industries, for example, policies that maximize trade usually emerge. Where labor unions are strong, either trade is heavily regulated or a substantial social safety net is constructed to protect workers from its effects.

Trade policy is also affected by the balance of power between the state itself and other domestic actors, because governments, which regard trade policy as a component of foreign policy, are more attentive to issues of autonomy, self-sufficiency, and national security than those who see only trade's impact on the domestic economy. Because nations more reliant on trade must often sacrifice assertiveness in foreign policy to avoid disrupting trade relations, states which aspire to autonomy generally seek to minimize trade dependence, especially in critical areas like food or weaponry. Naturally, the power of the state relative to other states also influences trade policy. Powerful states can tolerate levels of interdependence that would be considered dangerous by weaker ones. Finally, weak states may not be able exercise much choice in trade policy if foreign actors assert their power.

In sum, trade poses fundamental dilemmas involving choices between competing values, alternative income distributions, and disparate effects on state goals and capacities. For this reason, no single trade policy is unequivocally "best." Further, economic theory alone cannot be a reliable guide to either the most appropriate choice or the most likely one. Instead, each nation resolves the dilemmas of trade in its own way, as it responds to prevailing theories, the state of markets, and the balance of political power.

TWO

□ □ □

The Theoretical and Historical
Origins of Trade Issues

Two competing visions have dominated discussion of international trade for more than two centuries. These ideas, which linger beneath the surface of most contemporary issues, can be seen with greatest clarity in the context of the historical periods that spawned them. Examining the origins of these visions can help us to understand both how each resolves the three dilemmas of trade and why nations have adopted the trade strategies implied by them.

LIBERALISM AND MERCANTILISM

One vision is that of **economic liberalism**, which has been dominant in theoretical circles since the very advent of systematic thinking about economics. Economic liberalism was first articulated in precise form by Scottish political economist Adam Smith (1723–1790) in his brilliant masterpiece of 1776, *An Inquiry into the Nature and Causes of the Wealth of Nations*. This school of thought, which was advanced by a long line of British theorists including David Ricardo (1772–1823) and John Stuart Mill (1806–1873), now numbers most contemporary economists among its membership. Economic liberalism is often summarized by the answer it offers to governments seeking advice on how to deal with the market: *laissez-faire* (from the French "allow it to act" or "leave it alone").[1] Thus, liberalism holds that international trade should be conducted by private actors largely free of government control. That advice is predicated on the premise that the most important value to be maximized by the state is the consumption of its citizens, usually summarized by a nation's gross national product (GNP).

The second perspective derives from **mercantilism**, a body of thought that originated with the mercantile policy (i.e., commercial or trade policy) of European nations, especially England, from the sixteenth century to the middle of the nineteenth. Though the practice of mercantilism long predated liberalism, the best-known text in the mercantilist tradition is Friedrich List's *The National System of Political Economy*, written in 1841, half a century after Smith's death. List's counterattack against Smith's liberalism is better known than the original doctrine he defends, because the sophistication of Smith and Ricardo's analysis elevated the rigor of subsequent economic debate beyond that of the narrow and piecemeal writings left by the early pamphleteers who supported mercantilist policies.

Even today, mercantilism is not so much a theory as a bundle of ideas centered around the conviction that governments must regulate trade in order for it to further the **national interest**. Perceptions of that national interest have varied from time to time, from place to place, and from author to author, but most variants of mercantilism have emphasized the goals of national self-sufficiency, a favorable **balance of trade**, the vitality of key industries, and the promotion of the power of the state, especially in foreign policy. That is, mercantilists resolve the values dilemma by deemphasizing liberalism's focus on consumption and instead embracing various alternative values. They also resolve the state goals dilemma by elevating elements of the national interest involving security and self-sufficiency above liberalism's emphasis on the desirability of interdependence and cooperation. Because the national interest encompasses a multitude of different goals that must be judged by each nation in its particular circumstances, however, no universal policy advice is offered by mercantilism. Still, protection against imports and the promotion of exports is common to most versions.

Much of the early writing of both mercantilism and liberalism concerned the controversies surrounding the English **Corn Laws**, a series of protectionist measures that regulated the trade of agricultural goods, especially grain, between the fifteenth and nineteenth centuries.[2] Their repeal in 1846 ushered in a period of free trade that represented the triumph of economic liberalism over mercantilism, which had dominated both economic theory and political practice in England for most of the previous three centuries.

However, the history of international trade reveals that the mercantilist inclination to regulate trade, particularly in order to protect domestic producers, has been somewhat more commonly adopted by nations than has the liberal policy of free trade. Perhaps it is more accurate to say that no nation has ever completely accepted or completely rejected either view. Instead, governments have sought to encompass elements of both in fashioning their trade policies. This is understandable because both theories are "true," but neither is universally so. Each is rooted in a set of assumptions that are more valid in some instances than others and each addresses concerns that are more salient to some states' priorities in interests, values, and goals than others. As a result, national policies vary, but each is a compromise that reflects a different resolution of the fundamental dilemmas posed by trade.

In this chapter, I examine the debate over the Corn Laws because it so closely parallels contemporary contests between free trade and protection. The lessons of this period help us to understand some of the puzzles of our own era, especially why nations have selected such a great variety of different trade policies, despite liberal theory's ardent and universal advocacy of free trade.

MERCANTILIST TRADE POLICY

Early English mercantile policy involved three major elements: the promotion and protection of industry, the **Navigation Acts**, and the Corn Laws. All involved restricting the scope of markets in international trade, and each is remarkably similar to mercantilist policies widely practiced today.

The motivations for the promotion and protection of industry—we would call their modern counterparts "industrial policy"—continue to inspire contemporary advocates of trade limitations. One goal was the creation of industries that would foster the state goals of self-sufficiency and economic development. This drive was manifested in a variety of actions dating to the time of Queen Elizabeth's reign (1558–1603), including exclusive patents (legal monopolies) to develop domestic industries that could substitute for imports: sugar refining, salt production, glass manufacturing, soap production, and others. Many industries were also introduced into England by government policy that encouraged the immigration of foreign workers with special skills. Once initiated, these industries were then sustained by import restrictions in the hope that eventually they would develop sufficiently to be capable of exporting. Support for **infant industries** is an integral part of all modern mercantilist policies, including the **import-substituting industrialization** (ISI) common to most of Latin America in the 1950s and 1960s and the postwar industrial policy of Japan.[3] Self-sufficiency and economic development were state goals given greater urgency by the concern that Elizabethan England lagged behind such continental rivals as the Dutch and the French in industrial development.

Exports were encouraged in part because they produced an inflow of **treasure**—gold or silver—to pay for them. Today, we would refer to this net inflow as a balance-of-trade surplus. The revenue earned from exports could be used to purchase goods from abroad that could not be produced at home, such as wine, tea, and spices. Treasure could also be accumulated for use at a later time. Given the crude monetary system of the age, the inflow of precious metals was also necessary to maintain the domestic money supply, especially as the nation shifted from an elementary agricultural economy dominated by barter exchanges and self-sufficiency to a more complex modern economy in which money and credit were needed to facilitate transactions. Exports were also desirable because once established they could be taxed to generate revenue that would support state interests, such as maintaining the navy or sustaining the power of the Crown against domestic challengers. Requiring exporters to secure government licenses also gave government officials the ability to earn revenues while playing favorites among license applicants.

Moreover, exports provided employment for workers and profits for industrialists, both of which fostered the growth of the economy as a whole. Rising employment increased the demand for food and thus benefitted the agricultural sector. The export trade helped to strengthen the merchant marine, which trained seamen for service in the navy, a vital factor in maintaining the power and security of an island nation like Britain. For all these reasons, exports were promoted, sometimes by bounties (subsidies) and sometimes by encouraging the cheap importation of raw materials necessary to manufacture goods for export.

At the same time, however, import restrictions were imposed on most goods. Trade regulations were designed to protect domestic manufacturing industries and their workers from a very early time. The first beneficiary in England, textile production, was protected as early as the thirteenth century, but a parliamentary law of 1337 is the first classic package of infant-industry protection. It included an **embargo** (i.e., prohibition) on the exportation of raw wool to prevent the textile industries of other nations from acquiring this important raw material to compete against English weavers. It also encouraged the immigration of clothworkers from abroad in order to build an English industry that would be capable of exporting finished cloth.[4] Most important, it added a prohibition against the importation of foreign cloth.

Import restrictions of this sort were designed for several purposes. First, they protected the employment of laborers and the profits of owners, considerations that motivate the bulk of import restrictions in the current era. Typical was the act of 1700, in which Parliament restricted the importation of silk textiles from India on the grounds that it would directly endanger the jobs of 250,000 employees in the English woolen-textile industry and indirectly lower the price of wool, threatening the prosperity of the landed interests supported by sheep grazing. Modern-

day analogues include the Multi-Fiber Agreement (MFA) and its predecessors, which have protected the U.S. cotton textile industry since 1961.

Second, import restrictions typically took the form of tariffs, which provided a substantial amount of government revenue. This consideration is
less relevant in the modern age among developed countries, but it remains central to many less developed countries for the same reason as in
early England: Revenues were difficult to raise through general taxation
because of the relatively low level of taxable domestic activity and the lo-
gistical problems of collection. The importance of this consideration is
shown by the necessity of reintroducing the income tax in England as
part of the package of import duty reductions between 1841 and 1846 that
culminated in the repeal of the Corn Laws. Even in 1994, final U.S. Senate
passage of the long-awaited **Uruguay Round** trade agreement was held
up by the need to find $14 billion to replace the import tax revenue that
would be lost when tariffs were reduced.[5]

Third, import restrictions were used as a tool of foreign policy, both in
order to induce other nations to open their markets to British industries
and to harm enemies while helping friends. For example, when Jean-
Baptiste Colbert raised French tariffs to levels that effectively prohibited
the export of English cloth to France in 1667, Parliament retaliated with
tariffs and prohibitions on French goods in England. A 1703 commercial
treaty imposed a lower tariff on Portuguese wine than on French wine,
thus diverting the lucrative wine trade away from France, which was
England's greatest political, military, and commercial rival. Retaliatory
tariffs designed to bring other nations to the bargaining table are now
commonplace; in 1992's "beer war" the United States imposed a 50 percent duty on Canadian beer to protest Ontario's environmental tax on
aluminum cans and warehouse charges for U.S. beer. Tariffs are still frequently used as a carrot and stick in other foreign policy areas, such as the
U.S. policy of threatening to withdraw the preferential tariff rate known
as most-favored-nation (MFN) status from China in order to induce
progress on human rights.

Domestic producers were also favored by another mechanism of protection, the domestic preference sentiment, whose modern expression is
found in the Buy America program and the propensity of Japanese consumers to purchase domestic rather than imported products. Then as
now, domestic preference was partly a matter of public sentiment and
partly a matter of government policy. For example, there was a period in
which woolen clothing was mandated for some occasions, including bur-
ial, in order to sustain the production of the domestic textile industry. The
consumption of herring to sustain the fishing industry was encouraged
by mandated "fish days." For a time the importation of Indian fabrics was
prohibited by law; at another point, English textile workers took matters

into their own hands by throwing acid on women who wore clothing made of Indian calicos.[6] The latter scene anticipates the symbolic destruction of Japanese cars by Detroit autoworkers two centuries later. It also presents a vivid picture of the kinds of distributional trade-offs that liberal theorists remind us always attend import restrictions: The protection of English workers was paid for by English consumers, because the price of English woolens was about eight times higher than that of foreign textiles.

The national interest was also protected by the Navigation Acts, which date from 1381. Because defense of an island nation and, later, the maintenance of a far-flung empire required a strong navy, the Navigation Acts required that English grain be carried only by English ships. This prohibition was designed to stimulate shipbuilding and sustain the merchant marine, which, like the fishing industry, trained sailors in seafaring skills useful to the navy. The Navigation Acts were only one part of an extensive system of government control designed to strengthen naval power. For example, to guarantee that wood supplies for shipbuilding would be available, a 1558 act prohibited timber cutting for use in iron smelting within fourteen miles of the coast. Monopolies were granted by royal letters patent to encourage investment and innovation in the production of munitions and in the mining and smelting of metals required for their production. Thus we see that mercantilist trade policy complemented domestic policy; both were formulated in the pursuit of such nationalistic values as defense and national power. In the modern era, states subsidize national airlines and defense contractors for similar reasons.

THE CORN LAWS

However, neither the protection and promotion of manufactures nor the Navigation Acts were as controversial as the Corn Laws, which perfectly express the distributional, values, and state goals dilemmas inherent in all trade policy debates. The Corn Laws and proposals for free trade represent polar opposites that illustrate both the arguments that sustained mercantilism and those of economic liberalism that eventually defeated them. The Corn Laws were a complex series of mercantilist trade regulations enacted by Parliament over a period of several centuries in order to control the price of grain. Depending on domestic supplies and prices, both exports and imports of grain were restricted at various times. Sometimes they were discouraged with quotas or taxes, sometimes promoted with bounties or subsidies, and sometimes outright prohibited—but seldom was the market permitted to freely determine prices or trade volumes.

The Corn Laws were initially designed largely to protect consumers. For example, when poor harvests caused a supply shortage and high prices, grain exports were prohibited. Just as consumers required shielding from market forces, government policy recognized the need to protect producers as well. As early as 1463, for example, the importation of low-priced grain from abroad was restricted and producers were allowed to dispose of a surplus through foreign trade. Generally, exports were permitted only when prices were relatively low (thus signaling that supplies were adequate to demand and that domestic consumers were protected from shortages and "unjust" prices) and often only when licensed by the state. This power was contested by the Crown and Parliament, with the Crown preferring regulations that earned it revenue and protected consumers and Parliament tending to the protection of landowners and producers.[7] Prior to 1660, the predominant beneficiaries of government policy were the Crown and consumers, but the Restoration of 1660 increased the power of the landowners in Parliament and the Revolution of 1689 established the dominance of Parliament over the Crown. With these changes in the political balance of power, government policy shifted in favor of producers and against consumers.[8]

Over the next 150 years, the Corn Laws were contested terrain both in academic debates and in practical politics, especially because their differential effects on various groups posed a stark distributional dilemma. Parliament dealt with them nearly annually as weather-related fluctuations in supply drove prices to levels that threatened either producers or consumers. When prices for grain rose, consumer riots were often directed against the Corn Laws, which were thought to be exacerbating supply shortages by keeping out imports and encouraging exports. When prices fell, farmers who rented land would frequently find themselves producing at a loss and landowners would be obliged to lower rents, at considerable loss to their principal source of income. Parliament generally tried to strike a balance. On behalf of consumers, exports were prohibited or heavily taxed when domestic supplies were limited. On behalf of producers, plentiful domestic supplies would trigger not only a prohibition or heavy tax on imports but also a bounty (today we would call it an export subsidy) on exports. In this way, producers were encouraged to employ peasants and keep acreage in production in anticipation of years when such capacity might be needed to meet domestic demand.

Thus, an elaborate system of price regulation was maintained with tariffs and export subsidies triggered at a price meant to define the lower boundary acceptable to producers; import subsidies kicked in at a price meant to be the ceiling acceptable to consumers. This cumbersome system was frequently changed by Parliament in response to both annual market conditions and the intense political activity of landowners and peasants—with the petitions of the former being generally more effective than the riots of the latter. However, until the nineteenth century no one seriously advocated the abandonment of the mercantilist market-regulating approach altogether by allowing free imports and exports. The effects of food prices on a range of economic, social, political, and cultural outcomes were far too great to allow them to be determined by uncontrolled forces like market supply and demand.

The desirability of maintaining self-sufficiency in such a critical area as food production was the most consistent argument used by protectionists. Of course, this concern with national security was imbedded deep in the characteristic perspective of mercantilism. Thus, it is ironic that this argument was best stated in succinct form by Adam Smith, whose writing on behalf of free trade made him not only the foremost exponent of economic liberalism but also a much quoted opponent of the Corn Laws. He noted, simply and eloquently, that "defense is of more importance than opulence."[9] Protectionists frequently applied Smith's reasoning to support the Corn Laws even though these words were written in support of the Navigation Acts, which he regarded as necessary for the defense of the realm. (He opposed the Corn Laws, since he did not regard self-sufficiency in food as essential for national security.)

The widespread fear that abandoning agricultural protection would exchange self-sufficiency for a dangerous reliance on imports was founded in the economic and political conditions of the day. Because grain prices were often lower on the continent than in England, tariffs were thought necessary to protect English producers from European imports. Though cheap imports would benefit consumers in the short term, they would mean misery for English agricultural interests and could have detrimental effects for the nation as a whole in the long term. If English grain producers were not guaranteed a steady market, they would begin to shift their production away from these import-competing products or abandon investment in their land altogether. Indeed, a steady increase in sheep pasturing did impinge on the acreage held in grain production. Moreover, many landowners began to devote more time and wealth to investment opportunities in industry and commerce than to improvements in agricultural output. If this trend were to continue over time, protectionists feared, England would come to rely on foreign imports of grain not just in years of a bad English harvest but on a regular basis.

In this period, it is not surprising that such foreign reliance should make mercantilists nervous. It would leave the nation dangerously sensitive not only to weather and other harvest conditions in Europe but also to any disruption of trade. Further, the threat of disruption would reduce the freedom of action that the government of a self-sufficient nation could enjoy in conducting foreign relations.

It was feared that politically motivated disruption of trade could become an instrument of statecraft (or war) that would put England at a severe disadvantage in conducting its foreign policy. Certainly, Elizabeth had been well aware of the advantage possessed by England in its war with Spain: England was self-sufficient in food at that time, but Spain was not. More recently, England's great rival, France, had sharply controlled the export of its grain when it was in short supply at home. Although this was done principally in order to protect French consumers (as was common in England and most other nations), it was feared that such control might also be exercised in order to force foreign policy concessions from England under the threat of mass starvation. Thus, mercantilists sought self-sufficiency where possible. Further, for those products in which England could not achieve self-sufficiency, reliance upon trade with their own colonies, a trade not so sensitive to potential political disruption, was preferred to trade with rival continental powers.

The interruption of trade by large-scale war was also justifiably feared, not only because England was at war with France during most of the period from 1793 to 1815 but also because war had been a frequent occurrence in Europe for centuries. Indeed, between 1562 and 1721 there were only four years in which all of Europe was at peace.[10] Moreover, England would not want to be put in a position of actually aiding an enemy. Sir Henry Parnell's support of the highly protectionist Corn Law of 1815 called attention to England's heavy importation of wheat and flour from France in 1810, which had enabled Napoléon to both quell an insurrection in southern France and collect heavy export duties that were used to strengthen the French war effort. This resolution of the state goals dilemma—emphasizing market controls to protect national security, self-sufficiency, and state power—is characteristic of mercantilist inclinations even today.

The protection of agriculture to keep prices and land rents high also had a justification rooted in the values dilemma. The maintenance of a strong agricultural sector was a value synonymous with the preservation of a prosperous and peaceful rural community, which from time immemorial had been the heart of English society as well as the core of the economy. When debates required that a policy's effect on national prosperity be defined and measured, the usual method was to invoke the strength of the rural sector. In turn, this approach usually meant that the well-being of landowners—especially the level of land rents—was used as a criterion. John Locke gave expression to this widely accepted interpretation: "An infallible sign of your decay of wealth is the falling of rents, and the raising of them would be worth the nation's care, for in that . . . lies the true advantage of the landed man and with him of the public."[11]

Since the social ideals of the landed gentry dominated both Parliament and the national culture, it is hardly surprising that the vision of England that motivated national policy remained rooted in this traditional, romantic, and self-serving view. Similarly, the protection of rice production in contemporary Japan can be explained partly by its enormous symbolic significance for Japanese tradition and partly by the predominantly rural political power base of the long-ruling Liberal Democratic Party. Mercantilism represents both a choice among alternative values and a preference among distributional outcomes.

Given the material conditions at the time, equating national prosperity with the wealth of landowners did have considerable merit. It was the income derived by landowners from ground rents that fueled the entire economy. Most investment originated in the savings of landowners, even that which built the manufacturing sector that eventually transformed the nation. Government revenues depended directly on the wealth produced by ground rents, since taxes were largely raised from these same landowners. Of course, definitions of national prosperity were inevitably to change as the economy became more reliant on manufacturing for profits, for savings and investment, for employment, and for taxable income. In the process, industrial development allowed capitalists to offer an alternative vision of England just as the advent of political democracy allowed the masses to suggest an alternative definition of what constituted national prosperity. Values can seldom be wholly separated from economic and political conditions.

THE ROOTS OF MERCANTILISM

The mercantilist view that international trade should be sharply regulated cannot be understood in a historical vacuum. Indeed, far from an aberration, it is a natural outgrowth of then prevalent theoretical and ethical perspectives on *all* markets. Prior to the evolution of modern economic society, free markets were no more common in the domestic economy than they were in international trade. In fact, mercantilism thrived in an environment in which none of the three elements of economic liberalism identified earlier—individualism, private property, and the free market—were widely accepted in either theory or practice.

The absence of these three elements is best illustrated by the communal character of agriculture, the dominant sector of the economy, as it had been widely practiced in England for centuries.[12] The open-field system of production was marked by a collective "commons," joint labor, and production decisions made at the village level. In a typical village, an individual would own or rent several small strips of land, but they were seldom contiguous. Because they were so intermixed with the plots of others, because the boundaries between them were not fenced, and because the entire open field would be given over to communal pastureland after the harvest, independent decisionmaking—entrepreneurship—was impossible and collective cultivation was imperative. If individualism was thus limited, so too was the freedom to use private property as one saw fit. The overlapping network of obligations typical of feudal systems meant that land ownership was not absolute. Though economically inefficient, this system promoted equality and full employment among agricultural laborers while it served as the basis for social interaction. The well-ordered village was the ultimate expression of the values of the period: It was a stable collective maintained by an ethical system rooted in a strongly hierarchical conception of society. It was also more or less self-sufficient, with most local production consumed locally rather than being sold on a larger market.

Prior to the nineteenth century, reliance upon the unregulated market was also uncommon outside of agriculture. The reasons parallel the three factors introduced in Chapter 1 to explain the choice of foreign economic policy by any nation. First, ethical considerations that originated in medieval social and economic theory cast doubt on the justice of markets. Second, material conditions did not allow efficient markets to develop. Third, the most powerful actors of the period—the church, the Crown, and landowners—were satisfied with the regulated economic system.

In the medieval period, it was believed that commodities should be sold at just prices that would enable each man to "have the necessaries of life suitable for his station."[13] To engage in a transaction that did not meet that standard was to commit the sin of avarice, punishable by both the church and the state. For example, in order to guarantee just prices, the parliamentary act of 1552 severely regulated the activities of brokers or merchants, prohibiting supply manipulation designed to increase prices and the resale of grain at a higher price in the same local market.

This last regulation is a striking reminder that the ethical status of markets and the morality of activities that benefit from their operation was a highly controversial issue centuries before Marx's critique of capitalism. Among the most visible manifestations of the moral outrage generated by market operations is the famous Rusby trial of 1800. During a period of grain shortage that had driven up food prices, riots were commonly directed against the brokers who were blamed for much of the price increase. John Rusby, a London jobber, was alleged to have purchased a lot of oats at a price of 41 shillings and to have resold a part of it later that same day for 43 shillings. This action, which today would be considered profitable and altogether legal brokerage, was regarded in the medieval tradition as unethical "regrating" and prohibited by local regulations throughout much of England long before it was codified in national law in 1552. These specific statutes were repealed in 1772 and 1791, but the offenses were still punishable under the common law. More important, they were still considered unethical—a violation of common morality—by the bulk of the population, especially when seen to contribute to prohibitive prices in a time of food shortage and economic desperation. Rusby was found guilty and heavily fined—and a London mob intent on lynching him destroyed his house. Similar riots in sympathy occurred throughout the nation.

According to medieval social theory, a divergence was generally acknowledged to exist between private interests and the public interest. Because this divergence made it a duty of government to protect the community from the harmful effects of the market, commerce and industry were also sharply regulated during the entire mercantilist period. For example, in addition to restraints on brokers, market regulation to protect consumers also included a standard system of weights and measures for various consumer goods, especially food and cloth. Laws governing the size and composition of bread loaves had existed for centuries before being meticulously codified by the Tudors and Stuarts beginning in the sixteenth century.[14] In conformity with accepted moral law, it was said that "the most desirable course is that prices should be fixed by public officials, after making an enquiry into the supplies available and framing an estimate of the requirements of different classes."[15] To that end, prices were fixed for various commodities at various times, especially bread and coal but also sometimes cloth, ale, and tea, among others. The market might serve the private interest of the seller, but it was not trusted to yield the just prices that were deemed to be in the public interest.

Restrictions on financial and labor markets were even more severe. Moneylending at excessive interest rates was prohibited by **usury laws** that were not finally repealed until 1854. Indeed, not until 1545 was money lending at *any* interest rate sanctioned by Parliament. These laws merely codified accepted moral standards that went back to biblical times. Parliament also mandated that wages be fixed by local justices of the peace rather than established by the supply and demand for labor, though the practice does not seem to have been universally followed. Finally, a minimum-wage law to protect workers (in the woolen industry) first appeared in 1604.[16] Thus, the regulation of markets to guarantee justice and to protect both consumers and workers has been an established governmental obligation in the Anglo-American tradition for centuries.[17]

It is undeniable that government regulation of the market was rooted in the ethical values that the church successfully transmitted from the early ages of Christianity. But the condition of markets during this period was also a significant spur to government action in support of those values. Limitations of transportation, the relatively low level of commercial activity, guild controls, and modest standards of living combined to generate markets that were, in the vernacular of our age, "thin." That is, limited supply and demand left prices unstable and easily manipulated by unscrupulous profiteers. Thus, government control was directed not so much at the competitive markets extolled by modern economic theory but at the monopolistic or oligopolistic markets then most common.

The absence of individualism and free markets was especially striking in the area of trade, where the interests of powerful actors were as much an explanation as prevailing theory or the condition of markets. Initially, towns attempted to maintain self-sufficiency in key products, an effort that was mirrored in the drive for national self-sufficiency in later centuries. Moreover, trade between towns was sharply controlled by local merchant guilds as early as the twelfth century. Members of the guild were able to prohibit nonmembers from engaging in trade or to tax them for the privilege of doing so. In exchange, guild members were required to permit other members to participate in any transaction that they arranged and to share its benefits. Clearly, individual entrepreneurial activity was neither valued nor rewarded. As in the agricultural system earlier described, there were few opportunities for individual enterprise.

Mercantilist and Liberal Responses to Trade Dilemmas

Mercantilism	*Liberalism*
1. Value trade-offs	
Trade should be regulated to achieve social justice, national economic development, stability, and self-sufficiency.	Trade should be free to maximize efficiency, productivity, consumption, and freedom.
2. Distributional outcomes	
Trade should be regulated to shield consumers from high prices and to protect producers, landowners, and workers from foreign competition.	Trade should be free so as to benefit the most efficient (i.e., industrialists).
3. Effects on the state	
Trade should be regulated to achieve state power and wealth, national security, and autonomy.	Trade should be free to achieve interdependence and peace.

Unquestionably, economic liberalism could not thrive in such an environment; indeed, its principles could not even be clearly articulated.

Against this backdrop of suspicion of markets and their sharp regulation in the domestic sphere, it was natural that similar attitudes would prevail as trade expanded from the intertown to the international arena. The East Indies and Hudson Bay trading companies exerted an **oligopolistic** control of trade with British colonies analogous to that of the merchant guilds. It can hardly be surprising that international trade was also heavily regulated by the government in the mercantilist age.

In fact, mercantile trade policy represented a distinctive response to each of the three dilemmas with which this book began: those concerning competing values, distributional outcomes, and effects on the state. The government controlled markets, especially those in international trade, in order to affect specific distributional outcomes such as the protection of consumers and grain producers. Mercantile trade policy also pursued the values of social justice, national development, and self-sufficiency more consistently than the values of efficiency and profitability associated with liberal trade ideas. Finally, advocates of mercantilism saw unregulated trade more as a threat to state power, autonomy, and national defense than as a guarantor of international peace.

THE DEMISE OF MERCANTILISM AND THE BIRTH OF LIBERALISM

This variant of mercantilism evolved in response to existing conditions in the economy and foreign affairs, in tune with prevailing currents of social, ethical and economic theory, and in recognition of the realities of the distribution of power within and among nations. These three factors, sketched in the conclusion of Chapter 1, account for why mercantilism initially prevailed, but changes in these factors also explain its eventual demise: Even while mercantilist trade policy was dominant, the foundations on which it had been erected were crumbling. Initially, the rise of the market was driven by rapidly changing material conditions at the same time that the values impeding it fell into decline. As a result, English industry advanced more rapidly than its foreign competitors. Then, the advent of liberal theory justified government policies that further strengthened the role of markets, especially those in international trade. Finally, the rise of social groups that championed free trade dramatically shifted the balance of political power domestically. By examining each of these changes in turn, we will see why mercantilism was seen as a curious anachronism by the middle of the nineteenth century and as ill suited to meet the modern challenge.

But be forewarned: In the next chapter, I also trace the demise of the very free trade system whose ascent is about to be chronicled. Although classical mercantilism is necessarily rooted in time and place, analogous factors have produced neomercantilist forces that influence economic policy everywhere. Thus, the changes that swept away mercantilism—especially the abandonment of the Corn Laws in 1846—should be seen as paving the way for the amalgam of mercantilism and liberalism that has emerged in our own time. Today, variations among nations in prevailing theories, market conditions, and power balances explain why they have chosen trade policies that reflect different resolutions of the dilemmas concerning alternative sets of values, state goals, and distributional patterns.

THE RISE OF THE MARKET

Rapidly evolving material conditions lie at the hub of economic, political, and social changes. The center of economic life was shifting from the countryside to the towns in response to the major improvements in machinery and factory technique that we refer to as the Industrial Revolution. The rapidly growing population, much of it increasingly located in industrial towns, fueled a large increase in demand for grain. Dramatic improvements in domestic transportation systems were also permitting a much longer range exchange of goods, so that grain surpluses in one area could be more easily marketed elsewhere.[18] Improvements in transportation were making international trade easier as well, so that demand from abroad encouraged increases in production and the threat of supply from abroad motivated English producers to improve production techniques and lower costs.

The communal style of agriculture, which was so admirably suited to the milieu in which it arose, could not adapt to these changing needs because it was hopelessly inefficient. Thus, the **enclosure** movement, in which the open fields and commons were enclosed (i.e., privatized and permanently fenced), which had been under way as early as the late Middle Ages, accelerated dramatically and contentiously after 1765. By the early nineteenth century, the predominant form of agricultural production had become capitalist rather than communal; land was owned by individuals in much larger, more contiguous, and permanently demarcated plots and worked by either wage labor or tenants who paid rent.[19] The agricultural system became more attuned to the market and less reliant on communalism, accepted practice, and government control. Land was bought and sold on the open market much more freely than in the past, labor was hired at market-driven wages when needed and dismissed when no longer required, and production decisions concerning cropping and grazing were made by individuals with an eye toward maximizing profit. The result was a sharp boost in efficiency: Agricultural output increased and the labor required to produce it decreased.

But the enclosure movement produced enormous controversy and extensive violence. It did so precisely because it so vividly illustrates two of the dilemmas of relying upon markets, whether in international trade or in domestic agriculture. Free markets, though more efficient and productive, produce distributional consequences and compromise other values. Enclosure resulted in large-scale unemployment of agricultural laborers and their eviction from the land. The heart of the old society—the slowly changing, self-contained, communitarian village—was ripped apart. Social harmony was strained and public order was undermined by the riots that frequently accompanied enclosure. The attitude of the villagers toward forced enclosure expressed these dilemmas:

> True, our system is wasteful, and fruitful of many small disputes. True, a large estate can be managed more economically than a small one. True, pasture-farming yields higher profits than tillage. Nevertheless, . . . our wasteful husbandry feeds many households where your economical methods would feed few. . . . In our unenclosed village there are few rich, but there are few destitute, save when God sends a bad harvest, and we all starve together. We do not like your improvements which ruin half the honest men affected by them. We do not choose that the ancient customs of our village should be changed.[20]

At issue was a clash in ethical viewpoints. The traditional view regarded land ownership as principally a stewardship, an obligation to maintain a system that produced products for the public good and sustained gainful employment for the peasants who worked the land and constituted the village. The profit derived by the landowner was an important component of the whole organism—because he too had a right to the standard of living properly associated with his station—but the profit motive did not assume the primacy that it was to achieve in later liberal economics. The more modern view stripped from the ownership of property any obligation to use it for the public good and asserted that a fundamental right associated with the ownership of property—indeed, the very meaning of "property"—was the freedom to use it in whatever way its owner saw fit. It was not within the purview of society as a whole or the state in particular to judge whether that use was in the public interest.

These changes were symbolic of a larger transition in the realm of values and social theory, from a largely religious conception of society built upon an ethics of duties and obligations to a more secular vision that emphasized an ethics of rights—especially property rights—originating in natural law. It substituted for the communitarian vision of social organization an individualist conception, which reached its height with the British liberal theorists John Locke (1632–1704), who exerted such a powerful influence on the U.S. Constitution, and John Stuart Mill (1806–1873), whose passionate defense of the freedom of a citizen from the government still stands as the foremost statement of liberal thought with respect to civil liberties.

These transformations in values were brought about in part by the diminishing influence of the church as it became subordinated to the government after the Reformation and in part by changes in religious doctrine and social ethics associated with the Reformation itself. In particular, many theorists, most famously Max Weber in his 1930 classic *The Protestant Ethic and the Spirit of Capitalism*, have ascribed the "triumph of the economic virtues" to the influence of Puritanism, which not only tolerated profit-maximizing behavior that had been condemned by more traditional religious teachings but elevated such practices to the status of moral virtue. Weber's Protestant ethic was not merely a commitment to hard work in pursuit of a calling in order to glorify God but a drive for achievement that included sharp business dealings and canny calculation of the means to achieve wealth. With these changes came greater tolerance for market outcomes in which those with greater bargaining power benefitted at the expense of those with less.

Over time, the justification for profit seeking came to be rooted much more deeply in the secular utilitarian ideas familiar to us today than in any religious precepts. With this evolution a separation developed between the realm of ethics and the realm of business, with organized religion ceasing to have much to say about the latter.[21] It is no coincidence that the full elaboration of an economic theory relevant to the age arrived only after this division between ethical thought and economic management had become accepted. Liberalism emphasized the expansion of productive output as its goal and reliance upon individual entrepreneurship and market forces as the means to achieve it. Both were too discordant with the older Christian tradition to have been tolerated in the earlier society, which was organized around the ethical precepts of that tradition.

This attitude change, like the increased prominence of the market in determining social outcomes, was neither universal nor complete. Not surprisingly, it was centered among the commercial and merchant classes that benefitted most from it, whereas those who suffered from the insecurity and inequality inherent in impersonal market forces longed for the protection afforded by social institutions that embraced values other than the maximization of material profit. Thus, the enclosure movement proceeded not only because of the efficiency gains it promoted but also because its distributional consequences were favorable to political forces

---

Contemporary Parallels

Increasing reliance on markets induces distributional changes and value clashes.

As the communitarian state-controlled economy in Russia has given way to an individualistic market-based system, unemployment and inequality has grown. A recent poll in Russia revealed that 48% would prefer an economic system based on "state planning and distribution" and 35% "private property and the market" (*Economist*, December 18, 1999, p. 21).

In Africa, leaders like Tanzania's Julius Nyerere and Ghana's Kwame Nkrumah rejected capitalism and sought to build a traditional African collectivist economy that extolled human dignity, often centered around the traditional village.

---

that were on the rise. In particular, enclosure was beneficial to the landed gentry, both because it produced greater profits and because it divorced the rights of landowning from its customary obligations to maintain stable employment for the peasantry. Because the Crown was more deeply committed to the values of the traditional village than to increasing agricultural production, the government at first opposed the commercialization of agriculture, the enclosure movement, and the transition from crops to pasture. However, with the coming to political power of the landed gentry after 1660, government policy began to change. As the Industrial Revolution shifted the demand for labor and food after 1765, public law strongly favored enclosure and the production changes it permitted. These changes were both inevitable and, on balance, desirable: The huge improvements in living standards of the masses and the emergence of Britain as a world power would have been impossible without them.

Many of the same forces that led to greater reliance upon free markets in agriculture also brought about laissez-faire policies in other areas of the domestic economy. For example, domestic price regulation, which was opposed by increasingly powerful industrialists, had begun to fade by the middle of the seventeenth century. As early as 1437 Parliament moved to limit the interference with free markets by craft guilds.[22] The merchant guilds that controlled domestic trade disappeared long before their counterparts in international trade.

A critical factor was that the Crown, which had been the principal agent of market regulation, was too weak after the Restoration to maintain control of a complex, expanding economy. Merchants and industrialists were restive and intolerant of a government regulatory system that constrained their activities, created artificial monopolies in the interests of political favorites, and induced inefficiency and corruption. The limits of government control had been surpassed, perhaps most vividly in the Corn Laws themselves. The balancing act between keeping prices low enough for consumers but high enough for producers had always been difficult; the unwieldy system of prohibitions, sliding-scale duties and bounties, and trigger prices required frequent amendment and even more frequent temporary suspension in the face of changing market conditions. As increased demand and larger-scale trade induced even greater price fluctuations, it became evident that government could not control even this relatively simple market. Effective management of more complicated arrangements seemed unlikely, especially in labor markets, financial markets, and long-distance trade.

Thus, laissez-faire principles slowly came to eclipse government regulatory arrangements. Wage control was abandoned in the woolen industry, the core of the emerging industrial sector, in 1756. Employers were no longer required to maintain employment for workers during a depression. The apprenticeship system of the craft guilds was also rapidly in decline when finally abolished in 1835. Consumer-protection laws that regulated production standards for cloth disappeared.[23] It was in this environment that free trade theory emerged.

THE ADVENT OF FREE TRADE THEORY

In 1751, Charles Townshend wrote a pamphlet on the Corn Laws that foreshadowed later liberal arguments. He attacked import restrictions and export bounties that raised the price of grain not because of their impact on agriculture but on the then novel grounds that they injured English manufacturing industries. He noted that when food prices increased, the wages paid to manufacturing workers had to increase in order to cover their "necessaries." The resulting price increases in finished goods made English industry uncompetitive with that of other nations. These effects were especially damaging because English import restrictions had exactly the opposite effect on nations with whom England competed: Preventing foreign farmers from exporting their grain to England tended to keep grain prices low abroad, just as it kept grain prices high in England. This enabled foreign wages to remain relatively low and finished products, correspondingly cheap.

This basic argument, strengthened, as we shall see further on, by the later elaboration of Adam Smith, was central to parliamentary debate in

1791, which for the first time featured explicit arguments for free trade derived from theoretical ideas. It was also during this debate that the first major clash occurred between the landed interests that dominated Parliament and the growing commercial and manufacturing cities of the Midlands and North. Prior to this time, arguments for free trade lacked the gravity they would later attain due to the changing economic structure (especially the dominance of the manufacturing sector), social structure (especially the growth in size of the cities), and political structure (especially the importance of the capitalist class). Nor had the theoretical ideas themselves developed sufficient cogency until presented systematically by Adam Smith in 1776.

With agricultural interests still dominant in Parliament, the last highly restrictive Corn Law was adopted in 1815. The passage of this law, with the debate that attended it and the way it operated, marked the high point of both agricultural protectionism and the class antagonism that increasingly attended these issues. During the parliamentary debate of 1813 to 1815 fierce rioting against the proposed legislation occurred, since most Londoners were convinced it would mean higher food prices. Further, the class bias in favor of landowners manifested so clearly in this bill was also evident in the debate surrounding it. As a result, all of the ire of the lower classes over food prices, which had long fallen on brokers such as Rusby, was now directed against the Corn Laws and the landed members of Parliament who supported them. It was against this law that the agitation for free trade was directed in the following thirty years, bequeathing to us such a rich literature on theoretical and practical considerations.

The arguments for free trade, which had surfaced in a less systematic way at least a century previously, became imbedded in the evolving theoretical edifice of economic liberalism, championed most visibly by Adam Smith and the English economic theorist (and member of Parliament) David Ricardo. Smith's argument for free trade rested on the concept of **division of labor** and drew a parallel with the argument concerning specialization in the domestic economy that was at the time better known and more widely accepted.

By the end of the eighteenth century, a reasonably extensive domestic division of labor had already developed: Individual peasants did not make their own shoes, grind their own grain, bake their own bread, weave their own cloth, or tailor their own clothing. With the growth of the town and specialized artisans, it became apparent that considerable savings could be achieved by concentrating one's efforts on producing that good which took advantage of the skills and productive resources at hand and by contracting through domestic trade for the other necessaries of life. For example, the skilled artisan was a better weaver than a peasant, owing to his more extensive tools, better access to quality materials, acquired skill, and other advantages of specialization. It was more practical and profitable for all parties to enter freely into the division of labor—that is, to specialize and trade—than to maintain self-sufficiency.

This argument was key to gaining ethical acceptance for the role of the market. Liberal theory contended that free markets would serve the highest moral purpose by maximizing aggregate consumption and thereby maximizing the welfare of the entire society. This position was wholly compatible with the emerging materialist conception of welfare and utilitarian ethical standards, though it remained at odds with the prior ethical tradition.

Smith applied the division of labor logic more broadly. The birth of modern international trade theory can be traced to his memorable phrase, "What is prudence in the conduct of every private family, can scarce be folly in that of a great kingdom."[24] If local trade between the artisans of a town and the peasants of the surrounding countryside can benefit both, if interregional trade between the grain-producing regions of England and areas where the land is more conducive to sheep grazing can be mutually beneficial, why cannot international trade that capitalizes on the respective blessings of different nations be equally advantageous? Thus, nations, like families, should specialize in some products for sale (exports) while acquiring others through purchases (imports).

The important intellectual breakthrough supplied by liberal thought is its blurring of the distinction accepted in medieval economic theory between the public good and the private good. Indeed, liberalism in its rawest form virtually dissolves that distinction. In this famous passage, Smith maintained that the pursuit of maximum profit by individuals inevitably steers them—as if guided by the so-called invisible hand of self-interest—toward behavior that maximizes the benefit of the community as a whole:

> As every individual . . . endeavors as much as he can both to employ his capital in the support of domestic industry, and so to direct that industry that its produce may be of greatest value; every individual necessarily labours to render the annual revenue of the society as great as he can. He generally, indeed, neither intends to promote the public interest, nor knows how much he is promoting it. . . . He intends only his own gain, and he is in this, as in many other cases, led by an invisible hand to promote an end which was no part of his intention. Nor is it always the worse for society that it was not part of it. By pursuing his own interest he frequently promotes that of society more effectually than when he intends to promote it.[25]

Inherent in this logic is the assumption that because all individuals are best equipped to make production decisions concerning their own skills and circumstances, they will naturally specialize in the production of the good in which they have a competitive advantage. Applying the same principle to international trade, Smith thus contended that trade barriers limit not just the private benefits but the public benefits of the gains from trade that accrue to the nation as a whole.

The most elaborate expression of this gains-from-trade argument appeared in Ricardo's 1817 classic, *The Principles of Political Economy and Taxation*, written forty years after Smith's masterpiece and building considerably upon it. Ricardo's famous example of the gains to be achieved by trading British cloth for Portuguese wine remains a powerful statement of the liberal position for free trade.[26] He began with the supposition that the climates, lands, and skills of the people were different in England than in Portugal and that the requirements for successful production of goods such as wool and wine were thus better met in one than the other. Because of this combination of what Smith earlier had called "natural advantages" and "acquired advantages," England was an efficient producer of wool cloth and Portugal an efficient producer of wine. Ricardo observed that each had an advantage in the production of one of the two goods, which he expressed in the form of the amount of labor required to produce each good in each country.

The example displayed in Table 2.1 is in the spirit of Ricardo's original, though the numerical exposition has been simplified to ease the application. Suppose that given the climate, soil, and manufacturing capital available in England, a worker would be capable of producing either two yards of cloth or one gallon of wine per hour. Suppose further that a worker in Portugal could produce only a single yard of cloth but two gallons of wine in the same time. England would be said to have an **absolute advantage** in the production of cloth, and Portugal to possess an absolute advantage in the production of wine.

To see that trade between them would be profitable to both, consider the levels of production in the absence of trade, assuming that both countries chose to produce the same amount of cloth as wine. In England, 100 hours devoted to the production of cloth and 200 hours to the production of wine would produce 200 yards of cloth and 200 gallons of wine. In Portugal, that same production—200 units of each good—would require that 200 hours be devoted to cloth and only 100 to wine.

But suppose that each producer observed these relative advantages and chose to specialize in the production of only one good and to trade part of that production for the other. The English worker, specializing completely in cloth, could produce 600 units of cloth and the specialized Portuguese worker could produce 600 units of wine. If they then agreed to trade 300 units of one for 300 units of the other, each nation could consume 300 units of both goods, whereas in the absence of specialization

TABLE 2.1   Gains from Trade with Absolute Advantage

Production Possibilities			Productivity per Hour	
	Labor Hours		Wine	Cloth
England	300		1	2
Portugal	300		2	1

Without Trade	Hours X Productivity		Production		Consumption	
	Wine	Cloth	Wine	Cloth	Wine	Cloth
England	200 X 1	100 X 2	200	200	200	200
Portugal	100 X 2	200 X 1	200	200	200	200

After Trade	Hours X Productivity		Production		Consumption	
	Wine	Cloth	Wine	Cloth	Wine	Cloth
England		300 X 2		600	300	300
Portugal	300 X 2		600		300	300

and trade, each could consume only 200 units of each good. The gains from trade consist of the increased consumption made possible by each producer allocating his resources in the most efficient way.

But Ricardo saw beyond Smith's idea of absolute advantage, illustrated in Table 2.1. He observed that profitable trade could occur between the two countries even if the worker in one country was more efficient in the production of both goods than the worker in the other country. This idea, illustrated in Table 2.2, is Ricardo's enduring legacy to contemporary international trade theory: the theory of **comparative advantage**. Here, England is more efficient than Portugal in the production of both goods: An English worker can produce 3 units of wine and 6 units of cloth per hour, and the Portuguese worker's efficiency is the same as before—2 units of wine and 1 of cloth. Although England has an absolute advantage in the production of both goods, Portugal is said to have a comparative advantage in wine because its workers can produce more wine than cloth, and the reverse is true in England. As a result, trade can still be profitable.

In this example, without trade England would divide its 300 labor hours so as to produce (and consume) 600 units of both wine and cloth, while Portugal, with 600 labor hours in this case, would produce 400 units of each. With the prospect of trade in mind, however, England completely specializes in cloth—the product in which it holds a comparative (as well as an absolute) advantage—producing 1800 units. Portugal shifts all 600 of its labor hours to the production of wine—the product in which it holds a comparative (but not an absolute) advantage. Not only does

TABLE 2.2 Gains from Trade with Comparative Advantage

Production Possibilities		Productivity per Hour	
	Labor Hours	Wine	Cloth
England	300	3	6
Portugal	600	2	1

Without Trade	Hours X Productivity		Production		Consumption	
	Wine	Cloth	Wine	Cloth	Wine	Cloth
England	200 X 3	100 X 6	600	600	600	600
Portugal	200 X 2	400 X 1	400	400	400	400

After Trade	Hours X Productivity		Production		Consumption	
	Wine	Cloth	Wine	Cloth	Wine	Cloth
England		300 X 6	1800		700	1100
Portugal	600 X 2		1200		500	700

this represent a considerable increase above the total production without trade, it also permits the two nations to exchange 700 units of wine for 700 units of cloth. When they do so, each nation consumes more of both products after specialization and trade than when self-sufficient in both. Thus, we can see that trade can be profitable even if one country possesses an absolute advantage in both goods. (That does not mean that both nations profit equally, but assessing the relative gains requires far more sophisticated analytic tools than this example provides.)

This simple statement of the gains-from-trade argument remains the most vivid demonstration of Ricardo's theory of comparative advantage. And it is the theory of comparative advantage, itself merely a subset of the more general theory of economic liberalism, that gives such intellectual force to the drive for free trade. It is cited as frequently in the trade controversies of the late twentieth century as it was in the Corn Law debates more than a century and a half ago.

But the liberal argument for free trade is far from timeless: It depended for its force on particular historical developments of the modern age. For example, efficient allocation of resources among different economic sectors is not an idea that could arise in a relatively stagnant medieval economy with only one dominant sector. Similarly, it would have been imprudent to rely upon trade when transportation systems were technologically backward and politically fragile. But Ricardian theory is especially modern in its acceptance of a vision quite at odds with mercantilist ideas: that maximum aggregate consumption is the proper central goal of national policy. Economic liberals assume that national prosperity is the dominant element of the national interest and that it consists of the aggregated welfare of all the individuals that make up the nation. Welfare, in turn, is identical with consumption. Economic liberalism thus embraces a secular, materialist, individualistic conception of national welfare quite distinct from earlier emphases on a stable, organic, and collective social whole. It is implicitly far more attentive to the welfare of the masses than notions of national prosperity that emphasize the status of landowners or the power of the state. If it is not yet explicitly egalitarian or democratic, it uses a language that can more easily accommodate these more progressive ideas.

In another sense, too, liberalism was born to a moment: Although liberal theory had undeniable analytical merit, it was the changing balance of political power that was decisive in bringing about the demise of the Corn Laws.

THE POLITICAL CONFLICT OVER THE CORN LAWS

Indeed, Ricardo's brilliant theoretical ideas were translated into the free trade policies of the 1840s by somewhat surprising political forces. The trade policy preferences of various groups reflected their perceptions of the dilemmas of trade, but the resulting political alignments did not follow precisely the expectations one might derive from Ricardian theory. In particular, although liberal theory identifies the major beneficiaries of free trade as consumers, whose welfare improves when declining trade barriers allow the competition from imports to push prices down, the fight for free trade in grain was actually led by industrialists.

One reason, of course, is that industrialists were permitted to vote and the working class was not. Another was the special skill of the Anti–Corn Law League, which was headed by Richard Cobden and John Bright and centered among the manufacturing interests of Manchester. Through its influence on parliamentary leaders such as William Huskisson, William Pitt the Younger, and Sir John Peel, the Anti–Corn Law League was the principal architect of the drive for repeal from the end of the 1830s to eventual success in 1846. These industrial interests were motivated by both philosophical and practical considerations.

Philosophically, laissez-faire arrangements would give a great deal of freedom to capitalists, who were becoming increasingly restive with the government regulations that constrained their entrepreneurial behavior. Unlike mercantilism, which placed the state at the center of economic development, Smith's "invisible hand of self-interest" analogy made it clear that a sound economy must be propelled by the creative activities of the capitalist entrepreneur. In liberal theory, it is the private individual—not the government—who discovers comparative advantage, invests in the export sector, and engages in trade. Government's only role is to stay out of the way. Such a doctrine would obviously have enormous appeal to an entrepreneur, who not only welcomed the freedom from government control but no doubt appreciated that his profit-maximizing behavior—once castigated as the sin of avarice—could be portrayed as the act of a patriot.

Though liberal theory certainly held its intellectual attractions for industrialists, the repeal movement was largely motivated by practical opposition to the Corn Laws themselves. Hostility stemmed from the conviction that, whatever their original rationale, these laws had long since degenerated into simple import barriers designed to protect landowners. This conviction was justified: The provocative Corn Law of 1815 was openly designed to benefit the landed interests in utter disregard for its impact upon consumers. Unlike earlier versions dating back centuries, the 1815 law suspended all the restrictions on exports, which were designed to keep prices down, but imposed high tariffs on imports, which served to restrict grain supplies and drive prices up by keeping foreign grain out.

Capitalists feared that if grain-producing nations in Europe and America could not sell their products in England because of the Corn Laws, they would have no money to purchase English industrial products. They speculated that the repeal of the Corn Laws would stimulate demand abroad and that English manufacturers would benefit by capturing at least a portion of that expanding market. Following that logic, they also argued that nations unable to acquire British manufactures would launch industry of their own. Moreover, since British trade barriers would encourage them to erect retaliatory tariffs to protect these fledgling industries, such industries could eventually become global competitors. Repeal of the Corn Laws could avoid this scenario by encouraging other European nations to remain specialists in grain production in order to serve the English market.[27]

But it was the effect of food prices on the production costs of British industry that lay at the heart of both the theoretical debate and the political controversy. Capitalists argued that repeal of the Corn Laws would lower food prices because grain could be imported from Europe more cheaply than it could be grown at home. In turn, that meant that wages in British industry could be lowered—without diminishing the standard of living of workers. Finally, this lowering of wages would permit British manufacturers to be competitive with foreign firms, because the wage savings could be passed on to consumers. At the same time, of course, lower food prices meant that consumers would have more money to spend on the manufactured goods being produced by British industry. Capitalists thus expected to sell more products at home as well as abroad after the repeal of the Corn Laws.

The most obvious opposition to the Anti–Corn Law League, the landed gentry who benefitted directly from agricultural protection, were unmoved by the liberal arguments. Whatever the gains from trade might be, they certainly would not accrue to landowners, who would unequivocally lose in a free competition with cheaper grain producers in North America and Europe. Thus, the chief political battleground concerned two groups of workers with seemingly different interests: urban workers, apparently tied to the health of the manufacturing sector, and the peasantry, presumably tied to the sectoral interests of agriculture.

It is the latter group whose concerns were addressed most directly by Ricardian arguments, because the unique contribution of liberal theory lay in its response to the protectionists' contention that free trade would injure workers in agriculture, the previously protected sector of the economy. The liberal position, illustrated by the Ricardian example of wine and cloth, offered a rebuttal to concern for the fate of agricultural laborers if repeal of the Corn Laws brought about the expected demise of grain production in England. Although Ricardo granted that employment in the production of wine might indeed decline or even disappear altogether in Britain, he maintained that there was really nothing to fear, even for workers in the wine industry, because the decline in wine production would be accompanied by a compensating expansion of cloth production, so that total employment would remain the same.

Following Ricardo, liberals argued that the repeal of the Corn Laws would not decrease employment but only shift it from the inefficient agricultural sector to the manufacturing sector, in which England had a comparative advantage. Liberal theory insisted (as it still does) that it is far better to tolerate these short-term dislocations—these transition costs—than to protect an inefficient industry, because total national consumption will increase with a more efficient allocation of resources.[28] The liberal argument for the North American Free Trade Agreement was identical: U.S. workers losing their jobs to Mexican imports were expected to find employment in industries that export to Mexico.

How is this key argument generally received? Those likely to immediately gain from free trade—the British cloth industry in the Ricardian example and the manufacturing sector in the case of the Corn Laws—can be expected to grant the logic of the free trade argument. After all, those in the most competitive sector have much to gain *personally* and nothing to lose, even if the liberal contention about *national* welfare should turn out to be wrong. They will typically urge those who will immediately lose—agricultural workers or wine producers—to patiently wait for growing employment opportunities in the most competitive sector to trickle down to them.

But those who will immediately suffer the dislocation are more concerned with the distributional effects of free trade than with its aggregate effects. They are likely to be more skeptical of liberal theory, simply because for them the stakes are so much greater. And they will be as attentive to the short term as to the long term, worrying about how long and painful the transition may be even if the future is fully as bright as liberal theory promises. After all, it is far easier for a theorist to move a column of figures from "wine" to "cloth" than it is for a worker who has devoted his life to farming to pack up and move to a strange town in the hopes that he might find a job in an unfamiliar industry that requires skills he does not possess. He will not be persuaded by the liberal theorist's contention that his loss of income is temporary or that his loss of security and way of life is illusory because it can not be measured in terms of the aggregate consumption that defines "gains from trade." Skepticism that the dislocations to individuals are warranted by aggregate gains are given credence by modern analysis. Dani Rodrik noted that "in the standard models used by international economists, the distributional consequences of trade typically dwarf its net contribution to national income. Under typical parameters, lowering of a trade restriction will result in $5 or more of income being shuffled among different groups for every $1 of net gain."[29]

In the case of the Corn Laws, the natural opposition of agricultural workers to a removal of protection for their sector seems to have been overcome by three factors. First, they were cross-pressured by their dual roles as both workers and consumers; in the latter capacity they appeared to benefit from lower grain prices. Second, they were not convinced that the benefits of agricultural protection had been passed down from landowners to agricultural workers. The Anti–Corn Law League was especially effective in persuading much of the peasantry that higher grain prices enriched only landowners because higher prices enabled them to increase the land rents paid by peasants. Third, they were reasonably optimistic that job opportunities existed in the industrial sector for workers displaced from agriculture. Because British industry was by far the most productive in the world during this period, and its output was increasing rapidly, industrial employment opportunities were growing. It was possible for peasants to envision a relatively brief transition with a relatively small risk. Confidence in the future of the dominant economy and the dominant industries in the world made the Ricardian arguments seem plausible.

The industrial working class was ambivalent. On the one hand, it had little use for the landowners, and the fall in food prices expected from free trade would be very welcome. However, it trusted neither of the two principal protagonists in the debate; the motivations of the Anti–Corn

Law League in seeking lower food prices attracted particular suspicion. Supporters of the Corn Laws cited the "iron law of wages"—the contention that desperate unemployed workers always compete for scarce jobs by offering to work for lower wages until eventually wage rates fall to the subsistence level (that is, just high enough to keep workers alive). Thus, any decline in food prices brought about by repeal of the Corn Laws would lower the wages necessary to provide subsistence, but that would not benefit workers, because wage rates would be driven quickly to that new, lower level.

A placard posted in Manchester conveyed the essence of a position that would be at home in the debate over NAFTA: "Why do these liberal manufacturers bawl so lustily for the repeal of the corn laws?—because with the reduced price of corn they will be enabled to reduce the wages of working men so that they may compete with foreigners who live upon potatoes."[30] Because industrialists did portray lower prices as necessary to meet the competition of producers abroad, the motivation implied by the placard seems well founded. Certainly the sentiment it expresses has been widely shared by workers in more advanced countries: fear that their living standards will suffer when forced to compete with foreign workers whose wages seem to them indecently low. Indeed, after the repeal of the Corn Laws, identical reasoning underlay the rallying cry of protectionist forces in the United States: "Protection against the pauper labor of Europe."[31] Many even doubted that lower wages would be passed along in the form of lower, more internationally competitive prices for final goods; instead, they believed that lower wages would mean only greater profits for capitalists.

The capitalist leaders who led the drive for free trade were not viewed as friends of the working classes because of their strident opposition to acts such as a child-labor law, poor laws to provide relief to the unemployed, regulations to limit the workday, and the legalization of collective bargaining for wages. Particularly during the 1840s when the Anti–Corn Law League directly confronted the Chartists, a working-class organization that favored full manhood suffrage, worker antipathies to capitalists were somewhat greater than toward landowners. However, it appears that mass opinion marginally favored repeal of the Corn Laws by 1846.

It is by no means clear that the position of the working class was decisive, though it unquestionably had some impact, even in the absence of democratic representation. Nor had the capitalist class displaced the gentry in parliamentary membership.[32] However, even landed members of Parliament (MPs) had to respond to constituents whose interests were increasingly concentrated in industry and commerce, not agriculture. Agriculture had lost its political clout, because with the expansion of the manufacturing sector and the growth of towns, it ceased to be the driving force of the economy and the principal source of government revenue.

Still, the final repeal of the Corn Laws owes much to the power of the arguments themselves. In particular, opponents of the Corn Laws were able to counter two claims of fairness raised by protectionists in all debates over free trade, including those of the present era. The first questions the value of free trade policy in one nation when other nations do not reciprocate. The second challenges the validity of eliminating protection for some while retaining it for others.

Protectionists used the **reciprocity** argument to question the real benefits of *unilateral* free trade. Liberals assumed that repeal of the Corn Laws would bring an increase in both imports of grain and exports of manufactured goods, but Sir Henry Parnell's speech in the House of Commons in support of the 1815 bill noted that neither linkage would occur unless Britain's trade partners would reciprocate by emulating the free trade stance. Parnell thus argued for free trade only on the "supposition that all the nations of Europe should adopt the same common policy."[33]

This reciprocity objection is a common feature of all debates over free trade, but liberal economists are unanimous in finding it to be totally without merit because protection always hurts consumers by increasing the prices of imports. Thus, although Smith acknowledged that "revenge naturally dictates retaliation," he found the policy unwise: "It seems a bad method of compensating the injury done to certain classes of our people to do another injury ourselves, not only to those classes, but to almost all the other classes."[34]

The sole exception to the principle that retaliation is self-defeating is the allowance that temporary measures designed to induce others to eliminate the objectionable barriers may be justified. On how far in this direction it may be safe to go, sage judgment cannot be found in the analytical ability of the economist, said Smith, but in "the skill of that insidious and crafty animal, vulgarly called a statesman or politician."[35]

The second fairness contention challenges the validity of eliminating protection for some sectors while retaining it for others. Observing that the very manufacturing interests that led the opposition to agricultural protection were heavily protected by tariffs themselves, Parnell challenged them directly: "If all those who are concerned in manufactures and commerce will consent to adopt the system of a perfect free trade, those who are now advocates for restraints on the importation of corn will willingly abandon on their part all claim to any such protection."[36] This point had a powerful internal logic and made a compelling appeal to fairness. In 1815, it carried the day: Because manufacturing interests were unwilling to give up the protection afforded by tariffs on industrial imports, agricultural interests refused to abandon agricultural tariffs.

The first step in breaking this deadlock was taken in the Petition of the Merchants of London, drafted by Thomas Tooke and presented to the House of Commons in 1820 by Alexander Baring. It called for an end to all protectionist measures (allowing, however, for customs duties necessary for government revenue), citing precisely the inevitability of the line of reasoning used by Parnell. Indeed, it went farther, noting that if British producers could be protected from foreign ones, the same argument could be made for each county and that free trade even within Britain would cease. Further, it observed that British protectionist measures were used as an example by other nations; until Britain embraced free trade, neither would others. Thus, Tooke's analysis engaged both of Parnell's objections and paved the way for the gradual dismantling of the protectionist structure of British commercial policy that occurred over the following three decades.

Explanations for Early Trade Policies

Early Mercantilism	Nineteenth-Century Liberalism
1. State of theory	
Religious and communitarian ethical theory assumed that to achieve the public interest in just prices required state interference in markets.	Materialist, individualist, and utilitarian ethical theory; economic theory emphasizes that comparative advantage enables free trade to increase the consumption of all nations.
2. State of markets	
Thin markets made prices volatile; unstable political relations made trade uncertain; and English producers feared foreign competition.	Lower transportation costs and reduced political risks make potential gains from trade large; technological improvements made English industry dominant over foreign competition.
3. Political power balances	
Parliament was dominated by the Crown, the church, and especially landowners.	Parliament increasingly influenced by industrial and urban interests.

CONCLUSION: THE TRIUMPH OF FREE TRADE

Modest movement toward free trade in industry was launched by the commercial treaty with France of 1786—which eliminated many prohibitions and prohibitory duties—but it accelerated dramatically after 1820. In 1824, the export of native wool was permitted after centuries of prohibition designed to protect the domestic textile industries. In 1825, the duty on foreign cloth was reduced from 50 percent to 15 percent. In 1842, all complete prohibitions were removed and duties on raw materials were reduced to 5 percent, on partially manufactured articles to 12 percent, and on fully manufactured goods to 20 percent. In 1846, the latter was lowered to 10 percent and the textile industries (except silk) ceased to be protected at all. During the same period, the Navigation Acts, which protected British shipping, were weakened in 1815, 1822, and 1825, before being finally eliminated in 1849. Agricultural protection in Britain ended in 1846 with the repeal of the Corn Laws.

THREE

□ □ □

The Politics of Protectionism

The repeal of the Corn Laws in 1846 symbolized the abandonment of mercantilism and the advent of the golden age of British free trade. Although by no means constituting complete free trade, British trade policy became the closest approximation to it that the world had yet seen.[1] The British example also contributed to the general decline of protectionism that occurred throughout Europe during the middle of the nineteenth century.[2] But from our historical vantage point, we can see that this change was neither complete nor permanent; instead, it was only one phase of the continuous cycle in which trade policy oscillates between relatively free and relatively protectionist.

CYCLES OF GLOBAL MERCANTILISM AND LIBERALISM

By the last quarter of the nineteenth century, the pendulum was already moving the other way, and during the 1930s, Britain was carried with the rest of the globe into a frenzy of protectionism that reduced global trade by two-thirds, with average tariff rates reaching 45 percent, not far from their peak prior to 1820. The cycle began again after World War II with a global movement back toward free trade led by the United States. Signs that mercantilist sentiment is again gaining strength have appeared since the late 1980s, but trade levels have continued to rise, fueled by explosive growth in the export-oriented economies of Asia that are the subject of Chapter 7. Indeed, by the end of the twentieth century, international trade and investment have reached a level that leads many liberals to celebrate the death of mercantilism and conclude that globalization is irreversible. They would do well to recall that the historical record casts doubt on any judgment of permanent resolution of the dilemmas of trade.

In this chapter, I seek to explain the cyclical pattern seen so far by returning to the central analytic question of why nations select the foreign

economic policies they do. The case of the decline of British liberalism in
the late nineteenth and early twentieth century is an especially intriguing
one because, for the most part, nineteenth-century free trade delivered on
the promises of liberal theory. With barriers to trade rapidly declining,
trade volume increased and total economic output grew with it. Despite
the dire predictions of landowners during the Corn Laws debate, even
English agriculture thrived until the 1880s. In part, this prosperity was a
tribute to the magic of the market celebrated by liberal theory: English
agriculture, facing foreign competition, became more efficient, especially
through the application of agricultural science and mechanization.[3] But
eventually the expected flood of imports did undermine English agriculture. By 1892, British importation of wheat and flour had grown to nearly
ten times its volume in 1846, constituting nearly three-quarters of domestic consumption.[4] As grain prices fell, English landowners shifted land
out of agricultural production and the volume of English arable land diminished by almost half.

Thus, exactly as predicted by liberal theory, free trade brought about an
economic restructuring based on comparative advantage. Britain ceased
to be self-sufficient in food as the comparative advantage of American
farmers derived from superior factor endowments (richer farmland) dictated the shift of English production away from agriculture. Meanwhile,
Britain experienced a rise in the production and export of the manufactured goods in which it had a comparative advantage by virtue of its
abundant capital endowment and its technical superiority over foreign
manufacturers.

But if the claims of liberal theory were validated by the growth of the
British economy, the doubts of protectionists persisted and, indeed, eventually emerged triumphant again. The tensions between mercantilism
and liberalism cannot be resolved by the temporary victory of one over
the other because neither can satisfy the objections implicit in the dilemmas of trade. In fact, the cyclical character of these alterations are rooted
in the excesses of each approach: As policy moves toward the pure form
of either mercantilism or liberalism, trade dilemmas become more starkly
perceived and inevitably draw a reaction that reverses the sweep of the
pendulum.

At the core of these policy reversals are changes in economic conditions, political forces, and social ideas, all of which influence how the
dilemmas of trade are perceived by different groups and different nations. In the following sections, the retreat from pure liberalism in Britain
is explained in terms that provide the lessons needed to understand contemporary instances of the competition between free trade and protectionism. First, the triumph of laissez-faire ideas brought a theoretical and
political reaction that sharpened the confrontation between the alterna-

tive values underlying mercantilism and liberalism. Second, the very economic development engendered in part by liberalism transformed the political power balance in Britain by reconstituting its class composition and governmental structure. The resulting political landscape contains the basic forces that compete for control over trade policy in the advanced industrial democracies of our own era. Third, the rapidly growing global economy altered the power balance among nations, thus changing attitudes toward trade in ways remarkably similar to the shifts we see at the end of the twentieth century.

THE REACTION TO LAISSEZ-FAIRE

Even while free trade emerged in the middle of the nineteenth century, key parts of the edifice that supported it were already crumbling. In particular, the leading theoretical challengers to the doctrine of economic liberalism were being born at almost the same instant that the repeal of the Corn Laws in 1846 signaled its highest triumph. The greatest of the neomercantilist works, *The National System of Political Economy*, was written in 1841 by Friedrich List (1789–1846). Karl Marx's (1818–1883) influential critique of liberal capitalism, which first appeared in *The Communist Manifesto* in 1848, was the forerunner of modern socialism.[5] Both reflected the reemergence of trade dilemmas, in the form of skepticism about the distributional consequences and the ethical basis of markets.[6]

The triumph of free trade in the nineteenth century followed from social and economic theories claiming that markets produced economically efficient and ethically acceptable outcomes. However, by the twentieth century, the limitation of markets and the ethical, social, and political dilemmas they produced were coming into ever sharper focus. At the forefront was the continuing development of the factory system that emerged from the Industrial Revolution.

Early in its evolution, there was little regulation of the industrial production process, especially with regard to the treatment of labor. It became apparent, however, that total reliance upon the market and total absence of governmental regulation had severe social ramifications. An excess supply of labor, signaled by high unemployment rates, drove wages near or beneath subsistence levels in conformity with the theoretical **iron law of wages**. Even factory laborers who worked twelve- to sixteen-hour days in miserable working conditions frequently lived in poverty. The market forces that held down wage rates were given free rein by labor laws highly favorable to capitalists, especially the notorious Combination Acts of 1799. These laws made it illegal for workers to act together in pursuit of economic interests: Trade unions were banned, strikes were outlawed, even holding meetings among workers was prohibited.

In this atmosphere, supply and demand for labor yielded abhorrent outcomes that undermined the legitimacy of the market. The exploitation of labor, including children, was rampant. Unregulated until 1819, the child-labor practices of that era were widely condemned, though they are a more grievous affront to modern sensibilities than to the standards of that age. The child-labor law of 1819, which was strongly opposed by capitalist interests, prohibited children eight and under from employment in cotton mills and limited those between nine and sixteen to twelve-hour days. Even after these prohibitions, children thirteen and under represented about 15 percent of the workforce in cotton and wool mills and nearly 30 percent in silk mills. In unregulated industries (that is, all but textiles), children as young as five or six years of age were frequently employed, sometimes as many as sixteen hours a day.[7] Women were not restricted to a twelve-hour day until 1844, and working hours for adult men were not regulated until 1908.[8]

These were the conditions that bred attempts to formulate an alternative ethic to that of the unbridled market. With the eclipse of an ethical theory rooted in medieval religious thought, workers sought an alternative source of protection from the vagaries of labor markets and the avarice of capitalists. They found it in the form of government regulation driven by increasing political power for the working class and informed by an economic and social theory—socialism—whose vision of economic life directly opposed that of economic liberalism.

Socialist ideas ranged from those of Robert Owen and Karl Marx to more moderate attempts to find a balance between the state and the market. The latter find expression in the British Labour Party and the various social democratic parties of Western Europe, which ushered in the mixed economy familiar to the twentieth century. Perhaps Joseph Chamberlain, a turn-of-the-century British cabinet member, put best the evolving understanding of the role of government and its place in regulating the market: "Government is the only organization of the whole people for the benefit of all its members; and the community may and ought to provide for all its members benefits which it is impossible for individuals to provide by their solitary and separate efforts."[9] It is no coincidence that Chamberlain was a leading figure in the movement to abandon free trade: Doubts about the legitimacy and efficacy of markets in the domestic sphere could not help but weaken the case for reliance upon markets in the conduct of international trade.

Similar concerns about the propensities of unregulated markets to yield undesirable outcomes, especially in labor markets, haunt less developed nations today. Horrible working conditions among unskilled workers in poor countries are often ascribed to the competitive pressures of international trade. However, the absence of government regulation of domestic markets, especially in nondemocratic political systems, clearly plays a major role as well, because most developed nations are at least as open to international trade without suffering these same excesses. The theoretical lesson is that free trade is difficult to evaluate in a vacuum because its effects are not universal and invariant, but rather vary from one nation to another. In fact, the post–World War II Western European experience— where the welfare state grew in step with the expansion of international trade—suggests a fundamental contradiction in the prescription of liberal theory: To achieve a balanced resolution of the value and distributional dilemmas, *free* markets in international trade may well require *regulated* markets in the domestic economy.

The reaction against laissez-faire was not based solely on normative considerations, of course. The experience with unbridled capitalism, particularly during economic downturns, had also eroded faith in the efficiency of markets. Alternative economic theories, most notably the market-interventionist views of John Maynard Keynes, challenged liberalism as an article of faith. His argument on behalf of an enhanced role for government spending to restore equilibrium and full employment has been influential in many countries, including the United States, since the 1930s. He also favored tariffs, international cartels, and state trading, all anathema to liberal theory.

THE RISE OF THE WORKING CLASS AND POLITICAL DEMOCRACY

Of course, social and economic ideas attain practical importance only when tied to political forces that can bring them into play. In the case of the reaction against markets in general and free international trade in particular, the catalyst was a growing, partially organized working class within the context of an evolving democratic political system.

An important consequence of the Industrial Revolution was the creation of a new and self-conscious social class, that of industrial labor. Because the increased scale of production led to the demise of the artisan and apprenticeship system and because the decline of agriculture limited employment possibilities in the rural sector, workers became completely reliant upon the market for industrial labor. The political arrangements of the period were such that the labor market was rigged in favor of business: Owners were permitted to collude in order to hold wages down, but workers could not organize to push them up. Together with the poor working conditions and generally low wages, this situation led workers to a feeling of alienation from capitalists and solidarity with labor. The result was a growing trade union movement that eventually was to transform the political structure of society. The act of 1825, which legalized trade unions solely for the purpose of regulating hours and wages, was the beginning of a steady advance in the power of organized labor and a broadening of the political role of trade unions.

These developments occurred within the context of a political system that was slowly moving toward modern democracy through the expansion of the franchise. Controversies over the right to vote extend back at least to the Reform Bill of 1832, which broadened suffrage somewhat to encompass much of the growing capitalist middle class.[10] Nonetheless, working-class support was critical to passage of the reform bill, as workers became persuaded that parliamentary reform would weaken the legislative stranglehold of the wealthy minority of landed interests. As anticipated, this reform did eventually aid the repeal of the Corn Laws. Many had also hoped that the reform bill would be a stepping-stone to their own enfranchisement. Although progress was slow, the working class did eventually achieve the franchise, with the first step being the doubling of the electorate from about 1 million to 2 million via the Reform Bill of 1867, sponsored by Benjamin Disraeli, head of the landed-gentry wing of the Conservative Party. In 1884, rural workers were added to the electorate, again doubling its size. In 1918, universal suffrage was finally granted to males over the age of twenty-one and females over the age of thirty. In 1928, that age gap was removed.

By the early twentieth century, these twin developments—the emergence of political democracy and the growth of labor unions—had come together to institutionalize political representation for the working class. The Labour Party was formed in 1900 by representatives of labor unions in concert with a group of intellectuals known as Fabian socialists. The latter included the noted writers George Bernard Shaw and H. G. Wells. By 1906, Labour had won fifty seats in Parliament and was well on its way to becoming one of two dominant political parties. Together with the declining political importance of landowners that resulted from the declining economic importance of agriculture, this development marked the beginning of a new era in British politics. The sectoral cleavage between industry and agriculture receded in importance, and the British political system came to be defined by the cleavage that is the mark of all modern political economies: a party of the right self-defined as pro-business and a party of the left self-defined as pro-labor.[11] It is tempting to define the resulting right to left continuum on politico-economic issues as lying between the extremes of complete trust in the market and complete trust in the state. Although this perspective contains some truth, it is a dangerous oversimplification, particularly concerning trade policy, because labor has sometimes been committed to free trade and business has sometimes preferred protectionism.[12] However, the growth of democracy and increasing power for the working classes certainly ensured that national policies would respond more vigorously to the perspectives of labor on the distributional dilemma than they had a century earlier. In any case, from this time forward, distributional issues centering on class—especially unemployment as an economic problem—were as prominent in trade policy debates as those centering on economic sectors or geographic regions.

This is not to say that capitalists and workers were always in disagreement over trade policy. To the contrary, it is precisely their broad agreement in Britain until World War I that sustained free trade. Furthermore, the successful movement toward liberalizing trade in Europe after World War II was also the product of agreement between business and labor, this time as part of an implicit bargain in which both could expect to be rescued from the vagaries of trade by a Keynesian welfare state. Businesses were mollified by an activist state that could counteract the most disruptive consequences of trade by using demand management techniques like counter-cyclical spending that would prevent the economy from succumbing to externally generated crises. A more powerful and ambitious state was also a helpful partner in forging competitiveness and profitability for a nation's firms, motivated by the recognition that in an open economy the national interest was promoted by success in international trade. For labor, a welfare state offered a social safety net to insulate workers from the employment insecurity implicit in relying upon the ever changing condition of international markets. Unemployment insurance and other generous welfare benefits eased the pain of adjustment when the restructuring of the economy in accord with comparative advantage entailed job loss. Liberated from this most dire concern about foreign competition, workers were more easily persuaded by liberal arguments about the long-term aggregate benefits from freer trade.

Of course, no state policy can eliminate the fundamental dilemmas of trade nor erase the political controversy over alternative responses to them. After all, to perform these tasks, the Keynesian **welfare state** requires high levels of revenue—on average nearly 50 percent of GNP in Western Europe—which necessitate high levels of taxation that please no one. This resolution of the values dilemma sacrifices higher disposable income for greater security and reduced inequality, a trade-off that surely appeals more to some than others. This resolution of the distributional dilemma also shifts income from many segments of society to recipients of state aid, never a noncontroversial action. Indeed, in the United States, where different value priorities and a different distribution of political power shapes policy, the state plays a much smaller role in ameliorating the impact of international trade.

Still, even this happy, if limited, coincidence of interests depends centrally upon the existence of a state that can be trusted to play its role in protecting the interests of both capital and labor. The impartiality of such a state, in turn, depends upon a rough balance in the political power of these two groups within a political system that grants each a voice in shaping government policy. These conditions did not exist prior to the emergence of political democracy and working class representation in Western Europe near the middle of the twentieth century. They do not exist today in the Third World. Thus, the relative political power of capital and labor continue to determine the shape of trade policy whenever conditions in international markets cast them into opposition to one another. Then their mutual opposition stems from the different stake that capital and labor have in trade. These distributional effects of trade can be seen with clarity only in the context of modern international trade theory, a topic to which I now turn.

MODERN ELABORATIONS OF LIBERAL TRADE THEORY

Since Smith and Ricardo, liberal theory has consistently advocated free trade, but its foundation has been elaborated and strengthened by subsequent theorists, especially Eli Heckscher and Bertil Ohlin, two Swedish economists of the 1930s. The Heckscher-Ohlin theory, abbreviated H-O or sometimes H-O-S to acknowledge the role of the American Nobel Prize winning economist Paul Samuelson in advancing it, is important here for two reasons. First, it reinforces free trade doctrine by specifying the precise economic conditions that constitute the sources of comparative advantage. In so doing, H-O clearly accepts the liberal tenet that governmental intervention is not required to steer the market to the gains from trade. Second, and more immediately, H-O leads directly to the Stolper-Samuelson theorem (explained further on), which exposes the class basis of the distributional effects of free trade. These distributional effects help to explain why contemporary controversies over trade policy, such as the debate on NAFTA, tend to follow a characteristic pattern in which some classes and sectors prefer free trade while others prefer protectionism.

Ohlin's classic work *Interregional and International Trade* remained squarely in the liberal tradition, but it advanced Ricardo's analysis by specifying in greater detail the sources of national comparative advantage. In the context of a simple economy, the early formulations of Smith and Ricardo were understandably rudimentary: They emphasized natural advantages such as climate or soil quality and acquired advantages such as specialized skills in weaving or metalworking. Ohlin went beyond these simple ideas to argue that a nation's comparative advantage lies in the relative abundance of some **factors of production** and the relative scarcity of others.

To reach this conclusion, he began by improving upon the simple labor theory of value that Ricardo used to demonstrate the gains from trade. Whereas Ricardo described the differences in the productive efficiency of a nation's industry solely in terms of the amount of labor required to produce any given level of output, Ohlin noted that production actually requires at least three factors of production: land, labor, and capital. All products require some quantity of each factor, but the proportion of each varies widely depending on the nature of the product and the processes used to produce it. For example, agricultural goods require large amounts of land (thus, they are dubbed land-intensive); heavy manufactures such as autos are considered capital-intensive because they require such large quantities of expensive plant and equipment; and light manufactures involving simple assembly or processing are labor-intensive because they rely on large numbers of unskilled workers. Ohlin claimed that differences in the factor intensity of various products would determine where they could be produced most efficiently.

Just as products differed in their factor intensities, Ohlin also observed that different nations possessed vastly different factor endowments. In the modern era, for example, capital is relatively abundant in the developed countries (such as the United States, Japan, and Western Europe), land is abundant in countries such as Canada and Australia, and unskilled labor is abundant in countries such as Mexico and the poorer nations of East Asia. Ohlin further reasoned that production of goods that used intensively any particular factor would naturally be more efficient in nations that possessed a relative abundance of that factor. Thus, land-abundant nations, for example, will have a comparative advantage in land-intensive products and capital-abundant nations will have a comparative advantage in capital-intensive products.

This theory of factor proportions and factor intensity perfectly explained Ricardo's classic example of British specialization in manufactured goods and Portuguese specialization in wine. Britain, with abundant supplies of capital, had a comparative advantage in the production of capital-intensive products, and Portugal, with its abundance of good land for the growing of grapes, had a comparative advantage in wine. Moreover, Ohlin's theory had broader application because it could be used to identify which nations would have a comparative advantage in which products: *Each nation has a comparative advantage in the production of those goods that use intensively the factor they possess in relative abundance.* It also was in accord with simple observations of the trade patterns among nations: Developed countries tend to export capital-intensive products while they import food from land-abundant countries and simple manufactures from labor-abundant countries.[13]

At the heart of this theory is the interaction between markets for final goods and the markets for the factors required for their production (land, labor, and capital). For example, in nations where labor is relatively abundant and land relatively scarce, the surplus supply of labor will cause wage rates to be relatively low, and the short supply of land will cause land rents to be relatively high. That is precisely why labor-intensive products are cheapest to produce in nations with an abundance of labor.

For our purposes, the consequences of trade are as important as its causes, and in this respect the contribution of H-O to understanding the interaction between goods and factor markets also is significant. That is because the distributional effects of international trade depend directly on how trade affects the supply of and demand for the various factors of production.

THE DISTRIBUTIONAL DILEMMA: THE IMPACT OF TRADE ON CLASS

To see how factor markets shape the distributional effects of trade, let us return to Britain at the time of the Corn Laws and stipulate that it is relatively abundant in capital and relatively scarce in land. That would imply that capital should be relatively cheap and easy to acquire in Britain and that land would be relatively expensive. If that is so, Ohlin would expect that Britain would be a relatively efficient producer of capital-intensive products such as manufactures but a relatively inefficient producer of land-intensive products such as grain. That seems to accord with the historical record of what happened when Britain adopted free trade: It became an importer of (land-intensive) grain and an exporter of (capital-intensive) manufactured products. Britain's food imports came largely from the United States, Canada, and Australia, all of which were abundantly endowed with land. Its manufactured exports went to nations with a relatively poor endowment of capital, including the land-abundant grain exporters.

But what were the effects of free trade on factor markets? The answer defines the distributional effects of free trade. We know that free trade led to the expansion of British manufacturing. That expansion required a considerable increase in investment in plant and equipment, which in turn increased the demand for capital. The owners of capital found that greater demand enabled them to charge a higher interest rate to manufacturers who wished to borrow capital to expand their facilities. That is, the increase in the production of capital-intensive products increased the return on capital. This result can be stated more generally as the first half of the Stolper-Samuelson theorem: *Free trade benefits the owners of the abundant factor of production.*

At the same time, the repeal of the Corn Laws caused domestic production of grains to decline in the face of foreign competition and the lower grain prices it engendered. With grain production less profitable in Britain, British landowners had to lower the rents charged to farmers to use their land; otherwise those farmers could not compete with foreign imports. British landowners, owners of the scarce factor of production, lost from free trade. Thus, the second half of the Stolper-Samuelson theorem: *Free trade harms the owners of the scarce factor of production.*

The political corollary to Stolper-Samuelson is now simply seen: Owners of the abundant factor of production will prefer free trade; owners of the scarce factor of production will oppose it. Because of this, debates over free trade frequently involve class divisions, and in a political system with class-based parties—that is, all modern advanced industrial democracies—trade policy frequently becomes a highly partisan issue.

THE DISTRIBUTIONAL POLITICS OF TRADE POLICY

We can now state more clearly the distributional dilemma of trade and the resulting political patterns that emerge in the debate over trade policy. These distributional effects—that some groups gain from free trade while others lose—can be described along three lines: economic sectors, socioeconomic classes, and producers versus consumers.[14]

Those sectors of the economy that rely upon exports will ordinarily favor free trade, especially if the firms involved are relatively efficient by international standards. Those sectors of the economy that compete against foreign imports will ordinarily favor protectionism, especially if the domestic firms are relatively inefficient. Sectors of the economy that utilize imports or import substitutes will, like any ordinary consumer, favor free trade because it is likely to lower their costs.

How individuals will react to these sectoral effects can be difficult to predict. Liberals urge most workers to ignore these considerations because they contend that any factor of production—including labor—that can no longer find productive employment in a sector damaged by free trade can simply shift to a sector that benefits from it. Protectionist sentiments arise from concerns about the costs and uncertainties involved in these sectoral transitions. For some, the transition costs are exorbitant because their highly specialized skills are adapted to a particular sector. Few middle-aged steelworkers are also skilled computer programmers, for example. Others find that personal circumstances such as the employment of a spouse or reliance upon family reduce geographic mobility. Nearly all will face temporary unemployment. Many may be averse to the risk that is inherent in predicting the uncertain future course of comparative advantage.

For example, at one time England was a low-cost producer of grains, though by the time of the last Corn Law its comparative advantage had shifted elsewhere. An alert worker, observing this shift, might well question where and when the next change might take place. Indeed, by the middle of the nineteenth century, the comparative advantage in textile production, the earliest and largest of the English manufacturing industries, was also beginning to shift away from England. Thus, protectionism can be comforting to workers who, though currently employed in a competitive industry, fear that they may be next to be displaced. This risk element helps explain why protectionism can be sustained politically even when it appears to benefit so few and harm so many. This argument carries even more weight in the modern era of more rapidly changing comparative advantage.

However, Stolper-Samuelson suggests that both these views, liberal and protectionist, will remain incomplete so long as they focus on the sectoral composition of the economy. Instead, a class perspective may be more appropriate because trade policy affects the owners of different factors of production very differently: Free trade benefits owners of the abundant resource and harms owners of the scarce resource. For example, since the United States is capital-abundant and labor-scarce relative to the rest of the world, Stolper-Samuelson predicts that wage rates for unskilled labor will decline under free trade just as the profit rates for capital will increase. This explains why American labor unions opposed NAFTA and protested the expansion of the WTO, whereas multinational corporations supported both.

Predicting the responses of individuals is further complicated because workers are also consumers—and their interests in these roles are often contradictory. Liberal trade theory emphasizes that consumers benefit from free trade because they can purchase goods more cheaply from those countries that have a comparative advantage than from inefficient domestic producers. From this vantage point, one would expect that consumers would be a major actor in the distributional politics of trade policy; indeed, they should be the strongest advocates of free trade. In fact, they usually are not.

There are several reasons consumers are seldom effective advocates of free trade. First, the costs of protectionism are ordinarily difficult for consumers to see because the trade barriers that affect the prices of foreign goods are not easily visible. Readers are invited to test this proposition for themselves: Can you identify the tariff rate presently imposed on *any* product by the United States?

Second, even if tariff costs were precisely known, they are seldom large enough to motivate any single consumer. For example, trade barriers in the textile and clothing industries are among the highest in any sector of the U.S. economy, yet they probably increase the price of clothing in the United States by under $100 per person per year.[15] Is this impact on your personal budget enough to persuade you to hire a Washington lobbyist to overturn the Multi-Fiber Agreement (MFA), which sustains these trade barriers?

Third, because those hurt by protection are geographically diffused and only marginally affected by trade legislation, they are unlikely to organize effectively to press for free trade. By contrast, because those who benefit from protection tend to be geographically concentrated and intensely affected by trade legislation, they are much more likely to organize effectively and use their political influence to achieve protection. For example, the Multi-Fiber Agreement provides $22 billion in benefits to U.S. domestic firms that employ more than 2 million American workers. Those firms and their employees have far greater motivation and opportunity to lobby in favor of protectionist trade policies than consumers have to oppose them.

All of these factors are commonly present in debates over trade policy, and they help explain why consumers were not in the forefront of the drive for repeal of the Corn Laws. However, for several reasons, consumers were actually a stronger force in opposition to the Corn Laws than is common in trade policy controversies, a fact that helps explain both why free trade achieved a rare triumph in 1846 in Britain and why it later faded.

Because the free trade issue was fought out over food, the welfare effects of the Corn Laws were much more visible than is usual for protectionist legislation. Since food occupied the largest share of the budget in most households and since imports constituted a significant share of food consumption, citizens were unusually attentive to the factors that influenced the price of imports. Thus one key to the emergence of free trade in England at this time is the unusually visible effect of the Corn Laws on an unusually large share of the population. Because the stakes were so large, so immediate, and relevant to so many, political action was easy to organize.

By the twentieth century, trade policy debates in Britain ceased to revolve around food prices, so consumers ceased to be a major factor in them. In most modern developed democracies, class-based political parties have been the major protagonists in the battle between free trade and protectionism. In most of those battles, the outcome is driven by the condition of markets, especially the relative efficiency of domestic and foreign producers.

THE EFFECTS OF MARKET DOMINANCE AND DECLINE

When an industry is confident that it is able to compete effectively against foreign manufacturers, it typically advocates free trade. An industry in doubt about its competitiveness seeks protection or subsidy. Workers ordinarily follow the lead of the industry in which they are employed; other citizens usually follow the industry dominant in their region. Thus it is for nations in aggregate: Liberal policies will suffice when a favorable balance of trade can be maintained without actions that encourage exports and discourage imports. Protection is the preferred policy when balance-of-trade difficulties signal declining competitiveness. That pattern was perfectly manifested in the period we have been considering.

Until the middle of the eighteenth century, the productive efficiency of British industry was not superior to that of its continental competitors. Indeed, in some important areas it lagged behind such early leaders as the Dutch. As we have seen, the government responded as early as the sixteenth century by encouraging the growth of key industries with a variety of subsidies, legal monopolies, and trade restrictions. Moreover, English manufacturers who lacked *economic* advantages over foreign competitors generally supported the measures that gave them *political* advantages: the colonial system, the Navigation Acts, and the great trading companies that monopolized trade with the colonies; the import barriers that enabled them to develop infant industries; and the restrictions on exports of raw materials, technology, and skills designed to retard the development of competitors abroad.

However, the technological advances of the Industrial Revolution came a generation earlier to England (circa 1760) than to its continental competitors, giving British producers a natural competitive edge against others by the early nineteenth century. When English manufacturers became confident of their ability to compete successfully with foreigners on economic terms alone, they gave up their own tariff protection in exchange for the repeal of the Corn Laws.

Thus, it is no surprise that free trade was adopted more completely and for a longer period in Britain, the dominant economic power, than in any other nation: Competitive industries do not need protection, so the governments that represent them oppose it. Still, even Britain encountered protectionist movements during economic downturns (first the Fair Trade movement of the 1870s and then the Tariff Reform crusade of 1903), but unlike the less competitive nations of Europe, it retained its free trade orientation. The Great Depression of 1873–1896 produced increasing protectionism throughout Europe as nations sought to defend employment and profits, especially against the competition of the British. Thus in the 1920s, Britain still maintained among the lowest tariff barriers in the world. By the end of the 1930s, however, when the end of Britain's economic dominance left it unable to resist the global move toward protectionism, Britain had become as protectionist as any.

In the twentieth century this pattern remains clearly visible: The economically dominant nation advocates free trade, but challengers opt for mercantilism. Immediately after World War II, the United States, by then the most productive and cost-efficient economy in the world, took up from the British the mantle of the leading champion of free trade. Both Japan and most of Europe, recovering from the war, adopted a sharply mercantilist stance.

By the 1990s, the positions had changed again. The policy of the United States, whose share of world exports declined from 45 percent in 1950 to under 15 percent in 1997, has become increasingly protectionist (though its rhetoric remains mostly liberal). Moreover, the United States assumes very different stances with respect to different sectors of the economy. It is protectionist in declining heavy industries such as steel and automobiles in which it no longer enjoys a comparative advantage but adopts a very liberal position in those areas in which America still dominates, such as technology, services, and intellectual property.

Theorists have long contended that a policy of free trade may be beneficial for dominant nations but harmful for others. For example, List countered free trade doctrine on the grounds known to posterity as the infant-industry argument. It states that an industry in its early stages requires protection against its better-established foreign competitors. Only after it has benefitted from a protected domestic market can it achieve the maturity, efficiency, and **economies of scale** necessary to withstand foreign competition. Premature free trade will doom an economy to specializing only in those products the dominant power may choose to ignore, presumably because they offer little profit or limited growth opportunity.

List urged France to avoid free trade and the specialization in wine that would result from it. Because he doubted that wine production could fuel broad and diversified economic development, he instead advocated the creation of new French industries, even though they would require tariff protection against established British firms until they matured. He noted that centuries earlier Elizabethan England had similarly emphasized developing infant industries in order to augment its agriculture and had similarly protected them. From our vantage point in the early twenty-first century, we can add to the list of nations opting for this approach. A nearly identical choice faced the Japanese in the American-dominated post–World War II period. They too rejected free trade—and the specialization in textiles, their comparative advantage at the time, that it would have implied. Instead, Japan elected the mercantilist path of protecting the fledgling firms in its electronics and automobile industries.

Indeed, this gap between the rhetoric of the dominant nation and the self-interest of its challengers has produced more than a little bitterness. For example, in this passage, List wrote powerfully in defense of the proposition that free trade is the policy of the dominant power and protection is the policy of the challenger:[16]

> It is a vulgar rule of prudence for him who has reached the pinnacle of power to cast down the ladder by which he mounted that others may not follow. In this lies the secret of Adam Smith's theory, . . . as well as all of his successors in the government of Great Britain. A nation which by protective duties and maritime restrictions has built up a manufacturing industry and a merchant marine to such a point of strength and power as not to fear the competition of any other, can pursue no safer policy than to thrust aside the means of elevation, to preach to other nations the advantages of free trade, and to utter loud expressions of repentance for having walked hitherto in the way of error, and for having come so lately to the knowledge of the truth.

Although considerations of relative efficiency suggest that nations will choose quite different trade policies, specific historical events will often cause nations to respond more similarly. Indeed, both the dramatic collapse of trade in the 1930s and the rise of liberal trade in the 1940s were global phenomena.

TRADE AND THE GREAT DEPRESSION

The collapse of the global economy during the 1930s affirmed an important lesson: Liberal theorists advocate free trade even if a nation must adopt it unilaterally, but its greatest benefits can occur only if liberalism is practiced by all nations. The experience of the Great Depression reveals both an economic and a political reason for this.

The economic reason stems from the simple fact that one nation's exports must constitute another nation's imports. Since no nation can export unless another imports, free trade cannot be fully effective unless all nations approximate this ideal at the same time.

Parnell's role in the Corn Law debates also suggests a political reason that unilateral free trade policies are very difficult to enact: They impose painful adjustments that will be strongly resisted without assurance that other nations are experiencing similar disruptions. This demand for reciprocity is partly a natural psychological reaction against **free riders** who enjoy the open markets of others but refuse to open their own. After all, no nation wants to be taken advantage of any more than individuals do. Moreover, the cost of adjusting to free trade will exceed the benefits unless a substantial expansion of trade results, which cannot occur unless other nations reciprocate.

As a result, both free trade and protectionism usually occur as global processes. One dominant nation that champions free trade can sometimes induce others to follow suit, as happened under the leadership of Britain in the middle of the nineteenth century and again under the leadership of the United States after World War II. But when one nation moves sharply toward protectionism, others also tend to follow—sometimes with disastrous consequences. That is exactly what happened during a sequence of events that led to the collapse of world trade during the Great Depression of the 1930s. And that is why, in the mid-1990s, some feared a trade war between the United States and Japan.

Though protectionist sentiment had familiar domestic roots, international politics fanned its flames after World War I. British protectionism focused on accusations that Germany was undermining its rivals by **dumping** iron and steel. Britain claimed that German steel companies were using unfair trading practices to drive British steel firms out of business. Coming soon after the war and in an industry critical to war planning, these claims received greater credence than now appears to be justified by the facts.[17] British tariffs were also motivated by the need to grant imperial preferences to members of the British Empire, which presupposes tariffs from which the empire would be exempted. In all countries, tariffs were said to be useful in strengthening the nation's bargaining position in dealing with other nations who practiced—or threatened—protectionism.[18]

These national security and reciprocity aspects of the state goals dilemma produced a spiral of protectionism with competitiveness issues at its base. Initially, severe unemployment triggered political pressures in several countries to save jobs, but the extreme protectionism that resulted had two dire consequences. First, it exacerbated the economic downturn itself by sharply reducing the gains from trade. Second, it goaded nations to increase their own protectionist policies in retaliation. European protectionism against the onslaught of competitive American firms had been building for years; the Smoot-Hawley Tariff, enacted by the United States in 1930, overwhelmed the last supporters of liberalism even in Britain.

After Smoot-Hawley, more than sixty nations retaliated directly against the United States.[19] The resulting global trade war produced a spiral of retaliation that cut trade further, and the political relations between nations continued to deteriorate. In 1930, 85 percent of goods had entered Britain free of duty, but by April 1932 only about 30 percent did so. Meanwhile, the average tariff level had reached 45 percent in the United States, 41 percent in Germany, 38 percent in France, and up to 70 percent elsewhere in Europe.[20] By 1935, 70 percent of global trade also was subject to **nontariff barriers** (NTBs), mostly quotas.[21] In just three years global trade plummeted by 70 percent. The Great Depression and the global trade war fed on one another to produce the most devastating economic chaos of modern times.

Unemployment reached 22 percent in Britain and more than 30 percent elsewhere in Europe, America, and Asia. However, the consequences were not just economic. Unemployment exceeding 40 percent in Germany fueled the growth of Nazism, which in turn led to the outbreak of World War II.[22] Diminishing trade prospects strengthened militarism in Japan, which was already building toward a second locus of the coming global war. As economies nosedived, more than half of the republics of South America experienced revolts in 1930 or 1931. When unemployment in the United States grew from around 5 percent to more than 36 percent between 1928 and 1932, the popular vote for the Communist and Socialist Parties tripled. With unemployment constantly over 25 percent for nearly a decade—before the advent of unemployment insurance and other welfare programs to ease the burden—both the marriage rate and the birth rate declined by 25 percent in the United States.[23]

It must be emphasized that the Great Depression was not caused by protectionism: Many forces conspired to make the global economy of the

---

Why Liberalism Was Overturned by the 1930s

1. State of theory

Government intervention was justified by socialist theory (because markets produce unethical outcomes) and Keynesian theory (to relieve unemployment).

2. State of markets

Even English producers feared foreign competition; market intervention by other governments brought retaliation.

3. Political power balances

Domestically, organized labor achieved power through democracy; globally, there was no dominant nation to lead.

1920s vulnerable to a serious contraction.[24] Neither did global protectionism begin in the late 1920s: In fact, it had been on the rise for half a century. But protectionism did reach a frenzied peak at the onset of the 1930s, and the Great Depression was certainly deepened by the protection-inspired trade wars that followed.[25] Moreover, these events—the Great Depression, World War II, and the collapse of global trade—became so indelibly linked in the minds of policymakers in the 1940s that they created the **Bretton Woods** system, discussed in Chapter 4, in order to prevent a recurrence.[26] Their recent experience with depression and war made economic prosperity and international peace more compelling than alternative values such as national autonomy, employment security, and distributional considerations, which in other times had inclined nations toward mercantilism. Furthermore, ascendant liberal theory suggested that these values would be best achieved by practicing liberalism. As a result, they were frightened into constructing an international trade system built more upon multilateral liberalism than unilateral mercantilism.

CONCLUSION: THE SOURCES OF POLICY CYCLES

Classical mercantile trade policy evolved in response to existing conditions in the economy and foreign affairs, in tune with prevailing currents of social and economic theory, and in recognition of the realities of the distribution of power. By the middle of the nineteenth century, these foundations had crumbled—and liberalism was erected on the ruins. The process was repeated a century later when the chaotic protectionism of the 1930s yielded to the American-led liberal system of the 1940s and beyond.

It is striking that the two great liberal movements in modern times were both a response to the worst excesses of protectionism. It was the extreme and irresponsible Corn Law of 1815 that spawned a liberal reaction against the agricultural protection that had been sustained for centuries. Similarly, Bretton Woods was the product of **beggar-thy-neighbor** protectionism enacted in the 1930s as part of a mad drive to retain employment in desperate circumstances. It is doubtful whether a less radical protectionism could have so thoroughly discredited mercantilism, which in its sober, classical form had been well rooted in established values and consistent practice. Nor would a less severe implosion of the global system have generated the same enthusiasm for the supranational solution created at Bretton Woods.

Of course, liberal policies are no more immune to changes in prevailing theories and values, conditions in markets, and domestic and international power balances than was classical mercantilism. Indeed, just as mercantilism's inherent liabilities are most apparent when the state thoroughly dominates the market, liberalism is especially vulnerable when the market threatens to overwhelm the political functions of the state. Thus, liberalism was swept away in the 1930s when trade levels had reached historic highs, only to reemerge in altered form after World War II. After half a century of growth, trade has now surpassed those levels. Will the pendulum continue its swing?

FOUR

□　□　□

The International Politics of Trade

The discussion thus far has emphasized the domestic factors that influence the choice of trade policy by nations, especially the degree to which free trade is tempered by elements of protectionism and export promotion. The choice among these three strategies inevitably highlights the distributional and values dilemmas, most notably the extent to which nations pursue the liberal goal of maximizing aggregate consumption at the expense of alternative values such as equality and security. However, most contemporary trade issues also involve elements of the fourth strategy identified in Chapter 1, the effort to forge conditions abroad conducive to expanding exports.

At the center of those foreign policy efforts are the international institutions designed to facilitate trade, without which no national policy is likely to be very successful. But these institutions inevitably pose a dilemma concerning state goals because they prohibit members from adopting policies thought to negatively affect other members. This limitation on national autonomy may be necessary to secure the benefits of trade, but it is also strongly resisted as an intrusion on state sovereignty. The operating principles of these institutions must be understood because many contemporary trade issues concern the dilemmas embodied in them, most notably the 1999 "Battle of Seattle" in which protesters disrupted the most recent round of World Trade Organization (WTO) talks.

THE ORIGINS OF BRETTON WOODS

The foundation of the postwar international economic system was laid in July 1944 at a meeting of Allied ministers in Bretton Woods, New Hampshire. The institutions created there remain at the core of the global economy today: the International Monetary Fund (IMF), **the International Bank for Reconstruction and Development** (IBRD, but known as the

World Bank), and the General Agreement on Tariffs and Trade (GATT). They are collectively known as the Bretton Woods institutions, even though the GATT was actually created two years later to replace the abortive **International Trade Organization** (ITO) that was originally designed as the third leg of the liberal order. The legal document now referred to as GATT 1947 remains the basis of international law with respect to trade, though it has been much amended and extended, most recently in 1994. The ad hoc international organization which grew up around the GATT has been replaced by the World Trade Organization (WTO), a broader institution that commenced operation on January 1, 1995.

To appreciate the role that these institutions play today, we must return to the principles that motivated the architects of the Bretton Woods system. We will see that the foundations of Bretton Woods were laid directly over the fault lines between liberalism and mercantilism—and between the alternative responses to trade dilemmas advocated by different nations. Today's trade policy disputes are the surface rumblings of these older seismic forces.

The resolution of trade dilemmas embodied in Bretton Woods was profoundly shaped by the Great Depression and World War II. With respect to the values dilemma, these events made economic growth and global peace the twin values sought most ardently by policymakers, priorities most visible in the design of the GATT. By discrediting protectionism, they also strengthened liberal theory as a model of how to structure economic relations in order to achieve these values. With respect to the state goals dilemma, the disastrous state of the global economy—especially the collapse of trade markets—contributed to the belief that the international system required greater management along liberal lines, even if it meant sacrificing some national sovereignty. It also convinced policymakers everywhere that a prosperous national economy required a level of trade that would be impossible without a well-designed international monetary system, a conviction that underlies the birth of the IMF. Finally, World War II left the United States as the dominant global power, capable of mobilizing other nations to create such a global system and willing to provide the leadership required to make it a success. In short, the prevailing state of theory and values, the condition of markets, and the balance of power among actors produced Bretton Woods. Created in the wake of the most protectionist period in the modern era, it led to the most open global trading order the world had yet seen. Though it remained an amalgam of liberal and mercantilist responses to trade dilemmas, Bretton Woods was tilted quite heavily in a liberal direction.

Efforts to move the global economy back toward higher trade levels began with **bilateral** approaches in both Britain and the United States. However, because of protectionist pressures on national governments, it was widely acknowledged that free trade required powerful international institutions to ensure global cooperation and sustain stable financial arrangements. It was equally obvious that such a system would require leadership that could be provided only by a single dominant nation, called a **hegemon**. **Hegemonic stability theory** posited as the requisites of a world leader attributes possessed only by the United States: economic size, military might, political power, ascribed status, and the political will to lead.

HEGEMONIC STABILITY THEORY AND AMERICAN GLOBAL LEADERSHIP

The central tenet of hegemonic stability theory is that cycles of global liberalism and protectionism coincide with cycles of hegemonic leadership and decline.[1] As a hegemonic power is in its ascendancy, it pushes the system toward greater liberalism, but as it declines the system tends to revert to regionalism and protection.

Indeed, nineteenth-century free trade was initiated by the championing of liberal principles by Great Britain, tentatively in the 1820s and decisively with the repeal of the Corn Laws in the 1840s. Britain's leadership, which rested on its increasingly dominant economic and military power, contributed to global liberalization in several ways. British diplomacy induced movements toward liberalism in Europe through a series of bilateral agreements, beginning with the Cobden-Chevalier Treaty of 1860, which freed trade between Britain and France. Britain's success led other nations to emulate its open economy. Britain's open market for their goods, especially continental grains, encouraged growth in their exports. Finally, Britain provided the financing that would facilitate trade: Sterling became an accepted medium of exchange and the City of London offered extensive credit.

By the early twentieth century, however, the relative decline of British power eliminated the hegemon that had enforced the rules of global liberalism. The theory of hegemonic stability predicted the result: The system slipped slowly into protectionism and regionalism, then rapidly and violently into instability, depression, chaos, and war. A liberal system could not reemerge until championed by another ascending hegemon, a role played by the United States in fashioning the Bretton Woods system after World War II.[2] By that time the United States was three times larger than its nearest rival in total production, with twice the per capita income and trade volume of the next nation and seven times greater foreign investment flows than its nearest rival. In conformity with the central tenet of hegemonic stability theory, the United States assumed the mantle of global leadership, championing Bretton Woods in the 1940s and sustaining liberalism through the 1960s. Since the early 1970s, however, American dominance has declined, and as predicted by the theory, both mercantilism and regionalism have reemerged to challenge the expansion of global liberalism.

A global liberal regime backed by hegemonic leadership is needed to overcome the natural inclination of most nations to retain their own trade barriers while inducing other countries to lower theirs. Such a **free rider** can take advantage of open markets elsewhere to expand exports but avoid the painful (if ultimately beneficial) adjustment to import competition. Even though all nations would benefit from global free trade, very few will adopt it unilaterally without assurance of reciprocity. To break this logjam requires a hegemon to take the lead and induce other nations to follow. The hegemonic nation will usually have to subsidize the organizational costs and also offer recalcitrant nations a more favorable deal than strict reciprocity would require. In fact, a hegemon frequently offers side benefits in exchange for cooperation in creating an international regime, such as the massive infusion of foreign aid provided to Europe by the United States under the **Marshall Plan** in the late 1940s.

American hegemonic leadership was especially critical in this period because conditions were not favorable for free trade in most major trading nations. In particular, depression-depleted and war-ravaged Europe could not be optimistic about its competitiveness, especially vis-à-vis the United States. Nor were the free-trade tenets of liberalism unchallenged. One dissent emerged from within liberal theory itself. Known today as the **optimum tariff** argument, it shows that a tariff can sometimes improve national income by forcing foreign producers to lower their export prices.[3] However, this benefit, which comes at the expense of trading partners, accrues only to countries whose large market gives them leverage on total global demand. Following Keynes's influential analysis, many also contended that protectionism could "export unemployment," contrary to the assumption of full employment used by Ricardo to generate the gains from comparative advantage. Together these arguments refuted the free traders' contention that the gains from protectionism were illusory, a position strengthened by recent analyses suggesting that British protectionism actually benefitted the British economy. Moreover, government control over trade was a logical corollary to then prevailing sentiment in Europe, which favored government supervision of the domestic economy, especially during its transition from a wartime orientation to a peacetime equilibrium.

Furthermore, although prosperity and peace were dominant values in the post-Depression, postwar world, two devastating wars within twenty-five years also inspired a desire for national security and autonomy. Europe feared economic dependence on the United States, particularly because of the widely held view that the Great Depression had been caused by poor management of the American economy. Since another U.S. recession would also spill over into other economies, Europeans insisted that the ITO include a full-employment mandate to prevent the contractionary policies to which the United States seemed prone. Thus, together with the ever present distributional implications of trade policies, these dilemmas ensured that global liberalism would face opposition.

However, several factors unique to the era made it easier for the United States to foster agreement. Most significantly, Europe was unusually susceptible to the side benefits that a global hegemon could offer. It badly needed the American market for its exports, American capital to rebuild its infrastructure, American dollars to finance trade and investment, and American military protection in the chaotic world of the 1940s. As a result of such undeniable dependence, European nations had little choice but to resolve the dilemma over national autonomy by accepting the constraints on its economic policies inherent in membership in the Bretton Woods institutions. The presence of the Soviet Union as a military threat and global communism as an ideological threat reinforced the common interests of Western nations. Not only would Bretton Woods strengthen Western forces against the Soviet Union by promoting rapid recovery and cementing closer ties, it would also reduce the appeal of communism at the same time that it highlighted the attraction of democracy, capitalism, and alliance with the United States. A final factor was especially conducive to founding a liberal regime—the conviction that **multilateral liberalism** and the resulting **interdependence** would lead to peace.

LIBERAL INTERDEPENDENCE AND PEACE

Policymakers saw several ways that an institutionalized liberal trading system could promote peace among nations. The growth of global institutions could weaken the hold of nationalism and mediate conflict between nations. Trade-induced contact could break down nationalistic hostility among societies. **Multilateralism,** since it involves **nondiscrimination,** would tend to prevent grievances from developing among states. Interdependence could constrain armed conflict and foster stability. The economic growth generated by trade could remove the desperation that leads nations to aggression.

Despite previous American indifference to international economic cooperation, this promise of peace inspired the United States to assume economic leadership and motivated Europe to follow it.[4] President Franklin Roosevelt's secretary of state, Cordell Hull, held an extraordinary belief in the efficacy of free trade as a guarantor of peace, largely because he ascribed to trade disputes a major role in promoting conflict. This view has been neatly summarized by the slogan, "If goods can't cross borders, soldiers will." As early as 1916, Hull even went so far as to contend that bitter trade rivalries were the chief cause of World War I. Though few historians would accord them such importance, economic tensions were certainly present: Between 1890 and 1914, tariff wars erupted between Switzerland and France, between Italy and France, between Germany and Spain, between Germany and Canada, between Germany and Russia, and between Russia and the United States.

Each was precipitated by discriminatory trade policies in which different quotas or duties were imposed on the products of different nations. Trade barriers became tools of foreign policy rather than economic policy. Preferences offered to one nation but not to others (i.e., positive discrimination) were used to create spheres of influence, as Germany did before World War I; to build empires, as Japan and Italy did in the 1930s; and to reinforce existing colonial ties, as Britain and France had done for years. Negative discrimination directed against particular nations was useful as an element of statecraft, but it created commercial rivalries and exacerbated national tensions. Such politicized trade could lead to tariff wars, but Hull believed that free multilateral trade would build bridges rather than create chasms between peoples and nations. As Harry Hawkins, Hull's deputy, said in 1944, "Nations which are economic enemies are not likely to be political friends for long."[5]

Indeed, even as late as 1938 Hull apparently believed that war could be prevented by negotiating a trade agreement with Nazi Germany. The Axis powers contended that discriminatory trading arrangements restricted their ability to export on equal terms, and because they were therefore unable to earn the **foreign exchange** necessary to purchase raw materials, they were forced to go to war to secure access to them. Thus, Hull championed the nondiscrimination principle, which had also been contained in the third of President Wilson's Fourteen Points for promoting peace at the end of World War I. In fact, because Hull's vision of the postwar order emphasized nondiscrimination in trading arrangements even more than expansion of trade volumes, multilateralism became the cornerstone of the GATT.

By contrast, the British valued free trade more than nondiscrimination, arguing that tariff reduction produced economic growth and that prosperity encouraged peace. Certainly interwar Europe illustrated that mercantilism could lead to economic failure, which in turn could generate dangerous levels of domestic instability. Such instability could foster antidemocratic and anticapitalist forces, as witnessed by the rapid rise of one-party governments throughout Europe in the early 1930s. Some of these governments were committed to economic and political programs—Nazism in Germany, fascism in Italy—that were bound to threaten international peace.

Liberals also borrowed an argument that had been developed a century earlier by Ricardo: that extensive trade among nations created a powerful incentive to avoid war that would disrupt it. Proponents of the Corn Laws had cautioned that to rely upon others for key commodities would compromise the autonomy of the nation's foreign policy, especially because one could not threaten war against nations that supplied essential food. Ricardo noted, however, that if free trade created a permanent need for England to import grain, then other nations would permanently arrange to produce a surplus to meet that demand. Eventually, England's reliance upon trade for consumption would be balanced by the other nation's dependence upon trade for export revenues, jobs, and profits. Therefore, domestic interests would exert enormous pressure on both governments to maintain friendly relations. Since then, interdependence theorists have used this argument to claim that free trade contributes as much to national security as self-sufficiency does.

For a combination of these reasons, policymakers in many nations came to share the view, expressed by President Roosevelt in a 1945 address to Congress, that an open trading system was necessary to make "the economic foundations of peace . . . as secure as the political foundations."

THE IDEALS AND INSTITUTIONS OF
THE BRETTON WOODS SYSTEM

Specific historical factors sharpened the appeal of liberalism by accentuating the values of economic growth and international peace that liberalism emphasizes. Because the primary threats to those values—instability, protectionism, and discrimination—emanated from uncoordinated national policies, the Bretton Woods institutions were created to impose on national governments a liberal discipline they were incapable of achieving on their own. That is, each nation agreed to some loss of national autonomy in exchange for limitations on those policies of other nations that were most harmful to them. Each institution was designed to prevent one of the three forms of beggar-thy-neighbor policies that abounded in the 1930s: tariff barriers (GATT), competitive exchange-rate devaluations (IMF), and capital controls (IBRD). Although a liberal trading order was the paramount objective of Bretton Woods, mercantilist concerns never disappeared, and as a result, the tensions and discontinuities embodied in these two visions became imbedded in the system itself.

THE PRINCIPLES OF GATT/WTO

The Bretton Woods conference envisioned an International Trade Organization that would facilitate negotiations to reduce trade barriers, govern trade
between negotiating sessions, and resolve other trade disputes. However,
its aggressive quest for trade expansion, which went well beyond dismantling direct trade barriers such as tariffs and quotas, brought it into conflict
with other national goals.[6] For example, the ITO charter called on nations
to maintain full employment policies, on the grounds that higher incomes
would result in higher trade levels. But powerful opposition, especially in
the United States, viewed this provision as a violation of national sovereignty, arguing that each nation should be free to choose its own domestic
economic policy. In America, this issue aroused great passion, and not only
because opponents feared that full employment policies would fuel inflation more than growth. They were also convinced that such Keynesian
policies were a product of European beliefs influenced by socialist values.
Thus, though the ITO charter was adopted at the United Nations Conference on Trade and Employment in Havana in 1948, it was never ratified in
either the United States or Britain, the two chief negotiators.

Because the ITO was never created, the GATT organization, originally
set up as a temporary secretariat to facilitate global tariff-reduction negotiations, assumed a somewhat larger role. Still, its principal activity was
the facilitation and supervision of a series of "rounds" of multilateral negotiations to reduce trade barriers, beginning with the 1947 Geneva negotiations, involving 23 countries. By 1949, the GATT had 33 signatories and
governed four-fifths of global trade. By August 1999, the WTO had 135
members, which together account for more than 90 percent of world
trade. Thirty others were in the process of negotiating accession, or entry,
among them China, Chinese Taipei (Taiwan), Saudi Arabia, Vietnam, and
several former Soviet republics, including the Russian Federation.

The ultimate goals of GATT/WTO are classically liberal—the expansion of trade and the maintenance of a trading system free of political
conflict—but the means used to accomplish them reveals an underlying
philosophy that contains both liberal and mercantilist assumptions. After
all, if nations accepted the liberal proposition that unilateral reduction of
trade barriers is beneficial regardless of the policies of trading partners,
negotiations would hardly be necessary. In fact, in contrast to the nineteenth-century British stance, the Bretton Woods philosophy assumes that
beggar-thy-neighbor trade barriers can sometimes benefit a nation more
than unilateral free trade, especially by exporting unemployment. This
possibility was seen as especially significant because the high unemployment experienced by all nations in the 1930s left policymakers wary of the
simple Ricardian models that assumed full employment. It also left them

unwilling to adopt free trade without some assurance that the expansion of exports would boost their employment as much as the growth of imports would erode it. Indeed, policymakers have come to think of employment growth as a more significant embodiment of the gains from trade expected of liberalism than lower import prices.

Thus, under the GATT/WTO, any nation that lowers an import barrier is deemed to have made a "concession," because reduced protection risks the loss of jobs and profits in that sector. That concession produces a benefit to other nations that can seize this export opportunity to expand production. Negotiations are necessary to induce one nation to grant concessions to others. The actual negotiating procedures were not laid out in the initial agreements and have varied considerably in the various rounds of negotiations.[7] However achieved, the negotiations must meet two basic principles of GATT—**nondiscrimination** and **reciprocity**—while allowing exceptions for the third basic principle, the freedom to retain certain **national safeguards**.

In theory, reciprocity is exceedingly simple: Each nation is expected to offer concessions equivalent to the benefits it derives from the concessions of others. For example, each nation's tariff reductions are expected to generate the same export revenue for other nations as the first will enjoy from the tariff reductions of others. There are at least two major drawbacks to bilateral bargaining under the reciprocity principle, however.

First, it would not permit tariff reductions when trade patterns were "triangular." Suppose, for example, that Barbados exported sugar to the United States but not to Britain (because of shipping costs), that the United States exported computers to Britain but not to Barbados (because the demand was small), and that Britain exported autos to Barbados but not to the United States (because the steering wheel is on the "wrong" side). In such a circumstance, bilateral bargaining would fail because, although the United States would be willing to lower its tariff against sugar from Barbados, Barbados would have nothing to offer to the United States in return. Likewise, Britain would be willing to increase its imports of American computers in return for equivalent concessions by the United States, but in this example, it sells nothing in the United States.

Second, bilateral bargaining would lead to as many tariff schedules for each product as there were trading partners. The United States would charge one duty for Haitian sugar, another for Jamaican sugar, and a third for sugar from Barbados—with the rate calibrated to the concessions offered by each. This complex system would invite deception by misrepresenting a product's origin or even by transshipping it through a third party to secure the lowest possible duty. Moreover, it would violate the liberal precept that a product should be exported by the most efficient producer—not the best negotiator.

Still, if the only goal had been to increase trade, such a system would have been workable. However, there was a more fundamental objection to it: Charging different duties to different nations constitutes discrimination—and that would inevitably politicize trade. Recall that the nondiscrimination principle was crucial to Hull's vision of a trading order that engendered peaceful political relations as well as efficient economic relations. Indeed, the importance of this principle may be gleaned from its location at the very beginning of the GATT, where it is embodied in Article 1's most-favored-nation (MFN) clause: "Any advantage, favor, privilege or immunity granted by any contracting party to any product originating in or destined for any other country shall be accorded immediately and unconditionally to the like product originating or destined for the territory of all other contracting parties." In other words, each signatory nation of GATT is prohibited from discriminating against any other signatory—either positively or negatively—by maintaining different trade barriers for different countries.[8] Similar provisions had been contained in all American treaties negotiated bilaterally since 1934 and most treaties negotiated by European nations since 1860.

This system has undeniable appeal, but it considerably complicates the negotiation process. If a single tariff schedule applied to all trading partners, strictly bilateral negotiations could not be very effective because any concession granted to one nation would automatically be enjoyed by all the others as well. In effect, a nation would have an incentive to free ride by refusing to offer concessions that would meet its reciprocity obligations, because under the nondiscrimination principle it would still be able to benefit from the concessions granted by others. By contrast, without the nondiscrimination principle, reciprocity would be self-enforcing in the sense that nations unwilling to offer concessions would find themselves unable to achieve access to the markets of other nations. Though this free-rider problem never completely disappears, the unconditional MFN principle has been retained, in part because a certain degree of free riding has been considered preferable to enduring the economic costs and political consequences of discrimination. Since the hegemon is usually the principal victim of free riding, it can exercise either its tolerance or its power to mitigate the problem. Furthermore, various negotiating arrangements have been found to reduce the severity of free riding.

In the first five GATT rounds (Geneva, 1947; Annecy, 1949; Torquay, 1950–1951; Geneva, 1955–1956; and the Dillon Round in Geneva, 1960–1961), bargaining began with a series of bilateral negotiations using the principal-supplier rule to identify the parties to a negotiation. That is, each pair of nations would exchange requests for item-by-item tariff reductions on those products for which each was a principal supplier of the other. Each pair would then negotiate an agreement that achieved bilateral reciprocity by granting equivalent concessions to each side. Of course, because these tariff reductions would become available to all nations under the MFN clause, no nation could accurately assess the balance of concessions and benefits until all the preliminary agreements involving all pairs of nations had been concluded. At that point, the preliminary agreements would be amended through multilateral negotiations to take account of the indirect benefits received by each nation from the generalization of the bilateral agreements reached by other parties. This approach was adequate for the initial round in 1947, which achieved large nominal cuts (about 20 percent, covering about 78 percent of total imports), because many 1930s-era tariffs were too high to serve any real protectionist purpose and nations were thus willing to give them up easily.[9] However, the next four rounds produced very small gains (2–3 percent each, covering products that made up only about 10 percent of global trade) because the item-by-item approach permitted domestic interests to rally support for protection. The principal-supplier method resulted in a relatively low incidence of free riding, however. A nation that attempted to free ride usually found that tariffs on its leading exports remained high because other nations were not willing to offer concessions in exchange for benefits that they would share with a free rider. The last three rounds (the Kennedy Round, 1962–1967; the Tokyo Round, 1973–1979; and the Uruguay Round, 1986–1994) successfully used a formula approach that began with an across-the-board cut followed by negotiations of item-by-item exceptions.

Operating under the nondiscrimination and reciprocity principles, these negotiations achieved major declines in trade barriers within many product categories, but they yielded much less progress in the products exported by most poor nations. In particular, barriers to trade in textiles and tropical agricultural goods remained high, because the nations possessing comparative advantages in these products were too weak to force them onto the negotiating agenda. Most poor nations found it difficult to meet the obligation of reciprocity, since opening their relatively small markets offered minimal export opportunities for rich nations. As a result, rich nations felt little pressure to reduce tariffs on those products, instead concentrating their attention on the demands of nations who had more to offer in exchange. Thus, poor nations assailed the non-discrimination principle as a sham that used liberal rhetoric to disguise the role played by power politics in the institutional foundation of international trade.

Indeed, Bretton Woods is far from a pure free trade system. After all, the very definition of import liberalization as a concession under GATT's reciprocity principle is a mercantilist, not a liberal, conception. Furthermore, old tariff barriers remain because complex negotiations to remove them take time, and new **nontariff barriers (NTBs)** have arisen in recent years. Moreover, significant antiliberal features—exceptions to the nondiscrimination and reciprocity principles—were built into Bretton Woods from the outset.

In fact, the GATT contains so many of these escape clauses that they may be said to collectively constitute a safeguard principle, which acknowledges that certain national interests are so essential that no international agreement could—or should—prevent nations from defending them. Thus, GATT accommodated these deviations from liberal principles because few nations could have accepted the agreement without such assurances. Three of these provisions are especially striking—though none has much import today—because they permit behavior that was central to classical British mercantilism. Under the grandfather clause of Article 1, paragraph 2, the British were permitted to retain the imperial preferences of the old British Empire. In extreme **balance-of-payments** deficit situations, Article 14 allows non-tariff barriers (which otherwise would violate Article 11's prohibition of import quotas), even discriminatory ones (which would otherwise violate the MFN clause).[10] Under Article 21, a nation may take any action it "considers necessary for the protection of its essential security interests . . . in time of war or other emergency in international relations."

A more important exception to the nondiscrimination provision is found in Article 24, which permits regional tariff preference areas such as the European Union and the North American Free Trade Agreement. A member of such a regional organization may apply a tariff schedule more favorable than the most-favored-nation rate to other member countries, but these discriminatory arrangements must meet three conditions to be considered GATT-legal. First, they must lower barriers inside the region rather than raise those outside it. Second, they must be completed over a "reasonable amount of time." Third, they must cover "substantially all" products. Although no regional arrangement has ever fully met these standards, all have been tacitly permitted.

Other escape clauses include Article 19, which permits nations to "suspend the obligation [of the GATT] in whole or in part"—that is, they may reduce or delay tariff reductions—if imports threaten domestic industries with "serious injury." Nations invoking this clause must offer equivalent compensation to affected parties, who are free to take retaliatory measures if they do not.[11] Under Article 35, a member need not recognize GATT obligations toward new contracting parties, a provision originally included at India's request in anticipation of South African entry but used by fifteen nations upon the accession of Japan in 1955. Finally, Article 25 authorizes the contracting parties, on a two-thirds vote, to grant waivers of GATT obligations "in exceptional circumstances not elsewhere provided."

The sum of these exceptions compose a significant mercantilist element within a structure that is ostensibly liberal. Indeed, business interests in the United States opposed the Havana Charter in part because they felt that these provisions would have made the agreement "a step away from, not toward, the goal of multilateral trade."[12]

THE FINANCIAL INSTITUTIONS OF THE BRETTON WOODS SYSTEM

The financial institutions of Bretton Woods—the IMF and IBRD—were designed to facilitate this new trading order. To do so, they had to resolve the problems that led to a disintegration of the international monetary order of the interwar years, which in turn contributed greatly to the collapse of trade. For our purposes, the most significant difficulty concerned the inability of nations to finance trade through the easy conversion of their currencies into acceptable media of exchange, especially during periods when trade deficits were relatively large.[13]

Conventionally, economists divide the challenge of maintaining an adequate international financial system into three interrelated problems: **liquidity**, adjustment, and confidence. In order to finance trade, the international financial system must provide a medium of exchange, that is, some "liquid" asset that traders will accept as money. Without such liquidity, private actors could exchange goods only through barter. National currencies do not provide a complete solution, since firms resist accepting payments in a foreign currency unless assured that it can be easily converted into the currency in which they conduct most of their business.

Ordinarily, the central banks of individual nations provide this assurance—and thus facilitate trade—by exchanging national currencies for one another. However, they are willing to perform this exchange function only if they have enough confidence in the values of these currencies to hold sufficient stocks of them. Just like private firms, central banks are reluctant to accumulate foreign exchange unless they are assured that it is liquid, that is, that it can be easily exchanged at a reliable and predictable price. Unless the system provides some basis for this confidence, banks will not maintain a large enough inventory of currencies to provide the liquidity necessary to accommodate a large volume of trade.

From 1870 to 1914, the mechanism that solved these two problems was the **gold standard**; central banks accepted gold as the ultimate liquid asset and individual national governments guaranteed a fixed conversion rate between gold and their national currency. Since each nation maintained a reserve of gold to back its currency—each nation's central bank agreed to exchange its currency for gold at a fixed price—the system worked well to facilitate trade and investment transactions. In fact, so long as the supply of gold was adequate and confidence was high that national monetary authorities would redeem currency for gold as promised, even temporary trade deficits presented no problem because excess currencies would be willingly held by national treasuries, central banks, and even commercial banks and other firms. Any successful system must tolerate such temporary imbalances, because it is inevitable that levels of imports and exports will fluctuate in the short term as prices and other economic conditions change.

Of course, there are limits to the confidence one can have in national monetary authorities and thus limits to the tolerance for disequilibrium. These limits are a function of the size of the deficits that are accumulating, the size of the gold reserves nations maintain to settle those deficits, and the ability of national governments to adjust their economies in the event that it becomes evident that those deficits result from long-term rather than short-term factors. For example, if a nation's exports continually lag behind its imports—presumably because its production is not competitive with firms in other countries—it has available three methods of adjustment. First, it may lower the price at which it agrees to exchange its currency for gold. This devaluation of the exchange rate makes it more expensive to purchase foreign currency and therefore foreign products, so imports should decline. Devaluation also makes a nation's own currency cheaper for others to purchase, so its exports should grow. Second, a nation may erect barriers to inflows of goods (imports) and outflows of capital (foreign investment). Third, it may contract the domestic economy so that citizens have less money to spend and consequently purchase fewer imports. In all three cases, a new equilibrium should be reached in which imports and exports once again balance each other. Confidence in the system is better maintained if trade stability causes disequilibria to be temporary and small, if liquidity is high enough to make adjustment relatively rare, and if a hegemonic actor can force countries to adjust responsibly when adjustment becomes necessary. During the period of British hegemony, the latter role was played effectively by a combination of the political power of the British government and the economic power of the City of London, whose banks controlled a large portion of the world's gold supply and influenced a still larger portion of the capital available for investment and loans.

Responsible adjustment is important to the system because any form of adjustment by one nation is inevitably disruptive to all others. Rapid or massive exchange-rate adjustments undermine the predictability of transactions and discourage trade. Devaluations especially arouse the ire of foreigners who are holding a currency when its value declines—and makes them wary of holding it in the future. Other nations are also resentful of any form of adjustment that shifts competitiveness more than required to reestablish equilibrium. Of course, they are particularly opposed to forms of adjustment, such as import barriers and capital controls, that restrict their ability to trade.

The gold standard worked efficiently so long as the gold supply was adequate to the routine liquidity needs of the system, so long as confidence in the pound sterling was sufficient to augment that liquidity in an emergency, so long as confidence in the hegemony of Britain to manage the system was unquestioned, and so long as the imbalances to be financed were small enough in relation to gold reserves that adjustments were modest and infrequent. After World War I, none of these conditions held. Severe inflation eroded the purchasing power of gold so that it no longer provided enough liquidity to facilitate trade, let alone the enormous amount required for payment of huge German war reparations owed to European nations and massive war debts incurred by European nations to the United States. Aided by the dislocations of a global economic downturn and considerable speculation in currency markets, rapidly shifting supply of and demand for currencies left nations unable to maintain exchange-rate stability. The gold standard was abandoned, leading to a period of sharp volatility in the relative prices of currencies that discouraged trade.

Britain's ability to manage the system waned because its economic power declined. Further, international norms broke down as an increasing variety of national political systems arose—from the New Deal in the United States to fascism in Europe—each dominated by different values and committed to different economic theories. Nations selected adjustment policies in keeping with their own domestic needs, seemingly indifferent to the disruptions these adjustments caused abroad.

Specifically, nations adopted protectionist trade policies and beggar-thy-neighbor exchange-rate policies in which they devalued their currencies in order to encourage exports and discourage imports. These competitive exchange-rate devaluations, like the tariff increases and export subsidies that they mimicked, elicited retaliatory responses from other nations that soon degenerated into a spiral of chaotic rate fluctuations. The resulting instability in exchange rates increased the uncertainty and risk of trade, which in turn inevitably led to falling trade levels. Nations also restricted the external flow of capital, both to better control their exchange rates and to keep investment at home, where it was needed to rebuild the economy. Just as trade declined enormously, so did financial flows. Hence, the Great Depression had roots in monetary chaos as well as the collapse of trade. Further, national hostilities generated by beggar-thy-neighbor monetary policies exacerbated those stemming from trade disputes.

Thus, a new international financial system had to be created that would solve the problems of liquidity, confidence, and adjustment against the backdrop of new political and economic realities. Some of these economic realities—such as the increase in liquidity required by the meteoric rise in trade, investment, and loan levels—posed greater challenges, but the political reality of a powerful United States committed to hegemonic leadership offered a greatly enhanced capacity to meet them. The method chosen was the Bretton Woods system, centered around the dollar-gold standard, an IMF-enforced system of fixed exchange rates, and massive capital flows provided by the World Bank and the United States.

Liquidity was provided by a combination of gold and the U.S. dollar, which were linked by the U.S. Federal Reserve's commitment to freely exchange gold and dollars at the rate of $35 per ounce. Given the gold shortage, nations held most of their international reserves in the form of U.S. dollars, the system's reserve currency. This meant that the liquidity of the dollar-gold standard rested on huge U.S. gold stockpiles and the willingness of the United States to export enough dollars—through balance-of-trade deficits, investment flows, loans, and Marshall Plan aid—to maintain reserve assets and facilitate trade. Confidence in this system also rested on trust in the United States, because the dollar could be debased at any time through irresponsible action by U.S. monetary authorities or miscalculation of the system's liquidity needs. Hegemonic stability theorists correctly note that only the U.S. dollar commanded sufficient respect to guarantee the confidence of most observers and that only the United States had sufficient political and economic power to silence those that did not share it.

It was still necessary, however, to restrict the ability of nations to choose adjustment policies that harmed others, especially the trade barriers, capital controls, and competitive exchange-rate devaluations that had contributed to the collapse of the 1930s. In particular, the International Monetary Fund (IMF) was created to supervise a new system under which the **par value** of each currency was defined in relation to the U.S. dollar. Each nation was required to use its reserves in order to maintain this par value by buying or selling dollars in exchange for its own currency until supply and demand once again balanced at the agreed-upon rate. Furthermore, governments were prevented from undertaking a unilateral change in this exchange rate without IMF approval, since such a change was considered a means of last resort to resolve persistent balance-of-trade deficits. Neither could nations "adopt any monetary or general price measure or policy" that would threaten the balance-of-payments equilibrium of other nations without a four-fifths vote of IMF member states. Thus, in the hope of preventing the wild currency speculation, capital flows, and bank failures that were common during the Great Depression, the IMF was empowered to constrain extreme and illiberal macroeconomic policies of governments.

But the cost—in terms of sacrificing national sovereignty—was high. In practice, these restrictions encouraged adjustment to trade deficits by contractionary domestic policies, including high interest rates and either high taxes or low government expenditures. Although these policies would slow the economy enough to restrain imports and would restore equilibrium with minimal impact on other nations, they were also likely to promote domestic unemployment, slow economic growth, and diminish the resources of the state to respond to the social problems that resulted. Given the political sensitivity of these effects—which were bound to undermine the domestic popularity of governments and doom the political careers of leaders—it was no small compromise for states to willingly relinquish the authority to choose alternative means of adjustment. Only the extraordinary conditions of the time can explain this unprecedented trade-off of state sovereignty for the benefits of a stable international trading system. However, since these pressures on national governments were well understood, the system also provided means by which

Resolutions of Trade Dilemmas Embodied in the Bretton Woods Amalgam of Liberalism and Mercantilism

Mercantilism	Liberalism
1. Value trade-offs	
Other values must be pursued by domestic legislation that does not contravene Bretton Woods principles.	GATT liberalizes trade to achieve efficiency, maximum economic growth, consumption, and international peace. IMF promotes stability.
2. Distributional outcomes	
GATT's negotiating rules benefit powerful nations.	Liberalized trade benefits efficient sectors, owners of abundant resources, and competitive nations.
3. Effects on the state	
GATT's escape clauses and reciprocity principle accord some scope for national sovereignty.	National sovereignty is restricted by GATT's non-discrimination principle and IMF rules.

major adjustments could be delayed as long as possible, in the hope that the disequilibrium would prove to be temporary or that minor adjustments would work given enough time.

Those means involved short-term loans from the IMF and long-term loans for war-recovery purposes from the IBRD. The latter provided a financing facility to repay war debts, provide for reconstruction, and aid balance-of-payments difficulties. The motivation for the World Bank was not only to provide an option for nations tempted to control trade and investment; it was also predicated on the assumption that the loan-induced prosperity of Europe would contribute to trade that could raise the prosperity of all the nations of the globe together. The same logic later applied to the Third World, where the bulk of IBRD loans have been directed since the 1950s. Thus, the Bretton Woods system was an attempt to encourage nations to maintain liberal trade policies while allowing some measure of national autonomy.

For many years the system worked; global trade increased at an unprecedented historical rate and the global economy expanded rapidly. Since its founding, however, the Bretton Woods system has undergone major changes, especially with respect to finance. Confidence in the dollar eroded as the persistent American balance-of-payments deficits documented in Chapter 1 dumped more dollars onto international currency markets than could be redeemed by U.S. gold stocks, eventually forcing the United States to abandon the commitment. Just as the link between gold and the dollar was broken in the early 1970s, which compromised the only source of liquidity that could command any confidence, the increase in trade and, especially, the huge trade deficits associated with spiking oil prices, required even *greater* liquidity. Most developed nations, unable to stabilize their currencies' values, ceased to peg them to either gold or the dollar. Instead, most major currencies have been allowed to "float," that is, their exchange rates are determined by supply and demand in global currency markets, with minimal intervention by states.

Increasingly, however, the source of demand for currencies does not lie primarily in the need to finance trade. Instead, currencies are purchased in order to facilitate foreign investment and, especially, to speculate on the future values of the currencies themselves. These changes stem partly from the technological advances in communication and information transfer that permit instantaneous exchanges across the globe. They also reflect the rise of multinational corporations that generate large capital flows and the emergence of a class of capitalists who earn rewards from the transactions themselves. Underlying all of these factors, however, is the effect of the Bretton Woods institutions in spreading liberal ideas about the benefits of free markets and in dismantling barriers to flows of both capital and goods. These changes have had enormous impact on the ability of the state to insulate its economy from external forces. With states no longer able to control the value of their own currency, rates can fluctuate so wildly that trade—once the principal purpose of foreign exchange markets—is now impeded by them. Indeed, as we shall see in Chapter 6, the EU has responded to the trade disruption caused by fluctuating currency values among its members by moving to replace the various national currencies with the Euro.

All of the Bretton Woods institutions have adapted to changing circumstances, not least those they themselves have brought about. Changes in the trade dimension of Bretton Woods can be seen in the Uruguay Round of trade negotiations, which not only continued the process of lowering trade barriers, but also created a new institution to govern global trade, the WTO.

THE URUGUAY ROUND OF GATT

The eighth round of GATT negotiations, the so-called Uruguay Round, was launched in September 1986 with the Punta del Este Declaration. After the longest and most difficult bargaining in GATT history, the Marrakech protocol was signed in April 1994 by 123 nations. *The Marrakesh Agreement Establishing the World Trade Organization* and its annexes are comprised of twenty-nine individual legal texts and twenty-eight additional documents, altogether about 430 pages long. Most notable among them are the revised GATT (now referred to as GATT 1994), the General Agreement on Trade in Services (GATS), Sanitary and Phytosanitary Measures Agreement (SPS) and the Agreement on Trade-Related Intellectual Property Rights (TRIPs). These agreements are accompanied by more than 20,000 pages, which detail each member's schedule of tariff concessions and service commitments. The agreement entered into force in January 1995 after protracted ratification fights in several nations, especially the United States.

The difficulties and delays were due in part to a continuing deterioration in three conditions that had once been helpful in achieving trade agreements. First, the interests of the various parties have diverged. The major trading nations are now trade competitors rather than allies in either hot or cold wars. Further, they no longer share the values and theories that once underpinned both national policies and the multilateral system. Second, the distribution of power among nations has fragmented. The erosion of American preeminence has left the system without hegemonic leadership, and the ascendance of Third World nations to positions of greater competitive danger in markets has increased their influence. Negotiations became much more complicated as membership expanded from 23 to 123. Third, global growth has slowed and the political pressure on national governments to improve economic performance—especially when threatened from abroad—has correspondingly risen.

At the same time, the issues discussed produce greater rancor, especially because they touch the fundamental dilemmas of trade more deeply. In this respect, the trade liberalization process suffers from the legacy of its own success: Because the first seven rounds of negotiations had already accomplished the easiest tasks, the remaining ones represented challenges to the global trading system that were both profoundly different and substantially more difficult than those surmounted previously.

For example, the across-the-board tariff cuts that had formed the centerpiece of previous rounds did not occupy the core of the Uruguay Round negotiations. After previous GATT rounds had lowered tariff rates to about a 4 percent average on most industrial products, they were no longer a significant barrier in most products and in most markets. However, the tariffs that remain, which are concentrated in a few "peaks" surrounded by virtually zero rates on most products, are very resistant to further reduction. Because decades of negotiations have rooted out most tariffs, the remaining ones are invariably those that pose the most serious dilemmas and thus command the strongest political support. Thus, across-the-board tariff reductions were a high priority only in relation to a handful of newly industrializing countries (NICs), especially South Korea and Brazil, whose protectionist policies are no longer tolerated now that they compete effectively with more developed nations. Still, further progress was made, with average tariff reductions of 36 percent (including at least 15 percent in all categories) phased in over six years.

However, the Uruguay Round negotiations were dominated by two other agenda items. First, GATT principles and procedures were extended into sectors not previously covered, especially agriculture and services. Second, the rules of trade were clarified and the procedures to deal with disputes that arise under them were institutionalized by creating the World Trade Organization (WTO).

The extension of trade liberalization into new sectors reflects both changes in the nature of modern economies and shifts in the power balances among nations. For example, the inclusion of textiles and tropical products reflects the growing importance of less developed countries (LDCs), but U.S. bargaining power minimized the gains they were able to achieve.[14] At the insistence of the United States, the service sector, which now accounts for about two-thirds of the American economy, was addressed for the first time. Several areas were liberalized, especially accounting, advertising, computer services, telecommunications, engineering, and financial services. The United States achieved some successes in trade-related aspects of intellectual property (so-called TRIPs) but failed in others. Because pirating was estimated to cost Americans between $40 and $60 billion annually, the United States sought to guarantee that other nations would honor patents, copyrights, trademarks, and designs, especially in the software, chips, biotechnology, and entertainment sectors. For example, computer programs are now treated as literary works that require copyright fees. However, barriers to trade in services remain, such as French restrictions on the percentage of radio and television content that originates abroad or in languages other than French, restrictions that were challenged by Hollywood and by American rock musicians. The United States also pressed trade-related investment measures (TRIMs), contending that regulating foreign investment by multinational corporations unfairly restricts access to markets.

The most challenging new sector to be addressed in the Uruguay Round was agriculture. On the one hand, liberal theory makes an especially compelling case for free trade in agriculture: Agricultural policies in industrial countries cost consumers between $200 and $300 billion per year. However, trade dilemmas have also enlisted the support of an unusually formidable collection of political forces. Indeed, many countries wanted agricultural trade on the agenda, but only a small group of highly efficient exporters (headed by Canada's and Australia's grain-exporting interests) unequivocally supported free trade in agriculture. Most of the rest, including the United States, wanted liberalization only in their main export crops. As a result, agriculture produced the most difficult bargaining of the Uruguay Round, resulting in so many delays and missed schedules that many doubted that an agreement could ever be reached.

Agriculture presented a unique challenge because its special role in most political economies ensures that any liberalization in this sector will induce extensive distributional consequences and uncomfortable trade-offs with other values. Nearly all nations are committed to sustaining a healthy agricultural sector, because a relatively large, geographically concentrated, and occupationally inflexible population is dependent upon it. Many cultural and political issues also swirl beneath the surface, exemplified by the Japanese symbolic commitment to self-sufficiency in rice production and American reverence for the "family farm." Moreover, because agricultural policy in most nations is a complex combination of various subsidies and non-tariff barriers (NTBs), it is difficult to compute its actual protective effect. As a result, the agreement requires that all nations replace NTBs with equivalent (or lower) "bound" tariffs. This "tariffication" simplifies negotiations because it allows a better comparison of the protectionist effects of different national policies.

Tariff rates were reduced in all products, guaranteeing at least minimal access to even previously closed markets such as Japanese and Korean rice. Among developed countries, the rates on each product must be reduced by at least 15 percent, with an average reduction across all products of 35 percent after a phase-in period of six years. LDCs are permitted ten years to phase in reductions of at least 10 percent, with an average of 24 percent. Markets receiving $8 billion in U.S. agricultural exports were affected by the elimination of NTBs.

The principal protagonists in the dispute over agriculture—the United States and the EU—clashed with particular ferocity over subsidies. The United States, which itself subsidizes farmers in a variety of ways, nonetheless took a hard line because about 60 percent of U.S. agricultural exports face subsidized export competition. The EU, whose Common Agricultural Policy (CAP) has been described as "the acknowledged paragon of farm-trade lunacy," resisted strongly, not least because the diversity of interests among its twelve member nations made any agreement, even among themselves, exceedingly delicate.[15] Before the agreement, the United States spent about $1 in subsidy for every $100 in agricultural exports, and the EU spent about $25. The agreement requires a 36 percent reduction in budgetary outlays to subsidize agricultural exports, to be phased in over six years. As a result, the EU would cut subsidies by $5–$7 billion, the United States about $500 million. LDCs are permitted ten years to phase in minimum reductions of 14 percent by volume and 24 percent in total cost.[16]

In addition to tariff reductions, GATT 1994 and its associated agreements also clarified and tightened various trade rules. For example, distinctions are drawn more clearly between those subsidies that are prohibited and those designed to meet goals such as regional development, environmental protection, and improved industrial research, which are not. The use of "health measures" as protectionist devices was disciplined by requiring scientific evidence to support the need for an import restriction. Similarly, technical barriers to trade—the use of testing, certification, and other procedures as a protectionist measure—are now restricted. Finally, there are more precise rules for countervailing duties.

THE WORLD TRADE ORGANIZATION

Perhaps the most visible accomplishment of the Uruguay Round is the creation of a permanent trade institution, the World Trade Organization, which commenced operation on January 1, 1995, nearly fifty years after the proposed ITO was abandoned. The WTO is not a wholly new organization, of course. Its staff and building in Geneva are identical to that of the GATT secretariat it replaced and the GATT agreements remain at the center of the legal order it now supervises. Furthermore, although the WTO may be said to govern global trade, it does so quite loosely and with very limited resources. Its annual budget, about $80 million, is smaller than at least fifteen other international economic organizations and barely 5 percent of the largest, the World Bank. Its staff, fewer than 500, is similarly dwarfed by the World Bank's 7,000 and the IMF's 3,000. WTO staff have no enforcement powers and are authorized neither to interpret GATT/WTO rules nor to investigate violations of them.

Still, the WTO does represent an important milestone, only partly because its founding coincides with the adoption of GATT 1994 and other agreements that clarify rules (e.g., SPS) and extend them to other areas of trade (e.g., GATS). The WTO also gives new prominence to the Trade Policy Review Mechanism (TPRM) and, most importantly, strengthens the system of dispute settlement. The Trade Policy Review Board is responsible for conducting periodic surveillance of the trade policies and practices of all members. The largest nations are reviewed every two years; the remainder at wider intervals. Trade policy reviews were begun in response to an influential 1985 GATT report that concluded, "Governments should be required regularly to explain and defend their overall trade policies." Article 10 of GATT had always required members to publicly announce all changes in trade policy, but very few did so. The TPRM was designed to strengthen observance of WTO commitments by monitoring compliance "and by establishing a forum within which members can question one another's policies and practices."[17]

Although the TPRM may bring to light a nation's trade policies and practices, it is not a means to enforce WTO rules or even to investigate violations of them. Indeed, overt inconsistencies between a nation's policies and its WTO obligations can—and frequently do—continue indefinitely, until another nation lodges a protest. That complaint initiates the provisions of the dispute settlement system, the most significant and most controversial new contribution of the WTO. The process begins when one nation files a complaint with the Dispute Settlement Body (DSB) against the policy or practice of another nation. If consultations between the parties cannot resolve the matter, the DSB appoints a panel of three (sometimes five) experts to hear evidence on the legal question of whether the policy in question is consistent with the relevant provisions of GATT and the other agreements which constitute WTO rules. That panel report, which rules on the violation and recommends how the violator should rectify it, can be appealed to an appellate body, whose final recommendation will be adopted unless the entire WTO membership unanimously disagrees. If the guilty party refuses to make the recommended changes or to offer acceptable compensation, the DSB will authorize sanctions to be exacted by the complaining nation, ordinarily by suspending concessions (that is, by raising tariffs against products of the guilty nation).

This dispute-resolution mechanism has been the most controversial feature of the WTO, first during the ratification debate in the United States, and later by virtue of its early decisions. It has become a lightning rod for various criticisms of the WTO, because it is charged with applying to particular cases the contentious principles contained elsewhere in WTO rules, including GATT 1947. Under the old GATT procedure, disputes were investigated by a special panel, but because its rulings were subject to a consensus among all GATT members, every nation had a veto over any adverse judgment. The WTO panels are also more influential, both because they have been given a more explicit standard of review, which increases the predictability of action, and because investigating authorities are now required to provide public notice and written explanations of their actions. These improvements are long overdue; some enforcement mechanism is necessary if trade law is to be effective. The United States argued most strongly for the new rules because of frustration over the ineffectiveness of the old GATT mechanism, which it used more often than any other nation.

However, a surprising variety of American groups opposed the WTO as a violation of national sovereignty. Environmental groups such as Friends of the Earth, Greenpeace, and the Sierra Club were joined by consumer advocates such as Ralph Nader but, surprisingly, also by conservatives such as Ross Perot, Pat Buchanan, Jesse Helms, and Howard Phillips of the Conservative Caucus. They feared that a WTO panel would rule that various U.S. government policies constitute unfair trade practices warranting retaliation by others. A GATT panel had ruled previously that the U.S. Marine Mammal Protection Act was an unfair trade restriction because it prohibited the importation of tuna caught by nets that also kill dolphins. EU automakers also challenged the U.S. law that established standards for auto emissions and fuel economy. Buchanan said, "WTO means putting America's trade under foreign bureaucrats who will meet in secret to demand changes in U.S. laws. . . . WTO tramples all over American sovereignty and states' rights."[18] Because the WTO could not force a change in American law, GATT director general Peter Sutherland called this position "errant nonsense," but the WTO could authorize an offended nation to impose sanctions or withdraw trade concessions as compensation for the injury. Thus, in July 1994, attorneys general from forty-two states wrote President Clinton saying the agreement could jeopardize state sovereignty.

The first few years of experience with the WTO dispute resolution mechanism reveal that two GATT provisions are especially controversial, because they allow the greatest intrusion into domestic arenas usually thought to be within the sphere of national sovereignty. Both the "national treatment" principle and the "nullification or impairment" clause have been fundamental to GATT since 1947, but they have assumed greater importance under the WTO for several reasons. Most importantly, because dispute resolution panel decisions are now binding, states have a greater incentive to use these provisions to challenge the domestic policies of others. Of course, with tariffs much reduced, such domestic policies have much greater impact than when they were dwarfed by traditional barriers. Furthermore, the WTO applies these obligations much more broadly and with much greater precision than previously.

GATT's Article 3 establishes the "national treatment" principle, that "internal taxes, laws, and regulations should not be applied to imported or domestic products so as to afford protection to domestic production. Imports shall be accorded treatment no less favourable than that accorded to like products of national origin in respect of all laws, regulations and requirements." The WTO has heard numerous complaints turning on whether a domestic and foreign good should be considered "like products." It has ruled that the EU ban on meat treated with growth hormones is a violation, rejecting the EU defense that such treatments render U.S. beef a cancer risk (and therefore not a "like product" entitled to the same status as European beef). Citing the Sanitary and Phytosanitary Measures Agreement (SPS) negotiated during the Uruguay Round, the WTO panel found that the scientific studies relied upon by the EU to establish the health risk did not meet the required burden of proof, and it further denied the EU's request for a two-year delay to commission acceptable scientific studies that would do so. Canada has also used the SPS to challenge the EU's exclusion of asbestos products, which have been banned in the United States for many years as a carcinogen. The "like products" standard has also been invoked to challenge the U.S. prohibition against the importation of shrimp from fishing fleets that use techniques thought to trap endangered sea turtles. In this case, it was ruled that an adequate regulatory program did not exist to certify that the average rate of taking of sea turtles by foreign fleets was greater than those of the United States. The "like products" standard has also been used to challenge the conformity of domestic taxes to the national treatment principle. Japan was found in violation by taxing vodka at a higher rate than *shochu* (a vodka-like spirit), and similar cases are pending concerning Chile's taxation of *pisco* and Korean taxes on *soju*.

GATT's Article 23 allows any nation to challenge the domestic laws of another if they "consider that any benefit accruing to it directly or indirectly under this Agreement is being nullified or impaired" by them, regardless of whether the law had that intention. This provision has been the basis of some notable attempts to penetrate domestic practices. The United States has challenged Japan's Large-Scale Retail Store Law, which limits the establishment of large retail stores that might drive smaller competitors out of business and regulates the floor space, business hours and holidays of supermarkets and department stores. The United States contends that it is difficult and expensive to market American products to the thousands of small retail stores in Japan and that it would be much easier for them if Japanese law and regulatory practices allowed large chain stores that were open longer hours to operate more freely. As evidence that these domestic practices "nullified and impaired" the market access to which American producers were entitled by virtue of Japanese commitments under GATT, the U.S. observed that Kodak photo film accounted for over 40 percent of the market in Europe and elsewhere, but only 7 percent of Japanese sales. A WTO panel rejected the claim but the U.S. has continued to press the point in **bilateral** negotiations with Japan.

The United States has been the most active claimant in WTO cases. For example, the WTO Annual Report for 1998 records that seven of the eight adopted panel reports concerned claims initiated by the U.S. Five of the fifteen new panels convened in the previous year originated from U.S. complaints, and twelve of the thirty-six other requests for consultations, a first step toward the convening of a panel, were brought by the United States. Among them were U.S. contentions that aspects of the income tax law of five different nations as well as French government loans to develop a flight management system for the Airbus aircraft amount to export subsidies. The United States also disputed the EU's classification of Local Area Network (LAN) adapter equipment as "telecommunications equipment" rather than "automatic data processing machines" (which enter under a lower tariff) and protested Canadian patent protection, which lasts only seventeen years, rather than twenty as required under the TRIPS agreement.

The United States has also been the defendant in a number of complaints. The U.S. laws that have been challenged include a 1996 Massachusetts Act that prohibits state officials from procuring goods or services from any persons who do business with Burma (Myanmar), in protest of its human rights record. Complaints have also been filed over the Helms-Burton Bill, which discriminates against Cuban products and firms that do business with Cuba, the Harbor Maintenance Tax (said to discourage trade), and the U.S. Copyright Act, which permits, under certain conditions, the playing of radio and television music in public places without the payment of a royalty. The most significant complaints, however, are those described in Chapter 5 concerning American unilateral actions under sections 301–310 of the Trade Act of 1974 and the Anti-Dumping Act of 1916, actions which impose penalties for alleged trade violations without recourse to WTO dispute settlement.

CONCLUSION: TRADE DILEMMAS, INTERNATIONAL INSTITUTIONS, AND THE "BATTLE OF SEATTLE"

These controversies surrounding the WTO boiled over in December 1999 when its 135 members met in Seattle. The summit conference was designed to build momentum for free trade by launching the "millennium round" of trade negotiations, the ninth since 1947, but instead it raised the profile of public resistance to the WTO. Unlike the previous Uruguay Round, which began amid obscurity and public apathy in the sleepy seaside resort of Punta del Este, this one attracted a massive display of public opposition that culminated in the "Battle of Seattle." Led by environmental activists and labor union members, tens of thousands of protesters with disparate and sometimes contradictory perspectives brought unprecedented discord to the debate over the rules of international trade. National delegates displayed the same diversity in national interests that prevented them from agreeing on an agenda in preparatory meetings. The talks collapsed in acrimony, revealing that contemporary international institutions are replete with trade dilemmas that must be confronted both by citizens as political issues and by nations in making policy choices.

On the one hand, the familiar liberal benefits of trade are too huge to be dismissed, even if U.S. trade representative Mickey Kantor's prediction that the Uruguay Round would yield $1 trillion in gains over ten years is disputed by the much smaller estimates of the World Bank, the Organization for Economic Cooperation and Development (OECD), the Institute for International Economics, and the Economic Policy Institute. On the other hand, these benefits must be balanced against other effects that become increasingly apparent to the public as the volume of trade expands and the institutional operations required to sustain that expansion become correspondingly more intrusive. The Battle of Seattle demonstrates that the WTO has become a focal point for a diverse set of anxieties about the dilemmas of international trade, not all of them directly related to the WTO itself.

Liberalizing trade produces winners and losers, both among nations and within them. For example, the World Bank identified Africa as a net loser of the Uruguay Round because its costs for food imports would rise and the prices of commodities exported by African nations, such as tea, coffee, and cocoa, would fall. Nevertheless, most developing nations continue to support trade liberalization, even as they strongly object to facets of WTO decisionmaking processes that give priority to issues that disproportionately benefit rich countries and burden poor ones. They point out that the world's largest trade barriers continue to be found against the goods in which they have a comparative advantage—labor-intensive manufactures like textiles and tropical agricultural products—whereas the proposed agenda for the "millennium round" focuses instead on issues that are of little relevance to them (e.g., e-commerce) or that actually directly threaten the interests of poor countries. Among the latter are intellectual property rights issues, such as the failure of African countries to honor the patents of Western pharmaceutical firms for expensive medicines. In the United States, the distributional dilemma of trade has been raised by industry groups ranging from corn growers to steel producers, triggering protectionist actions under American anti-dumping statutes that other countries see as violations of free trade.

Even more significant are issues in which the distributional dilemma is intertwined with value trade-offs and sovereignty concerns, each of which is judged differently by groups around the world. In Seattle, the largest demonstrations were by U.S. labor organizations, who succeeded in pressuring President Clinton to endorse proposals that would include highly controversial provisions for labor standards in future WTO agreements. Previously, the preparatory committee had considered various proposals under a so-called **social clause** that would exempt from WTO benefits any exports produced by slave labor, child labor, workers prohibited from organizing and bargaining collectively through labor unions, or those denied a minimum wage or health and safety protection. Such proposals are unlikely to be accepted, however, because they seek agreement where none is possible: Not all nations share the values implied by these provisions, which would also affect different groups very differently.

Human rights groups strongly support labor standards on value grounds. U.S. labor unions agree, not only standing in solidarity with workers facing exploitative conditions abroad, but also seeing their material interests threatened by imports produced cheaply because of lax labor standards. Multinational corporations oppose such restrictions, which would increase their labor costs, and many Third World governments line up with them, noting that cheap labor is the source of their comparative advantage. They accuse developed countries of hypocrisy in blocking trade based on cheap labor while advocating free trade for products using rich countries' comparative advantage in technology. Poor countries see these proposals as self-interested protectionism, cultural imperialism, and violations of national sovereignty under the guise of humanitarianism. In response, left-leaning groups around the world decry the WTO as the agent of big business and its allies among political elites, especially in nondemocratic governments. As one placard carried by Seattle protesters put it, "The WTO kills people. Kill the WTO." Clearly, the underlying issues go far beyond the WTO, but we have seen before that trade often crystallizes conflicts among alternative theories, values, and interests. The WTO may not have created these conflicts, but it must resolve them if international trade is to be governed by an institutionalized set of rules.

Of course, not all see the dilemmas concerning the effect of trade on the state, especially matters of national sovereignty, in the same way. The case involving EU prohibitions against hormone-treated beef and genetically

Global competition. Danziger © *The Christian Science Monitor*

modified foods from the United States is perhaps the most revealing contemporary example. Surely the United States is correct in noting that free trade requires nations to refrain from using fraudulent health issues as a disguised means of protecting its inefficient industries. Further, the experience of several centuries makes it clear that the drive for free trade, which may begin with modest tariff reductions, leads inexorably to targeting aspects of national life that are more sensitive, controversial, and likely to provoke conflict. Finally, it is hard to deny the need for some institutional means to transform such political disputes into more easily resolved legal ones. Yet, surely the EU is also correct that the European citizens' right of self-determination includes the freedom to elect governments that pass laws to protect communities against health risks. That would seem to include the right to their own weighing of those risks, including the judgment that some foods may be dangerous, even though formal scientific studies have yet to prove it conclusively. Finally, it is hard to deny that the WTO finding has undermined the sovereignty of states and with it the freedom of citizens.

Environmentalists in Seattle made much of this concern, fearing both the substance and the process of future WTO actions affecting the trade-off of environmental and commercial concerns. Substantively, they observe that the WTO has made many decisions that seem as hostile to the environment as they are friendly to trade, on issues ranging from sea turtles to tropical forests. This bias is hardly surprising, they note, when key decisions that have multiple implications—for economic, environmental, social, political, and cultural questions—are made solely by experts in trade law. The insulation of trade dispute resolution bodies from public opinion and the lobbying efforts of advocacy groups strike at the heart of democratic ideals.

Trade inevitably poses such dilemmas. It is easy to see that some individuals, groups, and nations will differ with others on how to resolve them. The policy choices by nations concerning the institutions that embody these options reflect different theories and values, different power distributions, and different estimates of the effects of markets. Trust in trade-liberalizing institutions is likely to be greatest in those nations and among those groups with the greatest power to dominate them. As always, support for liberalization is greatest in nations with the most productive industries (and thus the greatest stake in removing barriers to trade), and with the highest weighting of trade benefits among its value priorities. Opposition is more likely from weaker states (which are more protective of their fragile sovereignty), from economies with more threatened industries, and from societies with a greater commitment to values other than aggregate growth.

Controversies over the various safeguard measures employed by nations pursuant to GATT's Article 19 also revisit this enduring problem of squaring the benefits of trade expansion with the compromises of national sovereignty required to achieve them. Thus, the very mercantilist exceptions that made the liberalism of Bretton Woods acceptable to nations have come under attack, revealing the inherent inconsistencies of the system. Indeed, the international trading order struggles with the co-existence of systemic institutions more liberal than mercantilist and national policies inclined to be more mercantilist than liberal.

FIVE

□ □ □

Neomercantilism and Bilateral Trade Issues

The Bretton Woods system achieved its goals of material prosperity and international peace, but these successes were neither complete nor permanent. International institutions can constrain—but ultimately cannot prevent—the adoption of national policies that disrupt market-based trade. When nations adopt policies that resolve trade dilemmas in different ways, trade between them is likely to create foreign policy friction. Nowhere is this more evident than in the conflict-ridden trade relations between the United States and Japan, the focus of this chapter.

U.S.-JAPANESE TRADE TENSIONS

The signs of trade-induced strain between the United States and Japan are evident in both formal diplomatic relations and in public opinion, with so-called Japan-bashing often heard on street corners and in Congress. More Americans (45 percent) see economic competition from Japan as a critical threat to U.S. interests than the military power of Russia (34 percent), Islamic fundamentalism (38 percent), or regional ethnic conflict (34 percent).[1] Polls show that only 43 percent of Americans have a favorable opinion of Japan and 53 percent believe that U.S.-Japanese cooperation is only fair or poor. It is revealing that only 25 percent believe that the American and Japanese people have a good understanding of one another.

U.S. complaints center on the bilateral trade deficit with Japan, which has hovered around $50 billion annually since 1985 and which approached $70 billion in 1999. Fifty-five percent of Americans attribute the imbalance to Japan's refusal to open its markets; only 17 percent cite the competitive weakness of American firms, while among opinion leaders those figures are 63 percent and 7 percent respectively.[2] Japan rejects culpability for the deficit: One poll revealed that 85 percent of Japanese felt that America unfairly blames Japan.[3] Furthermore, Japan complains that American efforts to reduce the trade deficit violate principles that are both imbedded in international law and regularly professed by American trade officials. As a result, the same poll found that only 45 percent of the Japanese regard America as trustworthy.

It is difficult to overstate the significance of this trade conflict between the globe's two largest national economies, which together account for about one-third of total world production. It jeopardizes their bilateral trade, which at more than $180 billion per year in the late 1990s exceeded that of any other pair of nations except the United States and Canada. Japan depends on U.S. markets to accept about 30 percent of its exports and on American products, which constitute nearly 25 percent of its imports.[4] The fallout from the trade dispute could also endanger other facets of the economic relationship. For example, the United States relies on Japanese capital to supply needed investment funds—Japanese investors hold more than $130 billion in foreign direct investment in the United States and a sizable share of the $725 billion in U.S. **Treasury bonds** held abroad—and Japanese investors depend upon the health of the American economy to generate returns on that investment. Furthermore, the credibility—perhaps even the survival—of the WTO, the centerpiece of the world trade order, may hang in the balance. In May 1995, the United States, which had been the chief sponsor of the WTO when created only six months previously, threatened sanctions against Japan that, if imposed, would have violated WTO rules.

At the heart of the dispute are complaints by American business that Japan exports too much and imports too little. Japan counters by pointing out that the allegedly low levels of Japanese imports look very different when seen on a per capita basis: The consumption of American products by the average Japanese citizen is greater than the consumption of Japanese products by the average American. Under this interpretation, the difference in population—the United States has twice as many consumers—explains the difference in import levels. Of course, applying this same logic to the export side would magnify American criticism, since Japan not only exports far more to the United States, but does so with only half as many workers. In any case, accusations of unfair trading practices have been accompanied by calls for the U.S. government to manage trade in order to ensure a level playing field for U.S. firms and workers. In fact, the phrase "fair trade" is now more often articulated as a goal than "free trade." U.S. labor has reacted stridently to the influx of Japanese products in the United States, arguing that imports steal American jobs. The bitterness is reflected in heated rhetoric, such as U.S. Representative John Din-

Friendly partners? Danziger © *The Christian Science Monitor*

gell of Michigan's declaration that "there's only one reason our automobile industry is hurting—those little yellow people." The view from the other side of the Pacific is different: Yoshio Sakurauchi, the speaker of Japan's lower house, opined that America can't compete because "U.S. workers are too lazy" and that "about 30 percent" of American workers "cannot even read."[5] It is difficult to avoid the conclusion that racism plays a role in the perceptions by each nation of the other, but real economic differences lie beneath the bombast.

The case for attributing the bilateral trade imbalance to unfair Japanese practices receives support from the observation that Japan has maintained a trade surplus with the rest of the world—not just with the United States. In fact, other nations have also denounced Japan's trade surplus, which exceeded $100 billion per year from 1992 to 1995 and averaged about 2.5 percent of its **gross domestic product** (GDP) throughout the 1990s. Indeed, Japan has had difficult economic relations for some time: Fourteen nations invoked Article 35 of the GATT in refusing to accord MFN status to Japan when it became a contracting party in 1955. In the 1980s, Japan was warned by the German economics minister that "trade should not be a one-way street" and by the British prime minister that the trade imbalance "cannot continue without threatening the breakdown of the free trading system."[6]

This antagonism is magnified because Japan runs large trade deficits with countries that supply raw materials and large surpluses with most developed nations.[7] In the latter countries, such as the United States, sectors that compete with Japanese imports constitute a strong domestic political constituency that is hostile toward Japanese trade. Ordinarily, protectionist pressures emanating from import-competing sectors are counterbalanced by liberal lobbying from the export sector, but the bilateral trade deficits that most advanced countries run with Japan translate into a deficit in liberal sentiment. As a result, Japan has been forced to reach agreements with European governments similar to those negotiated with the United States, such as export restraints on automobiles.

Nevertheless, with a **current account** surplus during the 1990s of over $700 billion, Japan has become the largest creditor in global history. Japanese ownership of foreign assets exceeded $2 trillion early in the 1990s and continues to grow each year, a pattern bound to alarm states who equate this accumulation of wealth with the power to influence the economies of others. The holdings of Japanese investors abroad, about 12 percent of the global total of foreign direct investment, dwarfs the ownership of foreigners in Japan, which amounts to about .7 percent of that total. In short, the U.S.-Japanese trade gap reflects forces at work in Japan's relations with other nations as well.

At the same time, however, Japan uses a similar logic in locating the source of the bilateral imbalance in U.S. economic policy, noting that the American trade deficit is not unique to its links with Japan. Indeed, the United States has become the world's largest debtor, after a decade of current-account deficits exceeding $1 trillion. Because the gap with Japan accounts for only about 40 percent of that, many feel that Japan is being used as a scapegoat for a broader American problem. They argue that the bilateral trade imbalance with Japan—and the related decrease in the value of the dollar from over 300 yen in the 1960s to under 100 yen in the 1990s—may be a symbol of American decline but not its cause. As one commentator put it, "To blame Japan for U.S. trade deficits is a lot like blaming your banker because you are in debt."[8]

Indeed, American fixation on the trade deficit with Japan is partly a reflection of anxiety about the loss of American hegemony. Although still the world's largest economy and exporter, the United States is no longer as far ahead of its competitors as it once was. In the early 1950s the United States accounted for about 45 percent of total global production (including 80 percent of the world's cars), held 43 percent of international reserves, and furnished about 20 percent of global exports. By the beginning of the 1990s, U.S. production and exports had grown significantly, but because that growth was not nearly as rapid as that in the rest of the world, U.S. production had slipped to about 25 percent of total output, international reserves were down to 6 percent of the global total, and U.S. exports made up less than 12 percent of international trade. American firms no longer produced 80 percent of the autos driven in the United States, let alone in the entire world.[9] Meanwhile, Japan's exports had grown from 2 percent to 10 percent of the global total.

Americans, having gotten used to global dominance, naturally assumed that something had gone frightfully wrong when their dominance began to diminish. Realistically, however, it is the 1950s that should be considered exceptional—U.S. dominance in the immediate postwar period represented the greatest concentration of economic power by any one nation in history. The global depression of the 1920s and 1930s, a massively devastating war fought on the territory of the other leading economic powers in the 1940s, and the unusually prominent role of the United States in Europe in the immediate aftermath of that war, all helped to propel the United States to a position of dominance that could not possibly be sustained after the recovery that eventually ensued.

Still, it cannot be surprising that such a steep relative decline would be psychologically disturbing to Americans. Furthermore, hegemonic stability theory reminds us that bilateral conflicts, along with the rising tide of regionalism and mercantilism that helps create them, are characteristic of any period of declining hegemony. Thus, because the 1990s mark the culmination of two decades of relative decline by the United States and five decades of remarkable growth in Japan, the contemporary strain in bilateral relations between these two powers should not be too surprising. Also, these conditions merely bring to the fore a conflict that is always latent among trading nations because it stems from an aspect of the state goals dilemma built into the way that international trade affects the state.[10]

THE EFFECTS OF INTERNATIONAL TRADE ON THE STATE

Despite liberal insistence that trade produces peace, the historical record shows that trade-related conflict is a common theme in international politics. Theorists such as Harold Laski and E. H. Carr argue that the expansion of trade frequently creates competitive struggles for markets, raw materials, and investment outlets. The hostilities that led to World War I have been attributed to national rivalries sharpened by a drive for colonies motivated by this competition. Both Japanese and German justifications for World War II cited similar goals in the drive for spheres of influence that ultimately became campaigns of conquest.

Common to these cases is a structural reality embodied in the state goals dilemma emphasized by mercantilists: States cooperate for economic gain, but they also use trade to compete for political power. It is ironic that this dualistic facet of international relations was portrayed most vividly by the liberal theorist Adam Smith:

> Being neighbors, [England and France] are necessarily enemies, and the wealth and power of each becomes, upon that account more formidable to the other; and what would increase the advantage of national friendship serves only to inflame the violence of national animosity.[11]

Thus, the attitude of a nation toward the economic success of a trade partner is torn between these two visions.

> The wealth of a neighboring nation, however, though dangerous in war and politics, is certainly advantageous in trade. In a state of hostility it may enable our enemies to maintain fleets and armies superior to our own; but in a state of peace and commerce it must likewise enable them to exchange with us to a greater value, and to afford a better market . . . for the produce of our own industry.[12]

A market perspective sees neighboring nations as potential customers, but the state must also see them as potential enemies. Which resolution of this state goals dilemma will dominate policy depends upon circumstances. If conflict seems likely—or even possible—the state must consider not only the absolute gains it receives from trade but also the power implications of those gains relative to the advantages it bestows on others. Following Smith's famous observation that "defence is more important than opulence," it may then be necessary for a state to refrain from trade that would be more advantageous to its potential enemies than to itself. As a result, conflict over trade becomes most likely when changes in respective power levels become visible, because that is when a nation becomes less concerned with its own absolute gain than with the relative gain of a rival.

Although few analysts expect the U.S.-Japanese economic rivalry to erupt into war, many do suggest that the United States should seek to strike a balance between these two considerations. That is, in recognition of the state goals dilemma, the United States should manage trade so as to minimize the long-term threat to national interests that the rapid ascendance of a rival may represent. In practice, that approach means insisting upon reciprocity in trade relations so that neither party gains more than the other, even if that policy requires limiting trade and thus sacrificing some of its benefits. It also means emphasizing trade with partners who are more likely to be allies than enemies, because trade may cement a friendly relationship, whereas it may intensify the conflict in an antagonistic one. Such a policy is a dangerous tightrope, however, because, as liberals note, interference with trade, especially in a discriminatory way, has often triggered major conflicts. Nonetheless, critics of American trade policy point to the persistence of the trade deficit as evidence that the United States has been less attentive than Japan to the long-term implications of trade for these power-related dimensions of the national interest.

Trade may also generate dilemmas for the state by conveying macroeconomic conditions such as inflation, employment levels, and interest rates from one nation to its trading partners. For example, during the 1930s, the American depression spread worldwide, in part because the decline of American imports meant unemployment for the export sectors of other nations. The consequences of such interdependence will be relatively benign if trade partners have similar macroeconomic goals, but if they do not, trade may be disruptive enough to produce foreign policy tensions.

Unfortunately, the United States and Japan pursue quite different value priorities, and the resulting divergence in economic policy brings injury to both. As Stephen D. Cohen has put it:

Domestically, the United States has embodied the cowboy spirit: an emphasis on consumption and recreation, the spirit of individual freedom and new frontiers to conquer, distrust of government, and the glory of the free market. Meanwhile, Japan has embodied the samurai spirit: an emphasis on production and the rewards of hard work, loyalty and subordination of self-gratification to group interests, respect for government authority, and the need for limiting the free rein of the invisible hand of the marketplace.[13]

In particular, the two countries display very different attitudes toward the values trade-off represented by the choice of consuming today versus saving for tomorrow. Japanese economic policy strongly encourages savings and discourages consumption, thereby reinforcing a preference that appears to be prevalent among Japanese households anyway. Restraining consumption carries the side effect of limiting Japanese imports, which constrains the exports and slows the growth of other economies, especially the United States. In response, other nations have pressured Japan to stimulate its economy through increased government spending, in the hope that the resulting rise in Japanese imports would also stimulate their economies. This pressure has been especially intense in recent years because the prolonged Japanese recession of the 1990s has been a drag on the recovery of the export-led economies of Asia from their 1997 collapse.

By contrast, the United States maintains an unusually low national savings rate. As a result, high levels of individual, corporate, and government debt require foreign borrowing, which limits the supply of investment funds available elsewhere in the world. Consequently, since the 1980s other nations—especially Japan—have urged the U.S. government to cut its **budget deficit**, anticipating that this action would diminish American consumption and thus lower imports and stem the disruptive flow of capital out of their economies. Despite considerable effort, neither state has been very successful in overcoming the proclivities of its respective economy. The U.S. budget deficit has disappeared, but private consumption continues to accelerate and record import levels have produced record trade deficits. The Japanese government has boosted spending to stimulate the economy, but in the process has incurred massive budget deficits without generating the increases in private consumption or import levels that would reduce its trade surplus.

The tensions created by such disruptive interdependence can be minimized if the injured party accepts a charitable interpretation of the motivations of the other, but such an interpretation is likely only when nations are already inclined toward friendship. For example, during the Cold War, the presence of the Soviet Union as a common enemy unified American and Japanese foreign policy interests and soothed economic tensions. Now, however, differences in culture and ethnicity reinforce lingering wariness from World War II, all of which inflame and complicate a conflict that remains rooted in a $50-billion-per-year bilateral trade imbalance.

Of course, Senator John Danforth has said that "the issue is not the size of the trade deficit; the issue is to make sure that both sides play by the same rules."[14] But that is precisely the problem: It is difficult to agree upon rules when judgments of what is fair are so deeply imbedded in such very different cultural and theoretical systems. Because the issues touch upon dilemmas of trade that are evaluated very differently on opposite sides of the Pacific, each party finds it easier to see the other as a competitor and an enemy than as a partner and an ally.

DIFFERENCES IN TRADE POLICIES

Simply put, major differences in the economic policies of the United States and Japan make a collision between them inevitable. In particular, American and Japanese trade policies have moved in opposite directions since the end of World War II, just as List predicted when he observed that dominant nations are typically free traders and trailing nations usually adopt a protectionist stance. Japan, which had lagged behind Europe and North America in productivity even before the war devastation, adopted a mercantilist trade policy that emphasized promotion of exports and protection from imports. Since about 1975, however, when Japan became fully competitive in global markets, its trade policy has moved away from mercantilist extremes.[15] Indeed, by the mid-1980s Japanese tariffs were comparable to those of the United States and the EU, though the actual level of imports remains lower in Japan than in other developed nations.

Meanwhile, as American economic and political dominance declined after the early 1970s, U.S. policy slowly drifted away from the liberalism it had embraced as a hegemonic leader. Though the United States remains committed to a liberal international system, American policy has become more aggressive in tone, more unilateral in spirit, and more mercantilist in substance. Despite its liberal rhetoric, U.S. trade policy now emphasizes a range of defensive tools that are seen as protectionist by others and as the *source* of trade tensions rather than an antidote to them. In short, most commentators still see American trade policy as predominantly liberal and Japanese trade policy as predominantly mercantilist, but the differences between them have dramatically narrowed in recent years.

Still, the differences between the trade policies of the United States and Japan are much greater than can be explained by the competitiveness of their firms in international markets. In fact, they lie in prevailing theories and values, the state of markets, and the balance of power among key domestic and international actors. Each of these factors helps to explain why the two nations have judged the dilemmas of trade so differently and adopted divergent policies that reflect their respective judgments.

JAPANESE TRADE POLICY

Though Japanese trade policy includes some components of classical mercantilism that were shared by American commercial policy for most of the republic's history, fundamental structural disparities in the American and Japanese political economies reflect the great differences in the historical forces that have shaped modern life in the two countries. The most striking differences stem from the divergent paths they followed in the immediate postwar period. One compelling characterization of their respective goals is that Japan sought to create a production machine, whereas as America emphasized a consumer society. In particular, Japanese economic policy since World War II has been shaped by an unusual commitment to rapid growth fueled by an export sector geared to the global market. It has also been fostered by an unusually dominant role for the state in mobilizing the energies of the private sector to fulfill that philosophy.

In one sense, this strategy needs no special explanation because less competitive nations are almost always mercantilist. But the ferocity of Japan's commitment to a trade policy that emphasizes national power over individual welfare and seeks future growth more than current consumption is explained by that country's unique position and history. The experience of World War II and the postwar American occupation illustrated graphically how much Japan lagged behind the rest of the developed world and how significantly that gap could affect Japanese life. The result was a national commitment to recover from the humiliation of this period and to restore national pride. At the same time, because Japan was very poorly endowed in oil, mineral ores, and other key natural resources, it had to maintain a significant level of imports. The need to sell exports to pay for them thus ruled out any form of autarchic development. Finally, unlike European nations, it was located in a region consisting of very poor economies that offered few marketing opportunities, so it had to orient its trade relationships to global rather than regional markets. Thus, it was imperative that Japanese firms be able to compete successfully in export markets against companies from far more developed nations that had a considerable head start.

Consequently, trade became the focal point of a far-reaching industrial policy through which the state shaped Japan's postwar economy. Policymakers sought to develop globally competitive firms in a few well-chosen sectors that promised long-term growth. The methods combined initial import protection—motivated by infant-industry arguments that date to at least Elizabethan England—with vigorous export-promotion programs centered around credit provided at very favorable terms by the state-run Japan Development Bank. Achieving rapid export growth required a complex set of policies that controlled credit and imports, permitted monopoly situations unthinkable in the American context, and deprived certain sectors (and consumers in general) to advance others. Direct subsidies, tax relief, and public support of research and development consortia, in addition to easy credit, fueled a huge expansion of investment.[16]

These efforts were coordinated by Japan's Ministry of Finance (MOF) and **Ministry of International Trade and Industry** (MITI). The unusually close connection between the government and private industry and the unusually prominent position of MOF and MITI within the government gave rise to the term **Japan Inc.** to describe the total social mobilization undertaken in support of these fledgling export industries. This could occur only because of the unique communitarian values, the rare national consensus, and the unusual structure of Japanese government. Bureaucrats attained high social prestige during the Tokugawa (feudal) period (1603–1867) and retained it as they led the modernization process under Emperor Meiji (1867–1912).

In the mid-1990s, MITI and MOF officials, who are mostly graduates of Tokyo University, Japan's most prestigious, remain a business elite. Usually career bureaucrats, they achieve considerable power to influence the behavior of private firms through "administrative guidance." When they eventually retire from government service to the private sector, they are said to "descend from heaven." The less lofty prestige of government officials in the United States is reflected in the comparable American colloquialism that they enter a "revolving door."[17] As a result, government efforts to steer the Japanese economy encounter little of the resistance from the private sector that is such a distinguishing feature of the American political system, especially during the current era dominated by antigovernment sentiments.

The propensity of government policy to intervene in markets is so central to its system that Japan scholars have suggested that the Japanese political economy represents a structurally distinctive system. In fact, Japan has been called a "non-capitalist market economy" by one and an example of "network capitalism" (distinguished from American market capitalism) by another.[18] Indeed, interference with the market mechanism is a core feature of the Japanese political economy and is by no means restricted to government intervention.

The so-called *keiretsu*, a network of firms linked through product markets, labor markets, and financial markets, exemplifies the prominent role played by nonmarket forces in the Japanese economy. These business empires had their origins in the family-controlled holding companies called *zaibatsu*, which prospered prior to the imposition of antitrust policy by American occupying forces immediately after World War II. The four largest of these zaibatsu accounted for about one-quarter of all capital in Japan in 1946 and controlled half of the financial markets and a third of heavy industry.[19] When holding companies were outlawed, many zaibatsu re-formed under a similar structure of cross-shareholding called keiretsu, centered around banks.

For example, the Mitsui keiretsu consists of twenty-four major companies linked together by stock in each firm that is owned by the others. In fact, more than 50 percent of the shares of these firms are held within the group. The companies also buy and sell from one another as well as share market information, provide credit, and cooperate in various other ways. Mitsui includes two banks, two insurance companies, a real estate firm, a shipper, a warehouse, an engineering company, a retailer, and producers of textiles, chemicals, mining products, and petroleum, as well as world-famous firms that produce electronics (Toshiba) and automobiles (Toyota). In the early 1990s, the six largest keiretsu accounted for about 16 percent of capital and profits in the Japanese economy and held about 25 percent of the outstanding shares on the Tokyo and Osaka stock exchanges.[20]

Naturally, these industrial structures shape the behavior of firms. Japanese companies are likely to respond to a variety of stakeholders—especially affiliated firms—whereas U.S. corporations are more single-minded in producing profit for shareholders. As a result, the planning perspective of Japanese companies is long-term and broad in scope; indeed, they may not even be profit maximizers in the same way that American firms are. For example, a company may pass up the lowest-cost supplier in order to buy from another member of its keiretsu, since as a shareholder in the latter it would earn part of the profit. Further, these large keiretsu often cooperate with one another to form an **oligopoly**, which, like monopoly control over a market, raises prices for consumers and increases profits for business.

Moreover, oligopolies are much more common in Japan than in the United States because antitrust policies, though by statute similar to American ones, have been weakened by amendment and are underenforced. For example, antitrust exemptions allow legalized cartels in declining industries (to cooperate in reducing excess capacity), among small- and medium-sized enterprises (to achieve economies of scale), and for "rationalization" (to improve an industry's overall performance), as well as to facilitate exports and limit imports. All these cartels operate under the principle that "excessive competition" can be injurious to a firm and an industry, thus undermining its competitiveness against foreign firms. By the 1960s more than 1,000 cartels had been explicitly exempted from the antimonopoly law by the Fair Trade Commission. Even when the Fair Trade Commission has attempted to discourage collusion and centralization, it has often been pitted against the more politically powerful Ministry of Trade and Industry, which helped to create and sustain many of these very same cartels. Further, no plaintiff has ever won a private antitrust suit in Japan.

State-based export-promotion policies have also been integrated with private efforts. Large general trading companies (*sogo shosha*) have formed to facilitate the entry of smaller firms into foreign markets by providing marketing expertise, transport facilities, and credit. The nine largest, each associated with a particular keiretsu, handle 47 percent of Japanese exports, 65 percent of imports, and 18 percent of domestic wholesale sales.[21] Aided by the government-run Japanese External Trade Organization, which maintains offices in more than fifty foreign countries, Japanese firms find it relatively easy to monitor foreign markets so as to compete more effectively. By contrast, U.S. firms lack such extensive help in marketing in Japan and often bear the further burden of ignorance of Japanese language, customs, and business practices. Every anecdote about Japanese government interference with trade—from minor annoyance to outright ban—can be matched with another tale of the difficulty of doing business in Japan without appreciating that the rules of business interaction in Japan are as different as the rules of social interaction.

It is not hard to see why these arrangements have aroused the ire of other nations, especially the United States. They diminish the role of purely market-based competition that is open to all in favor of cooperative networks of elites that tend to be closed to outsiders, especially foreigners. Not only do they encourage exports and discourage imports, they do so through nongovernmental processes that cannot be easily identified or targeted as outright violations of WTO rules.

For example, Japan's notoriously inefficient retailing system suppresses imports. Most retailers are small shopkeepers who must rely upon an extensive network of wholesalers to supply the goods they sell. However, these wholesalers are usually affiliated with manufacturers, who can legally prohibit retailers from selling the products of competitors. Furthermore, because retailing licenses are required and existing merchants can block the granting of new ones, it is difficult to establish large chain stores that would be less reliant upon existing wholesalers and more price competitive. All of these arrangements make it difficult for new producers or foreign firms to get their products onto store shelves, the central allegation made by Kodak against Fuji in a 1995 dispute over color film that brought the two nations near a trade war. Of course, by severely restricting competition this system also drives up consumer prices. The WTO ruled that Japanese practices did not constitute a GATT violation, and Japan has since passed a new Large Scale Retail Store Location Law, but the United States continues to issue a semiannual report "assessing Japan's implementation of the representations it made to the WTO regarding the openness of its photographic film and paper market."[22]

At the same time that these structural features of the Japanese political economy discourage imports, others tend to increase exports. For example, in keeping with the Japanese tradition of lifelong employment, companies do not usually lay off workers even when sales decline. This constraint shapes labor-management relations, transforms the trade-offs involved in pricing and production decisions by firms, and changes the nature of political pressures on government macroeconomic policy. It is especially prominent in motivating corporate behavior that is otherwise inexplicable; for example, American competitors contend that Japanese firms engage in "dumping," selling products in the American market at a price that does not earn a profit. Since workers will be paid anyway, Japanese firms have an incentive to continue production under market conditions that would make an American firm discontinue operations.[23]

Thus, under the influence of both overt mercantilist policies and more subtle influences built into the fabric of economic structure, the Japanese economy in general—and several specific export industries in particular—achieved great technical sophistication and market success. Specifically,

Japanese firms achieved global dominance in textiles in the 1950s, electronics in the 1960s, and autos in the 1970s and 1980s.

As the conditions that sustain this policy have changed, Japanese policy has moved in a markedly more liberal direction since the late 1970s. Industrial policy is now much less aggressive, allowing market forces to assume a considerably greater role. Further, import protection has assumed the pattern more common in other developed market democracies, emphasizing the support of declining industries rather than the expansion of those with growth potential. Though tariffs and most nontariff barriers have visibly declined, critics contend that protectionism has not diminished so much as the predominant methods of import control have shifted. They now include arrangements that are difficult to document, such as administrative guidance on the part of government officials designed to intimidate importers, incomplete enforcement of intellectual property rights, government procurement policies biased against imports, and technical barriers to trade such as misuse of customs procedures and product standards.[24] It is no coincidence that the Uruguay Round agenda included measures in each of these areas. On the evidence of actual import levels, which are much lower in most industrial sectors than in other countries, various structural impediments remain, especially involving restrictions on distribution channels for imports. For example, only 3 percent of autos in Japan are imported, but in most developed nations the proportion is between one-third and one-half.

American attempts to assess Japanese economic policy typically stumble over two major puzzles. How can such antiliberal policies succeed? Why have they been tolerated? Both questions arise because liberal theory contends that all of these structures that supplant the private market—keiretsu, cartels, vertically integrated retailing, import barriers, export subsidies, and other government intervention—sacrifice consumer welfare. It is certainly surprising that policies that harm consumers could persist so long within a democracy. The key to understanding the differences between Japanese and American trade policy lies in the recognition that they pursue different goals, each representing a distinctive response to the trade dilemmas that all nations must resolve.

Although a full explanation of these choices would carry us too far afield, it is essential to realize that foreign trade permits these apparent sacrifices of consumer welfare to be interpreted in ways that strengthen their appeal. Most important, trade provides a means to exchange some loss of current consumption for alternative values such as full employment (to minimize instability and inequality), Japanese national power, and future consumer welfare. For example, the foreign currencies earned by the trade surplus have been used to greatly expand Japan's foreign direct investment (FDI) abroad. Japanese FDI, which now amounts to about

---

Japanese and American Responses to Trade Dilemmas

Japan	*United States*

1. Value trade-offs

Trade should be regulated to achieve social justice, domestic stability, and future national power and prosperity.	Trade should be free to maximize individual consumption, global efficiency, and stable world order.

2. Distributional outcomes

Trade should be regulated to protect workers, benefit desirable sectors, and shift welfare into the future.	Trade should be free to maximize current consumer welfare and encourage efficient sectors.

3. Effects on the state

Trade should be regulated to enhance national power and autonomy.	Trade should be free to achieve interdependence and peace.

---

12 percent of the global total (up from 0.7 percent in 1960), continues to earn profits that can be enjoyed long after the trade surplus that gave rise to it has faded into memory. Moreover, Japanese economic policy—in both its domestic and international dimensions—rests on economic theory that directly challenges key assumptions of liberalism.

STRATEGIC TRADE THEORY AND POLICY

Like early English mercantilism, postwar Japanese trade policy was not erected on an edifice of formal economic theory. Whereas liberalism contains an integrated body of precise premises, refined logical arguments, and universalistic policy conclusions, **neomercantilism** has always consisted of fragmented practical wisdom derived from an eclectic mix of past policy successes, tactical judgments, and a smattering of theoretical ideas. However, economic theorists have always followed in the wake of successful practice, so in recent years a body of thought now called **strategic trade theory** has arisen to explain the most novel aspects of the Japanese neomercantilist approach.

Of course, many elements of Japanese policy reflect age-old motivations and well-known policy initiatives. The distinctiveness of the Japanese experience lies in its artful integration of domestic industrial policy with promotion of the export sector and protection against imports. Indeed, the administration of these policies has been so artful that many commentators—especially liberal theorists—doubt that such an approach can be made to work outside the special circumstances of postwar Japan. Few governments inherit the structural conditions and public consensus necessary to implement an approach that depends so centrally on trust in governmental institutions and sacrifice of current welfare for the promise of future payoffs.

Nonetheless, recent theoretical advances—stimulated in part by the Japanese model—make a compelling case for export promotion and industrial policies. Strategic trade theory, which breaks with liberal theory in several important ways, is a refinement of older economy-of-scale ideas. Most important, it provides a defense for two propositions that are antithetical to liberal and free trade canon, though they have been accepted by countless governments for centuries. First, comparative advantage is not discovered by the savvy investor but actually created by a powerful state. Second, export promotion may be as essential to some infant industries as import protection because in some sectors a firm cannot be sustained by the market of a single country. For both reasons, government intervention is sometimes necessary to trade successfully. To see how this alternative explanation for trade suggests a greater role for the state, we must review the liberal premises that strategic trade theory challenges.

The liberal counsel that the state should avoid intervention in trade flows naturally from the Heckscher-Ohlin (H-O) assumption that the sole basis for comparative advantage lies in national endowments of land, labor, and capital—which governments can do very little to affect. However, these endowments may play a smaller role in determining relative production costs of modern high-technology products than they did with respect to the simpler products considered by Smith and Ricardo. Further, factors of production are no longer immobile across national boundaries. For example, American capital is readily available to Mexican firms if they have the other attributes needed to be competitive, such as technology, consumer brand-name loyalty, marketing expertise, product innovations, and, most important for our purposes, favorable government policy (especially subsidies). Of course, government subsidies have always been capable of affording competitive advantage to domestic firms over those of other countries, but such a policy was regarded as self-defeating for the economy as a whole because subsidies require tax revenue to fund them.

However, government intervention would be appropriate if comparative advantage rested on some factor that could be provided at no net cost only by the state. Strategic trade theory suggests at least three such candidates: very large-scale capital, coordination among competing firms, and a credible commitment to aggressive export-promotion policies. To be successful, though, all require the existence of economies of scale; that is, the unit cost of production must decline as the volume of production increases. Of course, to some extent all products benefit from economies of scale. After all, it is hard to name a product that cannot be mass produced more cheaply than made one at a time. But most products reach a point where higher production volumes carry no further cost advantage because a very large organization becomes increasingly inefficient.

Economies of scale sometimes persist even at a volume that saturates the market, however, especially when the variable costs of production are low in relation to the fixed costs. For example, the major cost for Microsoft in producing its computer software—paying programmers for the creative process of writing it—is fixed regardless of how many copies are sold. Its variable costs—buying blank disks to distribute the software—are very small. Consequently, once Microsoft has sold enough copies to recoup its fixed costs, it can sell additional copies profitably at a price that cannot possibly be met by a new firm that produces a competing product in much smaller volumes.[25] Because comparative advantage in such industries resides wherever large-scale production is initiated, an industrial policy that subsidizes start-up may be beneficial to firms breaking ground in new technologies. Of course, subsidies will be absolutely essential to start-up firms in such sectors if foreign firms are already established. Subsidies need not cause a loss of consumer welfare but only a postponement of it, because the mature firm should eventually generate employment, profits, and tax revenue that repay the state for its initial support. If so, a mercantilist industrial policy may itself be a source of comparative advantage and a major national asset.

Critics of industrial policy correctly observe that the state is not the only source of venture capital to initiate such industries and that private entrepreneurs may be better at picking winners and losers than government bureaucrats. Nonetheless, when very large-scale capital is required for a risky venture, the state may be the only realistic source. That is especially true when economies of scale accrue outside the firm itself but inside the nation in which it is located. For example, the concentration of chipmakers and computer industries in the Silicon Valley of California makes it profitable for similar firms to locate in the same area, taking advantage of the skilled technicians and the research expertise of those already employed there. Because the original companies produce advantages enjoyed by new companies—pioneers such as IBM and Apple paved the way for countless others—it may not pay private investors to initiate a dynamic industry even though it would benefit the economy of the nation. In cases of market failure like this—that is, when the private market fails to provide adequate capital because of externalities—the state can play a pivotal role.

Furthermore, a state with an activist industrial policy can bestow sources of comparative advantage that no private market can provide, such as subsidies for pure research or relief from onerous laws and regulations (e.g., antitrust). But the most formidable weapon of strategic trade policy is the reputation of the state itself for aggressively supporting an industry and ruthlessly competing with rivals. The promise to subsidize firms (or benefit them in other ways) well beyond the capacity of an unsubsidized firm to respond can intimidate potential competitors in other countries. Indeed, if the intimidation is great enough, neither the initial advantage nor the economies of scale need be especially large. Certainly the reputation of Japan Inc. discouraged some American firms from competing in consumer electronics because they were convinced that the Japanese government commitment to capturing the American market would make their efforts futile and costly.

Thus, where economies-of-scale considerations loom large, government interference with the private market yields benefits not recognized by free-trade theory. But why has Japan been so much more aggressive than the United States in exploiting these possibilities? Why has Japanese trade policy been predominantly mercantilist and American policy more liberal?

THE DIFFERENT ROOTS OF AMERICAN AND JAPANESE TRADE POLICY

It is useful to recall the lesson contained in our analysis of early England: An intimate connection always exists between a nation's trade policy and the remainder of its political economy. The same forces that shape a nation's response to trade dilemmas—various strands of ethical, social, and economic theory, the state of markets, and prevailing power balances among key actors—also influence the evolution of the domestic economy.

The liberalism of American trade policy reflects a domestic economic policy that also avoids state intervention in the market. For example, Japan (and most European nations) adopted an industrial policy that confers government benefits on selected sectors in order to build globally competitive industries; in contrast, the United States has emphasized a competition policy that emphasizes antitrust actions to prevent monopolies or oligopolies.[26] In particular, the Federal Trade Commission prevents market dominance by blocking mergers or acquisitions that would lower the number of competitors beyond a critical threshold. This strategy exemplifies the liberal conviction that efficiency is best promoted by competition among multiple firms and that government need only prevent business collusion that would lead to stagnation in productivity enhancement, product innovation, and consumer welfare. By contrast, the Japanese approach de-emphasizes antitrust, instead relying on foreign competition to fill whatever gaps are left by the absence of domestic competitors. Japanese leaders recognize that concentration of market power, control over prices, and sharing of effort is necessary to compete against foreign firms, especially those not restricted by antitrust laws in their own countries.

The difference can be explained simply: Japanese policy evolved in response to foreign competition, and American policy has its roots in an era in which foreign competition was insignificant in the United States. During its formative period, the United States enjoyed relative autonomy from international forces. Because of the sheer size of the American market and a plentiful endowment of natural resources, the country could produce most of what it needed and could sell within its own borders most that it could produce. This made it feasible for the United States to limit trade to a degree utterly impossible for Japan, whose dearth of resources and smaller market prevented self-sufficiency. At first because of the protection offered by tariffs and by high transportation costs resulting from physical isolation from trade competitors, the U.S. economy evolved an internal orientation almost without precedent. Even the post–World War II liberalization did not threaten most American firms, which had become competitive abroad and so dominant at home that as late as 1960 imports made up less than 5 percent of U.S. GNP. In the face of these market conditions, it is hardly surprising that industrial policy did not arise but antitrust policy did: Industrial policy is motivated by the presence of foreign competition, whereas antitrust policy is imperative in its absence.

Even though persistent U.S. balance-of-trade deficits demonstrate that foreign competition became much more formidable after the mid-1970s, an American industrial policy still has not emerged. The U.S. government lacks the ability to engage in successful industrial policy because it has no counterpart to Japan's MITI, whose expertise in coordinating import protection, credit subsidies, research and development consortia, cartel formation, marketing schemes, and export promotion are indispensable tools. Strategic trade policy also requires a level of trust between government and business that exists in Japan but not in the United States, where the relationship between the public sector and private business is more adversarial.

This strategy is especially well suited to the Japanese business environment because it rewards firms that pursue market share rather than immediate profit. By underpricing the competition, a firm can acquire a dominant position in a foreign market, which provides the leverage to raise prices in the future when the competition has been weakened or driven out of business altogether. Achieving market share is a goal consistent with the long-term view characteristic of Japanese firms but is not common in the United States.

Moreover, these strategies require that consumers sacrifice immediate welfare, which is more compatible with Japanese values than American ones. The Japanese willingness to defer consumption is symbolized by both a high savings rate and a trade surplus; the American budget deficit, trade deficit, and consumer debt levels are all testimony to the propensity of Americans to demand gratification sooner rather than later.

In fact, cultural differences between the two countries extend to a broad range of ethical theories and value judgments that are reflected in divergent economic structures and policies. The more communitarian tradition of Japanese culture finds expression in a variety of economic forms: reliance on personal networks rather than impersonal markets, lifelong employment practices, and consumption decisions that give preference to Japanese products, among others. This tradition also helped Japan achieve a national consensus after World War II in favor of a comprehensive industrial policy designed to use trade to achieve national goals and shift welfare from the present to the future. The U.S. political economy—and the trade policy that follows from it—has far different roots. It is built upon a structure formed by liberal theory and the individualistic and materialistic values that sustain it, much like the liberal period in nineteenth-century Britain. Thus, liberal theory has become an article of faith in the United States but not in Japan, which embraces the precept that too much competition can be as injurious as too little.

At the same time, the political power of key actors in both countries has played a major role in policy choice. For example, Japan's political structure allows the farm vote—the single strongest source of support for import protection—to elect something approaching 25 percent of the Diet, the Japanese parliament. Further, so many individuals benefit from each of the exclusionary arrangements—keiretsu, import restrictions, retailing networks, lifelong employment—that a substantial constituency exists for the system as a whole. Finally, the political culture does not encourage the challenges to community consensus or government policy that are more common in the United States. As a result, the Liberal Democratic Party, which created and sustained Japanese trade policy, enjoyed a near monopoly of political power for most of the postwar period.

In the United States, some critics have suggested an emulation of Japanese or European industrial policy, observing that a liberal approach leaves American workers vulnerable to foreign competition, which is particularly alarming because welfare provisions in the event of unemployment are much less generous in the United States than in Europe. However, because the United States lacks the leftist parties centered around the strong trade union movement that marks the European social democracies, this argument has not been championed by an effective political power base. For a number of reasons, political power in the United States has been decentralized, and a sharp class-based cleavage has not appeared. As a result, the American state has been smaller and less active in promoting welfare benefits than the typical European state, and less powerful and interventionist in shaping the economy than the typical Asian state.

Because Americans have such strong faith in the market—U.S. producers have been among the most competitive in the world in all the leading sectors—and so little affection for government, it cannot be a surprise that American trade policy after World War II took on the same liberal orientation found in its domestic economic policy. Indeed, the United States sought to remake the global political economy in its own liberal image, confident that the burdens imposed on the country by the Bretton Woods commitments could be easily borne.

Explanations for Postwar Trade Policy

Japan	United States
1. State of theory	
Communitarian ethical theory; neo-mercantilist and state-directed theory of trade and industrial policy.	Materialist and individualist ethical theory; liberal macro-economic and trade theory.
2. State of market	
Dependent on global markets, but inefficient.	Industry dominant over foreign competition.
3. Political power balances	
Dominance by state personnel, keiretsu, and rural sector.	Private sector dominant.

CONTEMPORARY AMERICAN TRADE POLICY

By the middle of the 1970s, however, this optimism had faded; several key American industries, especially steel and autos, had lost their global dominance and a substantial share of their home market. Not surprisingly, these industries began to take a sharply protectionist view and an especially hawkish attitude toward trade policy with Japan. As theoretical conviction gave way to material interests, American policy slowly drifted in a more mercantilist direction, partly driven by the mercantilism of others.

American protectionism has taken several forms, some of which are fully in accord with GATT rules (and even consistent with liberal principles); others have exploited gray areas in the agreement. GATT allows nations to increase tariffs in response to sudden changes in imports that diminish the income of any economic sector, even if they arise naturally from market forces and are desirable for long-term aggregate welfare.[27] In the United States, Section 201 of the Trade Reform Act of 1974 implemented GATT's Article 19 escape clause. It charged the U.S. International Trade Commission with investigating petitions for import relief and recommending action to the president. Between 1974 and 1986, fifty-five cases were investigated under Section 201 and relief was provided in eighteen of them. During the 1990s, such actions were rare, with only one or two petitions per year.

Instead, the United States has preferred to rely upon the Trade Adjustment Assistance program (TAA) contained in Title 2 of the Trade Reform Act. Upon certification by the secretary of labor that unemployment has resulted from imports that reduce a firm's sales, the TAA grants benefits for retraining and relocation to workers displaced by foreign competition. In keeping with liberal theory, this approach facilitates adjustment to trade's effects rather than a cancellation of them, which would reduce the gains from trade and antagonize trading partners. Since 1975, more than 800,000 auto workers and over 400,000 textile workers were the largest groups certified for benefits, but 5 other industries had more than 100,000 beneficiaries each. During the 1990s, about 1500 petitions a year were initiated, with about two-thirds of them certified, covering about 100,000 workers per year. A special program provided similar assistance to 50,000 workers displaced by trade induced by NAFTA in 1998. About 200 firms a year have also received technical assistance in conjunction with import competition under the TAA.

More controversial has been the increasing American willingness to impose retaliatory tariffs against "unfair" trade competition. "Countervailing duties" are used to offset foreign subsidies so that American producers compete on a level playing field in the U.S. market. Remedial duties are used to protect American industry from injury caused by the dumping of foreign manufacturers, which consists of either selling a product abroad for below its cost of production or below the price for which it is sold in the home market. Antidumping charges were first filed by American television manufacturers against Japanese electronics firms in 1968, with the U.S. Customs Service finding that Japanese-made televisions were sold in the United States for as little as half their price in Japan.

Both measures are authorized under GATT 1947 and the clarifying agreements of the Uruguay Round, but other nations question whether the frequency of American use of them is consistent with the responsibilities of a liberal hegemon. Under the pressures of the massive trade deficit, both Congress and the United States Trade Representative (USTR), the executive official charged with trade policy surveillance, have been hawkish on trade policy since the 1980s. The WTO reported that at the end of 1997, 87 countervailing duty measures were in force among its reporting members, 52 of those by the U.S. Of 880 antidumping actions in force, 302 of them were by the United States.[28] The United States has also been the leading litigant in using the WTO dispute settlement mechanism—42 times since 1995. Critics charge that this behavior, a protectionist response to its own domestic economic interests, is inappropriate for a hegemon expected to be more concerned about the health of the global economy. Antidumping actions taken in 1999 against nations in severe crisis—Russia and the suffering Asian economies—added to this criticism.

Furthermore, the United States has used controversial provisions of Section 301 of the Trade Act, which authorizes retaliation against any foreign manufacturer found to be engaging in "unjustifiable, unreasonable or discriminatory" trading practices, in ways that less powerful nations have been afraid to emulate. The USTR has initiated 118 investigations pursuant to Section 301 since the statute was first enacted in 1974. The Super 301 provision of the 1988 Trade Act goes further, with an emphasis upon identifying the products and markets that offer the best potential for the expansion of American exports. It places pressure on the president to designate "priority foreign countries" who maintain "unfair" trading practices and to set a deadline for progress in correcting them. The major target was clearly Japan, but both 301 and Super 301 have been broadly used in recent years. Moreover, all such actions produce "procedural protection" by serving as an example to other foreign producers, who will avoid even the appearance of unfair competition so as to avoid the rigors of the U.S. legal process and possible retaliation. They also provide the teeth that encourage nations to seek bilateral negotiations with the United States over trade disputes.

In fact, before the Uruguay Round sharply restricted the practice, it had become common for nations—especially the United States—to require competitors to "voluntarily" reduce exports through bilateral voluntary restraint agreements (VRAs). Of course, when the United States asks another nation to restrict its exports and threatens retaliation if it does not agree, the agreement is voluntary in exactly the same sense that one hands over one's wallet to a gun-toting mugger voluntarily.[29] The first voluntary export restriction, in cotton textiles, was adopted by Japan in 1955 and replaced in 1957 by a more formal bilateral agreement. The most notable of the voluntary export restraints (VERs), however, arose from a conflict over automobiles that began in the 1970s and culminated in the early 1980s. In June 1980, the U.S. Senate adopted—by a vote of 90 to 4—a resolution calling on the Carter administration to send a signal to Japan by reviewing American import policies. However, significant American opposition to import controls came from consumer groups who valued the energy-efficient imports during a time of high gasoline prices and resented the lackadaisical approach of Detroit automakers to foreign competition from Japanese cars that were widely perceived to provide higher quality and lower prices.

Heated public debate in the United States was mirrored by heated negotiations at the industry and governmental levels. The Reagan administration, committed to free trade but alarmed by the decline of the American auto industry, sought a voluntary export restraint by Japanese automakers that would achieve the desired end—a limit to foreign imports—while saving face for both sides. The United States did not wish to impose limitations that violated free market principles and the Japanese wanted to avoid action that would imply wrongdoing on their part. Eventually in 1981, a VER was negotiated that limited sales to 1.68 million units per year with subsequent renewals occurring at higher volumes. However, the ceiling, at 2.3 million units per year, has not been reached since 1987, largely because Japanese manufacturers have shifted production to the United States, thus avoiding the limit.

Though narrowly successful in achieving their limited aims, these sector-specific talks have pleased no one. Liberals in both countries assail them for violating free trade and legitimating other nontariff barriers (NTBs) that interfere with market efficiency and lower global welfare. Consumers complain that U.S. NTBs, which were estimated to reduce American manufactured imports by about $50 billion in 1983 (around a quarter of actual imports), raise prices while protecting inefficient industries.[30] Japanese exporters contend that they are being punished for their own efficiency; the American firms they compete against feel that the protection offered is inadequate.

Critics fear that these gray-area measures undermine international institutions, observing that the WTO cannot adequately police—or even document—agreements that are informal, unwritten, and, technically speaking, voluntary. A GATT review identified forty-seven such arrangements, but the United States denied that many of these exist. Efforts to achieve a standstill of further policies that contravened the letter or spirit of GATT or rollbacks of existing violations were centered on the United States (which accounted for about half of the protests lodged). These developments have been especially distressing because as national policies have skirted the international institutions that constrain protectionism, nontariff barriers have mushroomed. Already more than a quarter of the imports of industrial countries are covered by NTBs, including 36.1 percent of agricultural goods and 16.1 percent of manufactures.[31] The result must be lower levels of trade and reduced consumer welfare.

Moreover, these arrangements dangerously politicize trade. This not only favors nations with greater bargaining power rather than those with superior legal arguments, but it also invariably engenders tensions among trading partners, none more prominent than those between the United States and Japan. Still, so long as the two nations cannot agree on either the general principles of what constitutes fair trading practice or the specific facts of the individual cases, no better means of resolving conflicts is evident.

RECENT TRADE DISPUTES

In the 1990s, the central issues in American-Japanese trade disputes have centered around the claims of each nation that the other denies it market access. The United States contends that its import barriers, described earlier, are necessary to counteract the unfair trading practices imbedded in Japan's systematic mercantilism. Japan denies that the failure of U.S. products to penetrate Japanese markets is caused by Japanese government policy and accuses the United States of preferring liberalism only in sectors it dominates while adopting ad hoc mercantilism whenever that would suit its interests.

The most heated trade tensions have revolved around American complaints about access to Japanese markets, even though liberal theory suggests that the main losers from Japanese import restrictions are Japanese consumers. For example, Japan's rice market is very heavily protected by quotas, and the United States is the second largest rice exporter in the world. In 1985, Japan produced and consumed about 15 million metric tons of rice at a total cost of about $21 billion. That same volume was worth less than $3 billion at prices prevailing in the United States and other global markets. Thus if free trade were to drive rice prices in Japan to global levels, the increased sales of rice exporters (in the United States and elsewhere) might benefit them by $3 billion but would benefit Japanese consumers by closer to $18 billion.[32] In manufacturing, where NTBs on U.S. products are estimated to be equivalent to a tariff rate of about 25 percent, complete trade liberalization might increase Japanese imports of U.S. products by $10–$15 billion annually, but these estimates are quite speculative.

As we have seen, however, these seeming losses are balanced by other benefits from the standpoint of the Japanese consumer. Thus, contrary to liberal theory, the loser in U.S–Japanese trade has been seen as the American worker, not the Japanese consumer. As a result, foreign pressure has played an unusually large role in shaping Japanese trade policy, with dispute resolution attempted at the unilateral, bilateral, and global levels. Unilateral efforts include Japanese initiatives in 1985 to designate October as import-promotion month, MITI's adoption of the motto "Spread friendship worldwide by promoting imports," and Prime Minister Yasuhiro Nakasone's urging each citizen to buy $100 worth of U.S. products.

At the global level, periodic attempts have been made to coordinate economic policies that produce trade disequilibrium, especially by the **Group of Seven** to stabilize the yen-dollar exchange rate. However, the WTO, which has been the most effective agency for dealing with other trade disputes, has been unable to deal with American complaints that Japanese markets have been effectively closed. In particular, WTO rules do not prescribe a remedy for the chief American complaints. Although GATT permits tariffs to protect domestic producers against imports that benefit from export subsidies by foreign governments, nations cannot use export subsidies to countervail foreign subsidies to import-competing industries. Thus, the United States could obtain no relief if American firms are prevented from exporting to Japan by subsidies to Japanese domestic firms. Nor could direct action be taken when export subsidies affect competitiveness in some third market. In both cases, the injured party could seek relief by appeal to the GATT Subsidies Committee, but in practice bilateral negotiations usually occurred instead. The WTO is intended to correct these deficiencies, but recent American actions to bypass its procedures suggest that even its chief sponsor doubts the effectiveness of dispute resolution by global institutions.

Indeed, most efforts to resolve trade conflicts between the United States and Japan have involved bilateral negotiations, mostly because they can more easily deal with the specific issues of market access that American trade officials attribute to Japan's unique economic structure and unusual consumer behavior. (Between 1993 and 1998, the Clinton administration negotiated 35 different trade agreements with Japan, mostly within particular economic sectors.) GATT was designed principally to reduce the overt barriers to trade commonly erected by all governments, but formal trade barriers like tariffs or quotas have ceased to play the major role in limiting American exports to Japan. Even direct government subsidies and technical barriers, which the WTO can address, have receded in recent years. Instead, American trade officials now focus their complaints on the private behavior of private actors and on the so-called structural impediments to trade that help shape that behavior. In doing so, they encounter more than the routine differences of opinion between nations that can usually be bridged by compromise—they confront a chasm formed by different philosophical positions concerning the fundamental dilemmas of trade.

Simply put, Japanese consumers and businesses appear to prefer domestic to foreign products. Japanese negotiators point out that the government is powerless to force consumers to demand imports, since consumer tastes cannot—and should not—be controlled by legislation. After all, they note, consumer freedom is an essential cornerstone of capitalism because it motivates the business competition that makes market-based allocation efficient and guarantees that citizen welfare will be maximized. They insist that the responsibility to reduce the bilateral trade imbalance resides in the private sector, principally with American businesses, which must either improve their products, tailor them more effectively to Japanese tastes, or market them more skillfully. Free trade, they contend, already exists.

This stance frustrates Americans, who insist that a refusal to buy foreign products cannot be considered fair trade, whether or not it conforms to classical definitions of free trade. Moreover, American negotiators point to a number of structural impediments that prevent Japanese consumers from realistically comparing domestic to foreign products. For example, the inherently exclusionary keiretsu arrangements act as formidable barriers to the entry of foreign firms, and the notoriously inefficient structure of Japanese retailing makes it difficult for foreign products to compete. One study estimates that for various reasons, the prices of selected American-made products are about 70 percent higher in Japan than in the United States.[33] Thus it is hard not only to generate the kind of free trade that the United States seeks but even to establish whether free trade exists when the very meaning of the term is contested.

These structural impediments to trade produce a conundrum in American efforts to open the Japanese market to U.S. firms. Eliminating formal trade barriers is an inadequate negotiating goal because it will leave intact those structural features of the Japanese political economy that tend to diminish imports. Standard approaches are no solution when a nation impedes trade through a societal rather than a state-based policy apparatus. However, any effort to attack these structural impediments forces a stark confrontation with trade dilemmas involving national autonomy and the preservation of alternative values. After all, asking for fundamental reform of the Japanese retailing system is equivalent to asking Americans to eliminate shopping malls.

As a result, negotiators have struggled with a variety of approaches to these inherently tendentious issues with very limited success. The most far-reaching negotiations were the structural-impediment-initiative (SII) talks, initiated in 1989. In attacking the structural arrangements that affect trade, these talks laid bare the dilemmas that arise whenever trade is linked to other aspects of national life. For example, the U.S. list of structural impediments to trade included Japanese savings and investment patterns, land policy, the distribution system, exclusionary business practices, keiretsu relationships, and pricing mechanisms. It was even suggested that because narrow Japanese roads discriminated against large American cars, they should be considered an unfair barrier to trade. The Japanese identified the chief impediments to imports of American products as the lack of U.S. investment in quality production methods, deficient worker training, and the poor American educational system. With an agenda like this, it is not surprising that the negotiations were acrimonious and unproductive.

Progress has been somewhat better when negotiations have focused on specific sectors of interest to potential American exporters, most notably telecommunications and electronics, forest products, medical equipment, pharmaceuticals, and, most recently, auto parts, air transport, and photographic supplies. In a series of so-called framework talks that covered automobiles, insurance, medical technology, and telecommunications, the United States sought to shift the focus away from formal trade barriers (because they are not the principal problem) and away from particular structural impediments (because they are difficult to measure or even identify with clarity). Instead, the United States has placed pressure on Japan to set numerical targets for imports by establishing "temporary quantitative indicators," a prediction of "what would happen in a particular sector if Japanese businesses and consumers made purchase decisions on the sole basis of commercial considerations."[34] The United States could then leave it to the Japanese government to find a way to import that quantity of American goods, thus shifting the pressure to identify and eliminate the unofficial import barriers to the Japanese government.

Japan has resisted, seeing this approach as a thinly disguised quota that smacks of managed trade—a direct conflict with America's professed commitment to free trade. The difficulty of papering over huge philosophical differences through such a voluntary import expansion (VIE) is exemplified by the semiconductor arrangement in which the Japanese government publicly stated that it "expected" that 20 percent of the semiconductors used in its computer industry would be imported from for-

The slow pace of U.S.–Japanese trade talks. Danziger © *The Christian Science Monitor*

eign firms (mostly the United States). However, the United States contended that this agreement should be considered a guarantee, and Japan rejected that interpretation of this "expectation." Thus, this approach, while sidestepping the most dramatic national sovereignty issues, invites misunderstanding and violates liberal precepts.

The two sides have been somewhat more successful in agreeing on quantitative measures of some structural impediments to trade. For example, in the auto area, the United States monitors the number of Japanese auto showrooms displaying American cars; Japan counts the number of American companies teaching the Japanese language to sales personnel or conducting seminars on how to do business in Japan.

However, U.S.–Japanese relations reached a new low in 1995, when the parties could not agree on provisions to increase Japanese purchases of American car parts. At this time the auto sector accounted for more than half of an escalating bilateral trade deficit. In frustration at the slow pace of negotiations, the United States announced plans to impose a 100 percent tariff on all Japanese cars priced above $30,000, which accounted for about $6 billion in sales in 1994. Japan, supported by the EU and most private economists in the United States, appealed to the WTO, claiming the retaliatory action brazenly violated the fundamental principles and specific rules of the WTO, which the United States had itself ratified several months earlier. Although American actions were consistent with U.S. law, they clearly violated the obligation to use the WTO's dispute-resolution mechanism, designed for exactly this purpose.

The stakes were high. As an American professor of international law put it, "America is flouting the core and central obligation since the beginning of GATT. This is just about the worst possible way to launch the WTO." Indeed, continued American defiance would squander the hard-won benefits of the decade-long negotiations over the Uruguay Round, which created the WTO, and if the United States refused to accept the WTO's judgment, surely other nations would cease to be bound by it. Furthermore, as the deadline for the imposition of these sanctions approached in June 1995, many cross-cutting retaliations in other sectors, especially air transport, were announced by both parties. A full-blown trade war, complete with a collapse in the legitimacy of the international institution that might otherwise contain it, could not be ruled out.

At the last minute, a settlement was arranged, but it was more a public relations achievement to allow both parties to save face than a compromise that actually settled any issues. Moreover, less than a week after this potential disaster was averted, a public brawl over color print film was instigated by the American firm Kodak and championed by the Clinton administration. The chief evidence for the existence of unfair practices was the claim that Fuji controlled more than three-quarters of the market in Japan, yet Kodak outsold them dramatically in every other national market in which they competed.

CONCLUSION: THE FUTURE OF AMERICAN-JAPANESE RELATIONS

There is some evidence that the problems in American-Japanese relations may be self-limiting. The Japanese priority on exports has diminished, and they now constitute a smaller share of GDP in Japan than in the United States. Japanese export performance has grown only at about the pace of its overall macroeconomic growth, which has been slowing, since the late 1970s.

Moreover, most analysts see a convergence in the two systems, as the inherent limitations of the Japanese system generate both internal and external pressure to harmonize Japanese practice with that in the rest of the developed world. Japanese citizens who work longer hours and face higher prices than workers and consumers elsewhere are tiring of these sacrifices. Japan has discovered that production cannot grow indefinitely without a greater increase in consumption. The long Japanese recession of the 1990s resulted partly from weak domestic demand associated with high savings rates and partly from weaknesses in the banking system that also had roots in the huge volume of savings. Thus, Japan has become less resistant to American pressures to deregulate its economy, though some of the changes have themselves contributed to Japanese troubles. For example, the gradual decline of lifelong employment has increased worker anxiety about job loss, leading to an even greater propensity to save rather than spend. At the same time, the United States has discovered that consumption cannot grow unabated without more energy directed toward production. In some areas American firms are moving toward the Japanese: in worker empowerment, just-in-time inventory practices, total-quality management, and greater integration and partnership among firms.

However, trade issues remain especially difficult for Japan because they dramatically expose the dilemmas involving distributional issues, effects on the state, and the trade-off between alternative values. Liberalization in general has been a divisive force in Japan, increasing the role of foreigners in a traditionally xenophobic society, diminishing the role of the bureaucracy, eroding the communitarian vision of the economy, and bringing into the open the conflicts among the interests of firms, consumers, and the government, between economic and political considerations, and between domestic and international goals. As a result, the consensus among policymakers responsible for the coherence of policy during the era of Japan Inc. has dissolved in recent years, with some agencies, such as MITI, favoring liberalization and others, such as MOF, more often opposing it.[35]

Still, convergence may be the ultimate answer to defusing trade tensions that originate in different economic policies, which in turn result from different values and economic theories, different conditions in markets, and different balances of political power in the two countries. The alternative, discussed in Chapter 6, is to use regional arrangements like the EU or NAFTA to encourage trade between similar nations and discourage trade among dissimilar ones.

SIX

□ □ □

Regional Integration

In response to the dilemmas of trade, most nations have fashioned some amalgam of mercantilist and liberal policies, seeking to capture the benefits of each approach without surrendering to the liabilities of either. One increasingly popular strategy is **regional integration**, which creates free trade within a group of nations but practices mercantilism toward nations outside that group.[1]

In this chapter I examine two variants of regional integration at very different stages of evolution: the European Union (EU) and the North American Free Trade Agreement (NAFTA). The NAFTA and the EU appear to foreshadow a global political economy of regional trading blocs that could signal an end to the multilateral (nondiscriminatory) structure that has defined international economic affairs since the end of World War II.[2]

THE EVOLUTION OF THE EUROPEAN UNION

The European Union was created in 1993 as the most recent of a progression of institutions that embody a vision of regional integration laid out in a 1946 speech by Winston Churchill: "I see no reason why, under the leadership of the world organization, there should not ultimately arise the United States of Europe, both those of the East and those of the West, which will unify this Continent in a manner never known since the fall of the Roman Empire, and within which all its peoples may dwell together in prosperity, in justice, and in peace."[3]

For nearly fifty years this image has guided a regional integration effort that has widened from six to fifteen nations and deepened from a narrow technical focus to an ambitious social, political, and economic agenda. The Treaty of Paris, signed in 1951 by France, Germany, Italy, Belgium, the Netherlands, and Luxembourg, founded the European Coal and Steel

Community (ECSC).[4] The treaty not only pooled and centralized the production of coal and steel, it also introduced the High Authority, the Council of Ministers, the Court of Justice, and the Parliamentary Assembly, all of which remain part of the institutional framework of the much broader EU that has subsequently evolved.

The Treaty of Rome, signed in 1957 by the same six nations, established the European Atomic Energy Community (EURATOM), and the European Economic Community (EEC), which greatly expanded the scope of the ECSC treaty by calling for the dissolution of barriers dividing Europe, the improvement and equalization of living and working standards, the abolition of restrictions on international trade, the removal of obstacles to concerted action among governments, and the enhancement of peace and liberty through closer relations among states. In 1967, the executives of these three European communities were merged. The Single European Act, which went into effect in 1987, was designed to create by 1992 the "single European market" that had been envisioned in the Treaty of Rome but had not been realized, "an area without internal frontiers in which the free movement of goods, persons, services and capital is ensured." In 1993 the Treaty on European Union, signed at Maastricht the previous year, entered into force, renaming the expanding web of institutions the European Union.[5] This institutional structure is increasingly statelike, with legislative, executive, and judicial branches (Parliament, Commission, Council of Ministers, and Court of Justice); economic institutions (Investment Bank, Central Bank, and Court of Auditors); and a variety of institutions that provide representation for the interests of various groups (Economic and Social Committee (ESC), Environmental Agency, Committee on Regions, Ombudsman, and many others). Meanwhile, Britain, Ireland, and Denmark had become members in 1973; Greece in 1981; Portugal and Spain in 1986; and Austria, Finland, and Sweden in 1995. As of 1999, thirteen additional countries have applied for EU membership and several others have reached trade agreements with the EU which give them some of the advantages of membership.[6]

Despite this growth, the future of the EU itself remains somewhat uncertain, because considerable opposition has arisen in many member countries. As integration has deepened, the dilemmas of trade have become more visible. A long-standing objection of critics is that European integration implies a substantial abdication of national sovereignty because it requires that national law be brought into accordance with EU law and because regional institutions are slowly eclipsing national ones as governing bodies. In fact, in response to this state goals dilemma the Treaty on European Union was initially rejected by a national referendum in one member country and survived very close votes in several others. Its most controversial elements were the call for a common defense policy and, especially, a monetary union with a single currency that would replace national ones.

It has long been apparent that the continuing liberalization of trade in Europe required a considerably more stable monetary arrangement than the system of freely floating exchange rates that had existed among all developed countries since the demise of the fixed exchange-rate system of Bretton Woods in the early 1970s. The most recent attempt at stabilization, the introduction of the currency called the **euro**, is discussed in greater detail later on. It illustrates that the dilemmas involved in trade, especially those concerning national sovereignty, carry over into the monetary arrangements required to facilitate it. Because of this concern over national sovereignty, not all the EU nations have joined the euro arrangement. Furthermore, because EU members fear that such intensive ties to nations with weaker economies would introduce too much instability, they established criteria for participation in the euro that many of the nations seeking EU membership would not meet. Regional integration is a strategy that attempts to maximize the benefits and minimize the costs of trade by carefully selecting partners in trade and in the institutions that must accompany it.

INTEGRATION: LIBERAL ON THE INSIDE AND MERCANTILIST ON THE OUTSIDE

Regional integration is best thought of as trade policy that is liberal on the inside and mercantilist on the outside. Within the community, free trade is encouraged by the elimination of trade barriers and the harmonization of economic policies. Trade barriers remain against the outside world, however, and the community achieves mercantilist goals of self-sufficiency and enhanced power that would be impossible for the constituent nations individually. Even the largest EU member, Germany, has a GDP barely a quarter of that of the United States, but the economy of the EU as a whole is slightly larger than the United States.[7]

Though liberals argue that both peace and prosperity could be achieved more fully through *global* free trade, regional integration may deal more effectively with trade dilemmas. First, regionalism dampens, though it does not eliminate, mercantilist worries about sacrificing national self-sufficiency and autonomy. Regional interdependence is less risky than surrendering control of the economy to the vicissitudes of global markets and the economic policies of 150 other nations, especially because regional nations are likely to share basic values and economic structures. Second, regional integration creates a level of governance above the nation that can soften the dislocations and resolve the disputes that inevitably arise from the distributional and values dilemmas of trade.

It is not wholly clear whether regional strategies like NAFTA and the EU are ultimately compatible with the ideal of global liberalism. The bicycle theory of trade policy argues that the two approaches are mutually supporting, because as long as free trade moves forward it stays upright, but it inevitably falls if it slows down or stops. Any movement toward free trade (even if regional) keeps the forward momentum going, thus resisting the natural drift toward protectionism that occurs whenever trade policy becomes strictly a national matter.

However, even though free trade areas are GATT-legal under Article 24, they contravene the liberal spirit of the nondiscrimination principle embodied in the most-favored-nation clause.[8] In fact, the term "most favored nation" has become a misnomer: The EU, for example, applies the MFN rate to only seven nations—the United States, Japan, Canada, Australia, New Zealand, South Africa, and Taiwan. Nearly all others are charged a *more* favorable rate. Free trade or preferential tariff rates apply not only to the fifteen EU members but to most other European nations (partners in the European Economic Area), twelve Mediterranean nations (EU associates), sixty-nine African, Caribbean, and Pacific countries (under terms of the Lomé convention), and all other developing countries (under the Generalized System of Preferences). As these arrangements multiply, the liberal foundations of the global order suffer severe erosion. A WTO study determined that by the mid-1990s 42 percent of all global trade flows were conducted under preferential agreements, but other studies have placed the figure as high as 53 percent. Nearly 75 percent of trade involving the EU is conducted under preferential arrangements, in contrast to about 28 percent in North America and 4 percent in Asia. In 1995 68 percent of the manufactured imports of EU nations came from other EU members and 59 percent of foreign direct investment was intra-EU. Thus, although the EU remains publicly committed to multilateral liberalism, its interactions have drifted into a pattern of discrimination more often associated with mercantilism.

The mix of liberal and mercantilist motivations for regional integration is most easily illustrated in connection with customs-union theory, which adapts Ricardian ideas concerning global free trade to the special case of regional trade preferences. Canadian economist Jacob Viner's classic 1950 book *The Customs Union Issue* identifies two effects of initiating free trade among members of a regional organization while continuing protection against the outside world.

Trade creation occurs when a customs union allows goods once produced domestically to be imported from a more efficient producer in a member country. The result is the familiar Ricardian gain from trade, in which both countries are better off and the rest of the world is not adversely affected. However, a second pattern, which Viner calls trade diversion, may arise if the establishment of a customs union shifts production from an efficient outside producer to a less efficient inside one. For example, suppose that Germany initially imports a good from its most efficient global producer, a firm in the United States. After the creation of a customs union between France and Germany, Germany would impose a higher tariff on the U.S. product than on the comparable French one. As a result, French imports could replace U.S. imports. This trade diversion modifies the positive liberal assessment of a customs union because it shifts production from a more efficient to a less efficient producer. Whereas trade creation benefits member states without affecting others, the benefits of trade diversion come to member nations at the expense of outside nations.

THE MERCANTILIST ROOTS OF THE EU

The presence of trade diversion makes it clear why outside nations typically see the mercantilist face of regional integration rather than its liberal face, which is turned inward. From their standpoint, regionalism not only furthers the classical mercantilist goal of protecting domestic industry, it does so through a classical mercantilist melding of foreign policy concerns with economic aims. Rather than erect trade barriers against all foreign competitors equally, the EU discriminates against nations outside the region, often because they are seen as a threat.

Indeed, from its beginnings, European unification has accelerated whenever threats from outside have been perceived. The early European Community (EC) was designed to protect Europe against the Soviet military threat posed by a large army and aggressive doctrine as well as the U.S. economic threat posed by large productive capacity and expansionist marketing plans. The Single Market initiative culminating in 1992—Carlo DiBenedetti called it "a deadline not to be dead"—was energized by the economic threat of rapidly growing productivity in Asia and the resulting "Euro-pessimism." Again we see that nations turn in a mercantilist direction when their industries fear more competitive firms abroad and when their states fear the rising power of rivals. The EU's goals are no different than those of Queen Elizabeth's sixteenth-century industrial development or Japan's postwar export promotion: Its uniqueness lies in the regional emphasis of its mercantilism, which can be seen most clearly by contrasting liberal and mercantilist viewpoints on trade diversion.

Whereas liberal theory disapproves of trade diversion because it compromises efficiency, mercantilism finds it perfectly acceptable if it helps to achieve other national goals. Since many values and goals conflict with efficiency, nations may prefer to trade with one country rather than another for several reasons. First, a nation may divert trade in order to benefit an economy whose resulting prosperity produces greater side benefits for it. For example, for reasons of physical proximity and economic integration, Germany is much more likely to gain from the prosperity of France than it is from the prosperity of a nation—for example, Japan or the United States—that is thousands of miles away. Second, trade diversion under regional integration is reciprocated: Germany diverts its trade toward France, and in exchange, France diverts its trade toward Germany. Third, most European nations are more comfortable with depending upon other Europeans than upon Japan or even the United States. Not only do they share more security concerns with their European neighbors but they also have more common views on issues that always arise in trade matters (e.g., dilemmas involving job security, welfare arrangements, and environmental protection). Furthermore, they can create regional institutions such as those of the EU to cope with whatever conflict may stem from differences in how they respond to trade dilemmas.

THE LIBERAL ROOTS OF THE EU

Despite these undeniable mercantilist motivations, the EU is also deeply rooted in liberal ideas, especially the gains from trade promised by Ricardian theory. For example, the Cecchini report (1988) was instrumental in gathering support for the Single Market initiative by estimating trade gains resulting in a 35 percent boost in GDP. However, gains from specialization and enhanced competition are not the only benefits of the EU seen by liberal theorists.

Economies of scale, which have always been a strong motivation for the smaller countries of Europe, were especially visible in the ECSC. Because steelmaking requires large-scale plants and equipment, which are efficient only when producing in large volumes, a steel industry could never emerge in a small country unless a firm could be guaranteed access to the larger European market. The ECSC provided that guarantee in the form of the pledges by European governments not to interfere with free trade in these goods. The result was a key industry with production facilities scattered among different countries, each dependent on other nations to provide both demand for the final product and part of the supply capacity. A side benefit of this arrangement was the fulfillment of the liberal dream of an interdependence that would prevent war by making it suicidal.

In fact, the EU's economic institutions were constructed for a political purpose. The mission of European integration, as stated in the preamble to the ECSC treaty, is to "substitute for age-old rivalries the merger of their essential interests; to create, by establishing an economic community, the basis for a broader and deeper community among peoples long divided by bloody conflicts; and to lay the foundations for institutions which will give direction to a destiny henceforward shared."[9] Thus, the ECSC was an innovative form of peace treaty, designed, in the words of Robert Schuman, to "make it plain that any war between France and Germany becomes, not merely unthinkable, but materially impossible."[10] In the aftermath of two devastating wars in the previous thirty years—which more conventional tools of international politics such as the European balance of power, the League of Nations, and international law could not prevent—European nations were willing to tolerate the erosion of national autonomy and self-sufficiency implied by interdependence in order to weaken the nationalism that had provoked so much violence.

THE POLITICAL ROOTS OF THE EU

Throughout its history, European integration has been seen as a means of escaping the liberal and mercantilist horns of trade dilemmas by providing a regional level of governance to deal with common problems that no single nation could solve. For example, the Common Agricultural Policy (CAP), born in 1962, embraced a concern with the distributional dilemma of trade that would have been at home in parliamentary debates of the eighteenth century: Its goals included "the assurance that those working in agriculture will enjoy a standard of living comparable to that enjoyed by workers in other sectors." Because it was evident as early as 1951 that this motivation implied an ambitious institutional design, the Treaty of Paris went well beyond limited economic objectives to create the executive and legislative institutions that remain at the heart of the contemporary EU. Later, the Treaty of Rome's social and political provisions—which included the creation of the Economic and Social Committee to provide a strong voice for workers, employers, consumers, and academics—made the EC much more than a mechanism for advancing free trade.

These arrangements were a direct outgrowth of the values and theories that influenced *national* economic policies in Europe, especially where working-class political parties of the left came to power—Labour in Britain, Social Democrats in Germany and Scandinavia, and Socialists in France, Italy, and Spain. Rooted in powerful trade union movements, those parties embraced values of egalitarianism that emphasized the welfare and security of workers, and shared the conviction that it was safer to entrust these goals to the state than to free markets. They erected welfare states to provide a level of institutional protection against the vagaries of markets that was quite distinct from the more laissez-faire arrangements in the United States. For example, vacations, maternity leave, and health insurance, which are all voluntary fringe benefits in the United States, are determined by law in most EU states. Furthermore, because some constitutions list the right to work among human rights, the ability of firms to hire and fire workers is sharply constrained. When European national governments spend an average of 25 percent of GDP on social protection, it is hardly a surprise that an agreement to increase trade would include a provision to compensate those who would lose in the resulting dislocations. Indeed, the Social Fund, created in 1951 to finance worker retraining and relocation necessitated by the ECSC and now charged with aiding trade-damaged geographic regions, has become the second largest expenditure in the EU budget (behind agriculture).

Liberal economists contend that compensating losers—though second best to laissez-faire—is preferable to protecting jobs through trade barriers, which are inefficient because the price increases they induce cut consumption and reward less efficient domestic producers. The second-best alternative is to augment free trade with programs that directly compensate displaced workers, such as unemployment insurance. However, because the taxes to finance such programs may be more visible to voters than trade barriers, protectionism may be politically first best though economically third best, at least where redistributive measures have limited philosophical support, as in liberal America. The European socialist tradition makes it easier to sustain much more generous welfare provisions, but such policies are not costless. They may be responsible for unemployment levels of over 10 percent throughout Europe in the 1980s and 1990s, which would be completely unacceptable in the United States, both because of the hardship on the unemployed and the tax drain of supporting them. By contrast, European polities would not tolerate the U.S. approach, which has always accepted "high risk and high reward, and left its losers to be pushed far from the economic and social mainstream," resulting in a "frisky, but cruel economy."[11]

However, it is difficult to maintain social protection—which inevitably imposes costs on business—when diminishing trade barriers force firms to compete with those in other countries that do not bear such burdens. For example, French firms demand a level playing field in competing with Spanish firms whenever the French government mandates employee benefits, health and safety rules, or environmental regulations more costly than those in Spain. In fact, free trade tends to harmonize many national policies, making it especially difficult for a nation to sustain different tax policies than its neighbors. Denmark, for example, found it impossible to maintain a value-added tax (VAT, i.e., sales tax) 8 percent higher than neighboring Germany's because Danish citizens could simply evade the tax by purchasing goods in Germany and bringing them across the border duty free.

Thus, some trade barriers must exist if nations wish to maintain different laws with respect to many aspects of economic, social, and political life. Of course, different nations do choose different policies, because they reflect different values and theories, different economic circumstances, and different balances of political power. Different tax policies, for example, reflect fundamentally different philosophies concerning how big the state should be, what functions it ought to perform, and how progressive taxation should be. In most nations, such key issues trigger mighty partisan battles over philosophical principles and the distribution of costs and benefits. In short, trade poses fundamental dilemmas, made more troublesome when nations tied together by trade view such dilemmas differently, as in the case of the United States and Japan. Indeed, regional integration is attractive to many nations precisely because it increases trade with regional neighbors—who are presumably similar in important ways—while retaining insulation from nations who are more distant not only geographically but in policy preferences.

Even in Europe, however, these dilemmas have been recognized but not resolved; instead, the battleground has shifted from national-level to regional-level politics. For example, workers fear that without regional coordination, diminishing trade barriers will tend to harmonize national policies by driving all nations to emulate those with the weakest social protection, an outcome called social dumping. Recognizing that national policies would increasingly converge, leftist parties successfully sought to foster harmonization in which the more laissez-faire countries emulate those with the most elaborate social policies. For example, the goal of the EU's Social Charter in 1989 was to promote "convergence between social protection policies to avoid . . . competition between the systems with the attendant risk of decreasing social standards." In particular, the European Parliament recognized "fundamental social rights which should not be jeopardized because of the pressure of competition or the search for increased competitiveness."[12] Of course, such a preference runs directly contrary to the values, theories, and political constituencies of more conservative parties throughout Europe, who prefer more laissez-faire arrangements.

The EU transformed this political contest between parties of the left and right into a controversy over the dilemma concerning effects of trade (and trade organizations) on the state, especially in Britain. In the 1980s, British labor unions recognized that the social legislation they preferred was more likely to be enacted by the EU than by a British government dominated by Conservatives. In effect, they preferred to have labor law written by the French Socialist Jacques Delors, president of the European Commission, rather than by Conservative British prime minister Margaret Thatcher. By allying with the Socialist Parties of Europe, the British Labour Party sought to reverse through EU legislation the conservative revolution that Thatcher had achieved through national legislation. Such calculations lead to controversies over how much national sovereignty must be sacrificed in order to achieve the gains from trade. Thatcher condemned the EU as an attempt "to suppress nationhood and concentrate powers at the centre of a European conglomerate."[13] She is certainly correct in that assessment, but one wonders whether her defense of national sovereignty would be as spirited if the majority of the EU were more inclined to support her brand of conservatism. In any case, citing national sovereignty, Britain opted out of the Social Charter in 1989, the social-policy annex to the Maastricht Treaty in 1992, and participation in the euro in 1998. In 1994, Conservative prime minister John Major blocked the election of the head of the European Commission because the leading candidate favored a larger role for the EU at the expense of the constituent national governments. The link between trade and other values cannot be severed.

Still, despite the loss of sovereignty implicit in economic interdependence, we can now see why regional trade liberalization generates momentum to create even closer forms of integration. In the liberal vision, every increment of liberalization hints at the greater benefits that lie ahead if integration progresses. For example, if free trade permits low-wage labor in Spain to produce products cheaply for the rest of Europe, free movement in factors of production such as capital would obviously enable Spain's comparative advantage to be exploited even more fully. As each barrier to trade is diminished, remaining ones become more visible and vulnerable to political pressure. In the mercantilist vision, regional integration also tends to generate momentum: Because each step increases interdependence, it is natural that each nation would welcome more intensive integration arrangements that impose greater constraints on the disruptive policies of other governments. As trade increases, the dilemmas it creates become more onerous and demands for institutions capable of dealing with them rise.

Thus, regionalism tends to progress along parallel tracks, one market-based, the other institutional. Even though the deepening of regional integration encourages greater integrative steps, it tends to sharpen political clashes over the form that it should take, especially the role it should play with respect to trade dilemmas. Liberals emphasize the economic dimension of free trade, in part because its tendency to undermine the capacity of national governments to sustain social protection could further the laissez-faire agenda of diminished state activity and an enhanced role for private enterprise. Fearing just such an outcome, labor accepts free trade only in exchange for the package of protection against the dilemmas of trade embodied in the social dimension. That is, it opts for an activist regional government to replace the increasingly impotent national governments.

However, greater levels of integration in Europe will require the precise resolution of ambiguities that, up until the early 1990s, were responsible for the acceptance of integration by groups with incompatible views. A key issue has been whether the leveling of trade barriers will arise from the opening of the most protectionist nations or the closing of the most liberal ones. The 1992 Single Market initiative was valued by some for its free trade face (Germany, England, Belgium, and Luxembourg); others were attracted by its protectionist face (France, Italy, and Spain).

The assessment by nations outside the EU will also depend heavily on the balance between trade creation and trade diversion. The real danger is that the complicated games among European governments and interest

---

The European Union Compromise on Trade Dilemmas

Liberalism	Mercantilism
1. Value trade-offs	
Trade creation within the region maximizes individual consumption and growth.	Trade minimized with nations having value differences; national and EU institutions achieve social justice and other values
2. Distributional outcomes	
Free trade within the region benefits efficient firms; most trade benefits are contained within Europe.	Workers protected by national welfare states and Social Charter; agriculture protected by CAP; poor regions compensated with EU funds.
3. Effects on the state	
Interdependence achieves European peace; trade diversion creates external tensions.	Severe erosion of national autonomy and state sovereignty; EU achieves power to counter United States and others.

groups will be resolved principally by shifting costs onto foreigners. The ambivalent U.S. attitude toward the EU has always been heavily dependent upon how protectionist it would become. However, the United States originally supported the EC as a means to European recovery at a time when Europe was seen to be more valuable as a political and military ally than it was seen to be dangerous as an economic competitor. The EC also tied West Germany to the West, discouraging a policy of neutrality or alignment with the Soviet Union in pursuit of German reunification. Now, however, the U.S. interest concerns its own exports, since about a quarter of them go to the EU and most of the rest face competition from EU firms. Further, because any preferential tariff area has the potential to become a heavily protectionist trade bloc, the behavior of the EU is continuously monitored by those who see it as the precursor of an international system composed of such regional arrangements.

Although the EU does appear to be moving in a liberal direction—its average MFN tariffs on industrial products fell under 3 percent by the turn of the century—in some areas of special interest to the United States that movement remains slow. Its agricultural tariffs still average over 20 percent, and import protection and the use of contingency measures remain significant in particular industrial sectors such as textiles, automobiles, and consumer electronics, where high tariffs co-exist with intense antidumping activity that also limits market access. As protection at the border is gradually reduced, internal obstacles to competitiveness and efficient allocation of resources become more apparent. Community subsidy programs remain sizable by international standards, and the opening of public procurement, which accounts for 12 percent of the Union's GDP, has so far had limited effect on external suppliers.

Within Europe, however, the major controversies concern the tensions provoked by the dilemmas of trade, an enlightening example of which is the chaos surrounding the collapse of the European Monetary System (EMS) and the subsequent creation of the euro.

THE DILEMMAS POSED BY EXCHANGE-RATE POLICY

Since the collapse of the European Monetary System's Exchange Rate Mechanism (ERM) in 1992, exchange-rate policy has been at the center of the trade dilemmas concerning national sovereignty that have threatened to derail further integration. As traditional trade barriers have diminished, the trade dampening effects of a system of multiple currencies have acquired increasing visibility. The most obvious effects are the simple transaction costs associated with currency exchanges: A consumer purchasing goods made in another country must pay the costs of exchanging the currency of his or her country for that of the nation in which the good was produced. Some costs are direct and visible, as when tourists pay a fee to a foreign-exchange broker; others are borne by businesses and passed along invisibly to consumers. In the mid-1990s, currency conversion alone cost European business $15 billion per year, and transaction costs associated with currency exchanges have been estimated to waste 2 percent of the value of trade. Firms also had to maintain accounting systems and bank balances in several currency units simultaneously and cope with multiple currencies in legal contracts, taxation, and strategic planning.

Moreover, when currencies are traded freely in foreign exchange markets, natural variations in supply and demand cause their values to fluctuate unpredictably, sometimes in wild swings of sentiment. This uncertainty concerning future currency valuations represented a major risk for businesses trying to operate across the European market. Long-term production and marketing plans were complicated because firms could not predict costs and revenues that were denominated in different currencies. In particular, firms feared that an increase in the value of their nation's currency would leave them suddenly uncompetitive elsewhere. This risk discouraged trade, because firms preferred to plan for the relative predictability of their domestic market. Indeed, as tariff rates among European economies declined, this system of floating currencies came to have a greater trade dampening effect than traditional trade barriers.

Thus, as a logical extension of the desire to increase trade, a single European currency to replace the fifteen national currencies has been a long-term goal of the EU for more than two decades. However, nations have strongly resisted giving up central elements of their national sovereignty: the rights to issue currency, to profit from the creation of a monetary asset, and to manage the economy by controlling the money supply. Any state harboring even a modicum of the mercantilist inclination to influence the economy—and all states do—would find the ceding of monetary policy to a regional authority an uncomfortable prospect. Moreover, a single currency would not be feasible until the various economies converged into a single market with similar levels of growth, inflation, and interest rates.

In the meantime, a less ambitious strategy was followed that preserved national currencies but restrained changes in their relative valuation. Early steps included a short-lived system of fixed exchange rates dubbed "the snake in the tunnel" in the mid-1970s. The European Monetary System (EMS), which launched the European currency unit (ECU) and included the Exchange Rate Mechanism (ERM), began operation in 1979. EU nations that joined the ERM pledged to maintain currency valuations within a mandated range, much like a regional version of the fixed exchange-rate system created under Bretton Woods. Whenever the value of their currency drifted beyond its agreed-upon bounds, they were obligated to use foreign-exchange reserves to buy or sell currency until supply and demand were once again in balance at the accepted value. When such actions were ineffective, however, governments were further bound to alter domestic interest rates or other macroeconomic policies in order to stabilize the values of their currencies.

It was expected that national economic policies and conditions would eventually converge, thus minimizing exchange-rate volatility and the need for governments to take extraordinary action to maintain their treaty obligations. In fact, however, different economic conditions in different countries—especially trade deficits, inflation, and interest rates—inclined foreign exchange markets to push the value of national currencies in different directions. Furthermore, because the priorities of different governments conflict, they often adopt policies that become incompatible with their obligation to maintain stable exchange rates. Thus, monetary integration poses the dilemmas of national sovereignty and value trade-offs, which is why only seven nations joined the ERM at its inception, while three others joined more than ten years later.

These dilemmas were brought home even more dramatically in fall 1992 when the ERM shattered and the prospects for further European integration consequently dimmed. At the time, Germany was suffering high inflation while struggling to unify formerly communist East Germany with capitalist West Germany. To restrain further price increases, German monetary authorities maintained high interest rates to slow the economy's growth. Meanwhile, both Britain and Italy, which were suffering high unemployment, sought low interest rates in order to accelerate growth. However, this disparity in interest rates induced British and Italian investors to transfer capital into Germany. As they sold investments denominated in the lira and the pound, the decreased demand for those currencies drove down their values, whereas the higher yielding Deutsche mark increased in value.

Under the terms of the ERM, Britain was required to sustain the pound at a value above 2.78 Deutsche marks (DM), and Italy was bound to maintain a value of 1,000 lira at DM 1.30. As the German central bank refused to lower its interest rates, both the pound and lira drifted to the bottom of their legal bands and finally sank beneath them. Britain spent more than $15 billion (half its total foreign-exchange reserves) to support the pound, and the Bundesbank spent nearly $50 billion to support the lira; but those sums were not enough. Italy was forced to acknowledge that it could not meet its treaty obligation to maintain the lira's value and withdrew from the ERM. Britain raised interest rates from 10 percent to 15 percent in a last futile attempt to remain in conformity but eventually abandoned the effort and similarly withdrew from the ERM. The pound quickly fell to DM 2.53 and the lira to DM 1.18 per 1,000. The Spanish peseta was also devalued by 5 percent and the Irish punt and Portuguese escudo soon followed. A few months later, the French franc was supported by over $10 billion of intervention in a single afternoon before the effort was abandoned. The ERM collapsed in a hail of recriminations that undermined faith in the ability of the EU to accomplish regionwide goals while simultaneously respecting differences in national-level priorities.

The ERM had succumbed to the same forces that had doomed the fixed exchange-rate system of Bretton Woods twenty years before—large capital flows that would destabilize currency values unless counteracted by policies that were politically unacceptable. It also foreshadowed the Asian financial crisis five years later, which is described in the following chapter. Economists refer to this interaction among interest rates, exchange rates, and capital flows as the Mundell-Fleming constraint: A nation cannot simultaneously maintain unrestrained capital flows, a stable exchange rate, and independent monetary policy. Yet the EU was committed to the free movement of capital by the Single European Act, the ERM mandated stable exchange rates, and domestic constituencies demanded monetary policies suitable to the unemployment and inflation conditions in their own country. In effect, to maintain the stable exchange rates that sustained free trade required nations to abandon the freedom to choose policies that would satisfy other goals, such as the reunification of Germany or the control of unemployment in Italy. Faced with this clear dilemma of national sovereignty, several governments chose policy independence over the regional arrangement to encourage trade.

In August 1993, the first attempt to rebuild the ERM acknowledged the Mundell-Fleming constraint, but accepted the primacy of national sovereignty. Nations were required to maintain their currencies only within a very wide band of 15 percent on either side of their central target, virtually an unmanaged float in comparison to the previous stringent requirement of 2.25 percent. The benefits of exchange-rate stability for expanding trade were thus sacrificed in this interim agreement so that governments could use monetary policy and even currency devaluations to better achieve domestic goals. But the fear of the disruptive impact of exchange rates that were permitted to move as much as 30 percent made this only a temporary expedient, chosen over two even less attractive options.

The first, a return to a real fixed exchange-rate system, was incompatible with independent monetary policy, even if it could be accomplished in the face of large-scale flows of capital. The need for independent monetary policy could be minimized, of course, if economic conditions were similar across all countries. But to more closely align economic conditions implied even greater constraint on the policies that produced them (the budget deficits that produced inflation, for example) and even greater sacrifice of national sovereignty.

The second option, the preliminary plans for which had been underway for some time, was to proceed with full monetary union by adopting a single currency. This option too required policy coordination, especially with respect to budget deficits, which could now produce inflation community-wide, and sacrificed even more national sovereignty because it eliminated *all* independent monetary policy. However, this single currency option, later to evolve into the euro, not only offered a more permanent solution to exchange-rate instability, it also transformed the national sovereignty problem that most irritated the French. France felt that the old ERM had degenerated into a system in which Germany would use its monetary policy to achieve its own goals—such as unification and the control of inflation—whereas the pressures of that decision would require that all other ERM members use its monetary policy to keep a stable link with the D-mark. Thus, Germany benefitted from a system that was being sustained by the sacrifice of national sovereignty by all the others. If European nations were to sacrifice economic independence, they preferred that it be surrendered to an independent Central Bank rather than to a long-time political, military, and economic rival such as Germany.

So was born the European Monetary Institute, established in 1994, to be transformed into the European Central Bank (ECB) in January 1999. Its mission was to issue a single currency, the euro, and thus to determine monetary policy for the entire region. The Euro was launched as an accounting unit on January 1, 1999, with eleven of the fifteen EU nations participating (all but Britain, Sweden, Denmark, and Greece). Euro notes and coins are to be issued on January 1, 2002, and all national currencies of the participating countries will cease to be legal tender on July 1, 2002.

Such an unprecedented ceding of autonomy over monetary policy entailed major risks, which required careful selection criteria of participating nations and strict limitations on the economic policies that could be enacted by them subsequently. Without monetary policies to insulate the national economies from the conditions prevailing in others, inflation and high interest rates induced by a budget deficit in one country could quickly spread to the others, for example. Thus, the Maastricht agreement established criteria for entry, the most constraining of which were that the budget deficit must be under 3 percent of GDP, the national debt under 60 percent of GDP, and inflation under 3.2 percent. In fact, these criteria were relaxed, with most nations qualifying only after obvious accounting tricks, but the effort to meet them did have a substantial constraining effect on national policies. Even more constraining is the "stability and growth pact," which requires that all participants continue to observe the 3 percent limit on budget deficits or face substantial fines.

In democracies where tax and expenditure levels are fiercely debated, the imposition of external controls undermines the ability of citizens to determine the most important policies of their governments. Moreover, the treaty explicitly forbids the European Central Bank to "seek or take instructions from Community institutions or bodies, from any government of a member state or from any other body." These arrangements may also unwisely prevent national governments from stimulating the economy during recession, a concern given greater weight by the statutory goal of the ECB. Unlike the Federal Reserve in the United States, the ECB is not required to take employment or output levels into account, but only to maintain price stability, which it has defined as inflation under 2 percent a year. Critics note that "in modern times, no major economy has hit such a target consistently over a run of years. . . . In short, a radically undemocratic institution has been charged to achieve, without compromise, an exceptionally demanding goal of virtually zero inflation." And the public support for such a massive transformation in authority remains precarious, with the percentage of citizens reporting that they feel well informed about the EMU well under 50 percent in all eleven euro countries and under a third in eight of them.[14]

Clearly, the EU represents an extreme example of one resolution of the dilemma of national sovereignty raised by the desire to achieve the benefits of free trade. Of course, the EU has other goals as well, many of which are not shared by the regional integration schemes that have sprung up all over the world in partial emulation of the EU. We now turn to the case of NAFTA, in which the dilemmas of trade manifest themselves in similar ways, but a very different type of regional trade arrangement has resolved them quite differently.

THE EVOLUTION OF THE NORTH AMERICAN FREE TRADE AGREEMENT

The North American Free Trade Agreement created a preferential tariff area among the United States, Canada, and Mexico beginning on January 1, 1994. However, the drive for regional economic cooperation had begun as early as 1851 with bilateral free trade negotiations between the United States and Canada. A free trade area involving the United States and all of Latin America was advocated by U.S. secretary of state James Blaine in 1881.

The first successful effort, however, was the landmark 1965 agreement that allowed duty-free trade in automobiles and original equipment parts between the United States and Canada. The resulting explosion of trade in the auto sector—from $625 million in 1964 to over $40 billion (about a third of total U.S.–Canadian trade) by 1984—motivated the Canada–United States Trade Agreement (CUSTA), which expanded free trade to most economic sectors beginning in 1989. Most of CUSTA's provisions were retained in NAFTA, which took effect in 1994 after ratification processes in all three countries revealed considerable public uneasiness over issues commonly associated with the dilemmas of trade.[15]

Although some of the motivations for CUSTA/NAFTA parallel those of the EU, both their provisions and the institutional structures that support them are vastly different. NAFTA is indisputably an economic agreement, lacking both the broader social and political sweep of the EU—it contains nothing resembling the EU's Social Charter, for example—and its more ambitious long-term goals for common foreign and defense policy. Thus, NAFTA has no parallel to the EU's web of executive, legislative, and judicial institutions, nor to its elaborate mechanisms for citizen representation. More narrowly yet, NAFTA is principally a trade agreement, with only limited provisions concerning investment and none addressing the monetary arrangements and economic policy coordination that are such a prominent part of the EU. The core of NAFTA consists of a phased elimination of tariff and most nontariff barriers over ten years, with a few sectors having a fifteen-year transition period. The remaining elements of NAFTA qualify this liberalization and provide a sparse institutional structure to implement the agreement and resolve disputes that arise under it.

Predictably, liberals lament that NAFTA does not go further in promoting free economic exchange. NAFTA attacks tariffs, but it does not prevent other barriers to trade such as subsidies and the procurement practices of governments. Some of these barriers pose the now familiar dilemma of competing values: Policies designed for other purposes—even Canada's government-sponsored national health insurance and America's defense-contracting practices—can be seen as trade barriers because they confer a competitive advantage on some firms. Negotiations on such matters were difficult because the structure of protection is so different across these countries, with the United States objecting principally to Canadian subsidies and Canada protesting that the United States used its trade-remedy laws to stifle legitimate competition.

Liberals also complain that NAFTA does not remove the barriers to movements of capital that prevent the most efficient combination of all factors of production. For example, a government review board is still required to approve foreign investment in some sectors of the Canadian economy, and parts of the energy sector remain off-limits in both Canada and Mexico. NAFTA also contains no provision to control fluctuating exchange rates, which can distort trade because an undervalued currency will "tax" imports by making them more expensive (because it makes foreign exchange more expensive) and "subsidize" exports by making them cheaper. During the CUSTA negotiations, the National Association of Manufacturers and the AFL-CIO contended that the undervaluation of the Canadian dollar acted as a protectionist measure, but exchange rates for the Mexican peso, which have fluctuated wildly, are potentially even more unsettling. For example, the value of the peso declined 33 percent in relation to the dollar during one week in December 1994, wreaking havoc in accurately pricing imports and exports. One year after NAFTA came into effect, the peso had declined by 43 percent; at the fifth anniversary, the peso had lost 70 percent of its pre-NAFTA value.

If NAFTA is flawed from the standpoint of liberals, its limitations are even more alarming to those concerned about the issues that arise from trade dilemmas. Provisions to deal with those concerns, which are prominent in the EU, are largely missing from NAFTA, in part because the motivations for regional integration were somewhat different in these two cases.

MOTIVATIONS FOR NAFTA

Like the EU, NAFTA is the product of multiple motivations, the importance of which differed across the three countries. Both Canada and Mexico were driven principally by liberal incentives, emphasizing the value of economic growth over equality, security, and sovereignty. However, NAFTA promised efficiency gains associated with Ricardian comparative advantage that amounted to less than 1 percent of GNP for Canada. Relatively few areas of factor-endowment-based comparative advantage remained unexploited because the U.S. and Canadian economies were structurally similar and already largely open. For example, nearly 90 percent of U.S.–Canadian trade faced tariffs of less than 5 percent even before CUSTA. The liberalization that produced trade expansion among EU members began from much higher levels of protection.

However, reminiscent of the ECSC's effect on smaller European countries, CUSTA/NAFTA offered Canada gains from economies of scale estimated at nearly 10 percent of GNP. Furthermore, because the agreement restrained U.S. trade-remedy laws, which produced forty cases of countervailing duties and antidumping sanctions between the United States and Canada from 1980 to 1987, Canadian firms can now exploit these economies of scale without fear that an economic downturn or a political campaign will trigger a disastrous protectionist turn in the United States. Such benefits were thought to be even more significant for Mexico because its smaller market ($214 billion compared to Canada's $572 billion) offered fewer opportunities for large-scale production. Mexico also would seem to benefit more from Ricardian gains from trade, even though before NAFTA its exports faced an effective trade-weighted tariff rate of only 3.5 percent in the United States (plus NTBs equivalent to another 1.3 percent).

Mexico's principal motivation, however, was to improve industrial productivity, both by exposing Mexican business to foreign competition and by encouraging foreigners to invest in Mexico. The Mexican economy had stagnated, especially during the 1970s and early 1980s, under the Mexican Partido Revolucionario Institucional (PRI), the ruling party for more than three-quarters of a century. The PRI's economic approach, said to constitute a third way between capitalism and socialism, had featured an activist state, sharp restrictions on foreign investment, and extremely protectionist trade policies. For example, in June 1985, Mexico's average tariff rate was 23.5 percent, import permits were required (and usually rejected) for products constituting 92.2 percent of tradable output, and official prices bound 18.7 percent of products. By the late 1980s, the PRI had undergone a revolution in economic policy, which came to emphasize privatization (selling 1,000 of the 1,200 state-owned companies, including the national airlines and the telephone company); budget deficit reduction (from 16 percent of GDP to under 1 percent); elimination of government price fixing; inflation reduction (from over 200 percent to under 30 percent per year); and import liberalization (by December 1987, tariffs averaged 11.8 percent and only 25.4 percent of goods required import permits).

NAFTA became the symbol of that revolution because it lent credibility to such a marked departure from historical practice, even though more liberalization occurred before NAFTA than was expected to follow its implementation. In particular, NAFTA encourages foreign investors to regard liberalization as permanent because it binds Mexico under international law to an agreement also enforced by the power of the United States. Otherwise, investors would not risk a return to the old policies that could make their investment unprofitable. Without an influx of foreign investment, capital from domestic sources would be inadequate to fuel the growth made possible by Mexico's cheap labor force and direct access to the U.S. market.

Judging U.S. motivations is more difficult, because the liberal gains that dominated the calculus of both Canada and Mexico were expected to be much smaller for the United States. Because of its much greater size, any gains in access to the markets of its nearest neighbors would have a negligible effect on the U.S. economy: In 1992, total trade with Canada and Mexico amounted to only about 2 percent of U.S. GDP. Obviously, the gains from economies of scale must be tiny, and reducing already low trade barriers promised little improvement in efficiently allocating resources.

These judgments were borne out by many macroeconomic models constructed to predict the effects of NAFTA on U.S. output and employment. The gains were difficult to estimate, but even the most optimistic assessment foresaw a positive U.S. trade balance with Mexico of only $7–$9 billion annually with a net increase of only 170,000 U.S. jobs, a little more than one-tenth of 1 percent of the U.S. workforce. The corresponding efficiency gains would be under $2 billion annually in an economy of more than $5,500 billion. These gains would have been so small that in a dynamic economy we would not have been able to verify them even after the fact. (As it happened, these predictions of a $7—$9 billion U.S. trade surplus with Mexico were entirely wrong; rather the United States ran a *deficit* of about $20 billion per year in its trade with Mexico in the late 1990s and from $20-$40 billion per year with Canada.)

Why the big push for NAFTA if the promised gains were so modest and uncertain? Some of the explanation centers on the indirect benefits the United States could expect to derive from the Mexican prosperity predicted to result from its recent liberalization—if NAFTA could make it permanent. Even if NAFTA created no net trade increases but only shifted some labor-intensive U.S. imports from Asian to Mexican sources, the trade diversion would benefit the United States, which would gain more from growth in Mexico than growth elsewhere. For example, about half of Mexico's export earnings during the 1980s went to repay foreign debt, much of it to U.S. banks. It was also argued that development in Mexico might help to stem the tide of immigration that is increasingly politically divisive, particularly in the U.S. Southwest, but it does not appear to have done so. Because nearly 70 percent of Mexico's trade was with the United States—and because Mexico seemed likely to run a trade deficit for years to come—Mexican prosperity promised to improve the U.S. balance of trade.

As it happened, by the end of the 1990s U.S. dominance of Mexico's trade had grown to nearly 80 percent, in part because Mexico raised its tariffs against the products of other nations while it was lowering the rate charged to U.S. goods, giving U.S. products about a 10 percentage point average tariff advantage. This discriminatory move perfectly illustrates regional integration as a trade policy that is liberal on the inside and mercantilist on the outside. However, although U.S. exports to Mexico increased, imports from Mexico grew much more rapidly, so Mexico has become the fourth largest source of U.S. trade deficits, after Japan, China, and Canada.

The United States was also interested in several specific sectors even though their aggregate effects might not be large. By opening the Canadian energy sector to U.S. investment, for example, NAFTA enhanced U.S. energy security, demonstrating that regional integration can secure a classic mercantilist objective by expanding the borders of a self-sufficient area. Domains such as financial services and intellectual property represent growth sectors in the global economy in which the United States has a comparative advantage.

U.S. motivations were also related to other strands in its trade policy. It may be no coincidence that the Uruguay Round of GATT successfully concluded only after NAFTA had been approved. Because the EU has always been able to fall back on regional free trade whenever global negotiations turned sour, the United States lacked the bargaining power to complete the deal until NAFTA demonstrated that the United States had a similar alternative. Moreover, NAFTA introduced innovations that became precedents for global agreements, including its dispute-resolution mechanism (particularly compulsory arbitration and surveillance of trade policies), its treatment of services, and its elaboration of specific rights and obligations concerning national treatment.

But the best explanation for U.S. interest in NAFTA may derive from the Reagan and Bush administrations' conviction that the ideal political economy is structured according to laissez-faire principles of deregulation, liberalization, and privatization. They hoped that the more competitive environment created by NAFTA would strengthen the case for pursuing a competitiveness strategy that emphasizes lower taxes, weaker labor organization, and a diminished welfare state. Thus, NAFTA constituted an external reinforcement for a liberal policy program whose internal elements had been under constant attack from critics as they were adopted piecemeal after Reagan's inauguration in 1981.

In Canada, too, NAFTA represented the culmination of a strategy of liberalization—both in the domestic economy and in foreign trade and investment—that commenced with the beginning of the Mulroney government in 1984. Liberal proponents expected that NAFTA would bolster the similar drive that had been underway in Mexico since the early 1980s by enabling the Mexican government to appeal to the necessity of competing with U.S. firms. They hoped that successful development there might serve as a liberal model for other Latin American nations as well. Many of these nations, like Mexico, have engaged in heavily protectionist import-substituting industrialization (ISI) in the past and, in the process, acquired large debts that are potentially destabilizing for their own political systems, hemispheric foreign relations and, perhaps most importantly, the U.S. banking system. In fact, negotiations are currently under way to expand NAFTA's liberal vision throughout the Western Hemisphere in a Free Trade of the Americas Agreement. To see what this liberal ideal entails, we must consider how the various trade dilemmas posed by NAFTA were viewed by political actors in all three nations.

THE DILEMMAS IN NAFTA AND THE POLITICAL RESPONSE

Public opinion concerning NAFTA divided along the familiar fault lines of nation and class, but national sentiment did not reflect analysts' expectations of relative gains. For example, most analysts believed that the United States would gain less than either Canada or Mexico—and some questioned whether there would be any trade expansion for the United States at all—but the objection to NAFTA on these grounds was negligible among the U.S. public. Apparently, asymmetrical benefits provoke little concern unless the nations involved are perceived as rivals; reciprocity is more important in dealing with Japan than with Mexico. Moreover, NAFTA was expected to have less impact on aggregate economic outcomes than on the issues raised by the dilemmas of trade. Thus, in the United States, the greatest protests emerged over NAFTA's effect on unskilled labor (in response to the distributional dilemma) and the environment (in response to the dilemma of competing values).

In Mexico, NAFTA initially escaped much of the criticism usually directed against the distributional implications of free trade policies, simply because the liberalization that preceded NAFTA had already drawn most of that fire. Mexico had been in the process of reducing trade protection and capital controls since the debt crisis of 1982 and more intensively since 1987. During that time trade levels had doubled, but in real terms GNP per capita at the introduction of NAFTA in 1994 remained below its level in 1981. Thus, it was thought that the dislocation costs had already been borne, and so most saw NAFTA as a means to capture with greater certainty and permanence the benefits that the unilateral policies of the previous five years had only promised. However, a peasant revolt that began in the southern Mexican region of Chiapas in 1993 was directed against the economic priorities of the PRI—especially its tolerance for adverse effects on the poor—which were manifested in both NAFTA and earlier liberalization policies.

Still, NAFTA attracted the usual litany of opposition to liberalization only when its first year of existence witnessed an economic collapse that culminated in the worst Mexican depression since the 1930s. This outcome dealt a serious blow to the liberal creed because economic prosperity was expected to be not only the chief benefit of NAFTA, but so great as to render acceptable the familiar sacrifices associated with trade dilemmas—adverse distributional consequences, diminished national sovereignty, and the erosion of alternative values.

In Canada, the evaluation of NAFTA was colored by the experience of the previous five years with CUSTA (especially the deep recession that initially accompanied it too), the long history of uneasy economic relations with the United States, and uncertainties about the future of the federal system of Canada itself. Anxieties about national sovereignty and the outlook for labor have weighed heavily in Canadian assessments of NAFTA; these assessments became a litmus test of attitudes toward the Conservative government, which negotiated both CUSTA and NAFTA. Antagonism toward free trade contributed to the October 1993 national election in which Conservatives were humiliated by losing all but 2 of their 169 seats in the 295-member Parliament and winning only 16 percent of the popular vote. New Liberal prime minister Jean Chrétien originally vowed to renegotiate NAFTA but later backed off from this position.

THE DILEMMA OF NATIONAL SOVEREIGNTY

International agreements that preclude certain national policies—as NAFTA prohibits most trade barriers—invariably involve some loss of national sovereignty. Although this dilemma has affected attitudes toward NAFTA in all three countries, the issue has arisen in a different way and with a different intensity in each nation.

In the United States, national sovereignty was a minor concern, subsumed by greater apprehension about the environment and job issues though related to both. For example, NAFTA shifts some economic and environmental decisions away from national legislatures to binational review panels created to resolve trade disputes. Environmental and other groups that have considerable influence on Congress but none on these panels contend that the transfer of authority to supranational bureaucrats undermines national sovereignty and deprives citizens of rights of access to officials through elections, lobbying, and open public debates. This same issue arose much more powerfully in the context of the WTO, apparently because Americans do not see Canada and Mexico as the grave threat to national sovereignty that a global institution might become.

Mexican concern about national sovereignty produced one major concession in the NAFTA agreement: the exemption of Pemex, the Mexican national oil company, from its investment provisions. Pemex, though inefficient and corrupt, has become a Mexican symbol of independence and autonomy that has resisted privatization and retains protection against foreign competition in some areas.

The national sovereignty issue acquired its greatest prominence in Canada, where closer trade with the United States has always triggered concern about maintaining national autonomy in matters of politics, economics, and culture. The continuing fear of U.S. domination is exempli-

fied by the fate of the 1911 U.S.–Canadian free trade treaty. During its ratification in the U.S. Congress, some proponents represented it as a first
step toward the annexation of Canada, an outcome vehemently opposed
by most Canadians. As a consequence, the Canadian government was denied reelection in a campaign dominated by the campaign slogan of the
opposition, "No truck or trade with the Yankees."

The source of these concerns is not hard to see. In economic terms, critics claimed that NAFTA would increase U.S. domination of Canada. Even
before CUSTA, exports to the United States constituted 75 percent of
Canada's trade and 20 percent of its total GNP. U.S. foreign direct investment in Canada was valued at $70 billion with 20 percent of Canada's 500
largest firms owned by Americans. About half of Canadian manufacturing was foreign-owned, most by Americans. By 1998, 81 percent of Canadian exports went to the U.S. and U.S. foreign direct investment in
Canada exceeded $100 billion. More Canadian manufactured goods are
exported to the United States than are consumed in Canada. Statements
like that of U.S. trade representative Clayton Yeutter to a Canadian news-
paper shortly after the CUSTA negotiations do not allay those fears: "The
Canadians don't understand what they have signed. In 20 years they will
be sucked into the U.S. economy."[16] The response is predictable; Shirley
Carr, president of the Canadian Labour Congress, remarked, "It is in the
interest of the United States to try to take over Canada. . . . They want to
disrupt and disturb everything we have and bring us down to their
level."[17] Of course, intensive trade with a more developed and more powerful nation has fed such anxieties since the days of Friedrich List, but regional integration can be especially troublesome in this regard. Indeed,
the dilemma of declining national sovereignty has even dogged the EU,
though Germany is much less dominant within the EU than the United
States is within NAFTA. U.S. dominance has been especially striking in
terms of culture: "Only 3 to 5 percent of all theatrical screen time in
Canada goes to Canadian films; 97 percent of profits from films shown in
Canada go out of the country, 95 percent to the U.S.; 95 percent of En-
glish-language TV drama is non-Canadian; Canadian-owned publishers
have only 20 percent of the book market; 77 percent of the magazines sold
here are foreign; 85 percent of record and tape sales are non-Canadian."[18]

In response to these concerns, CUSTA's Article 2005 states that "cultural industries are exempt from the provisions of this agreement,"[19] thus
allowing a continuation of Canadian protection and promotion of cultural industries that has existed for most of the twentieth century. It is interesting that this very same issue also arose in the Uruguay Round talks,
with French negotiators eventually winning protection from Hollywood
film producers they regarded as symbols of U.S. cultural hegemony.

THE DILEMMA OF VALUE TRADE-OFFS
AND ENVIRONMENTAL POLITICS

Most of the major U.S. environmental groups opposed NAFTA, especially the Sierra Club and Friends of the Earth, which (unsuccessfully) sought a court order to require the administration to file an environmental impact report. For three reasons, critics feared that a commitment to NAFTA's free trade principles would require a compromise with the value of environmental protection. First, the border region of Mexico has become an export platform for companies who want to sell products in the United States but evade U.S. environmental standards. Second, the availability of the border region to polluting industries produces social-dumping pressures on U.S. state and local governments to save jobs by lowering environmental standards. Third, NAFTA opens U.S. environmental regulation to foreign challenge because it can be interpreted as an illegal barrier to trade.

The direct environmental dangers are concentrated in the border area between Mexico and the United States, which hosts the maquiladora program. Countless reports and studies have documented the area as an environmental wasteland with threats to the human population on both sides of the border, especially from water pollution. The Rio Grande, which serves as the U.S.-Mexican border for much of its length, is heavily polluted with metals and raw sewage. It provides drinking water for a million people and irrigation water for a large agricultural area, but its fecal contamination levels "regularly exceed, often by a factor of a hundred, standards to protect public health."[20] The New River, which begins in Mexico and flows into the Salton Sea, California's largest lake, is known as the most polluted river in North America. Beaches within several miles of the outlet of the Tijuana River into the Pacific Ocean have been closed for ten years. In San Elizario, Texas, 90 percent of the population has contracted hepatitis by age thirty-five because of a polluted aquifer.

This pollution originates largely in maquiladora firms, fully 10 percent of which admitted that they had migrated to avoid U.S. environmental regulations and take advantage of the weaker environmental laws and notoriously lax enforcement in Mexico.[21] For example, the La Paz agreement of 1983 required that industries importing chemicals into Mexico return any resulting hazardous wastes to the country of origin, but a 1988 report of the U.S. EPA showed that only 1 percent of maquiladoras had done so. This record cannot be a surprise: In 1990, the Mexican federal government budget for environmental law enforcement was only $3.15 million.

Environmentalists also fear that NAFTA will trigger value trade-offs similar to those that have arisen from conflicts between various environmental policies and previous free trade agreements, including the WTO.

For example, the Bush administration successfully pressured British Columbia to end a government-funded tree-planting program because it was an "unfair subsidy" to the Canadian timber industry. Similarly, government payments to farmers to promote soil and water conservation could be interpreted as an unfair subsidy of agricultural exports. Export restrictions on lumber designed to enforce practices of sustainable forestry could be considered a violation of prohibitions against export restraints. Restricting imports of food contaminated with pesticides now banned in America can be grounds for foreign governments to sue the United States for establishing nontariff barriers to trade.

The most dramatic episode occurred in the 1994 clash known as "GATTzilla versus Flipper," in which a GATT tribunal ruled in favor of a complaint brought by the EU on behalf of European tuna processors who buy tuna from Mexico and other countries that use purse seine nets. The United States boycotts tuna caught in that way, since the procedure also kills a large number of dolphins, but GATT ruled that the U.S. law was an illegal barrier to trade because it discriminated against the fishing fleets of nations that use this technique.

Initial experience with CUSTA confirmed that such environmental trade-offs will arise under NAFTA. The first trade dispute under the free trade agreement involved a challenge by the United States to regulations under Canada's Fisheries Act established to promote conservation of herring and salmon stocks in Canada's Pacific coast waters. The provision to require reporting was struck down by the dispute panel. Similarly, the Canadian government challenged the U.S. EPA's regulations that require the phaseout of asbestos, a carcinogen once frequently used as a building material. A balance between environmental concerns and free trade principles could be achieved, but NAFTA, which lacks the EU's recognition of the social and political dilemmas of trade, does not do so.

THE DISTRIBUTIONAL DILEMMA AND THE POLITICS OF LABOR ISSUES

In both Canada and the United States, however, the most controversial issue concerned the impact of NAFTA on jobs and wages. Unlike the Corn Laws, which posed the distributional dilemma principally in terms of sectors of the economy, in NAFTA the dilemma emerged as a class issue. Opponents contended that NAFTA would produce a net loss of jobs, especially among the unskilled, who are least able to adjust; a decline in wages among the unskilled who remain employed; and a transition period involving disruption and risk that is excessive given the small and uncertain projected gains.

Liberal trade theory made a persuasive case for NAFTA's long-term benefits, including more job creation than job loss, though macroeconomic computer models generally showed the net effect to be quite small. Opponents of NAFTA questioned outcomes derived from such computable general equilibrium (CGE) models because they required unrealistic assumptions such as full employment, balanced trade, and capital immobility. It is especially noteworthy that the major fear—job loss—was assumed away by the CGE assumption of full employment. As one critic pointed out, "We might forgive the Ford employee for being less than convinced by a CGE model that crosses a deep ravine by *assuming* a bridge."[22] Arguments for free trade often appear most convincing to those who have no stake in their truth, but for the workers whose livelihood depends on the accuracy of the trickle-down models, the theories usually seem too flimsy to justify the risks.

Labor concerns arose from the recognition that NAFTA would destroy U.S. jobs as some U.S. firms lost sales to Mexican firms and others moved production facilities to Mexico. Opponents emphasized dislocations from NAFTA-related job loss estimated in the range of 150,000 to 500,000. The transition period can be long and painful: It was estimated that 40 percent of laid-off workers would remain unemployed a year later and that the remainder would suffer wage losses averaging 10 percent for service workers, 20 percent for manufacturing workers, and 30 percent for automobile and steel workers. Within five years, most workers would have recovered their previous wages; but 35 percent would never again make the same wages, and three-fourths of workers would not go back to the same type of job. The average cost of a job loss for a worker was estimated to be about $80,000 over a lifetime.

Proponents observed that NAFTA-related job-loss estimates were modest in relation to the 2 million Americans expected to lose their jobs every year for the next decade for reasons unrelated to NAFTA. Further, they noted that job loss to low-wage countries was inevitable even in the absence of NAFTA. Finally, they pointed out that some job gains from NAFTA were just as inevitable as some job losses. Indeed, the positive employment effects of increasing exports should equal or exceed the negative effects of increasing imports. It is no wonder that businesses emphasized their vision of an efficient, comparative advantage–based economy that would eventually result from NAFTA and that labor organizations emphasized the transition costs that would be borne before such a future could emerge.

Free trade always triggers labor's concern about employment, wages, and social dumping, but three considerations made the issue unusually acute in the case of NAFTA. First, huge disparities in wage rates and working conditions between the United States and Mexico increase the

Smith-Corona, last US typewriter maker, moves to Mexico.

NAFTA fallout. Danziger © *The Christian Science Monitor*

pressure on U.S. workers. With wages for unskilled labor roughly eight to ten times higher in the United States than in Mexico, U.S. firms have a strong incentive to either abandon production requiring unskilled labor or move it to Mexico. Negotiating under this kind of threat, U.S. workers may be unable to resist a decline in wage rates and living standards. "A Wall Street Journal survey of 455 senior corporate executives taken just after NAFTA was initialed, found that 25 percent would use NAFTA to bargain down wages and 40 percent would move production to Mexico." Furthermore, a 1997 study of 600 attempts by labor unions to organize workers or negotiate a first contract revealed that "62 percent of employers threatened to move their operations instead of negotiating with the union."[23]

The factor price equalization theorem, an elaboration of Heckscher-Ohlin, states that free trade will cause all factor prices, including wage rates, to equalize across nations. Supporters hoped that NAFTA would bring a growth boom to Mexico that would result in Mexican wages rising to U.S. levels rather than U.S. wages falling to Mexican levels, but such a result is, at best, a long way off. Labor surpluses and weak labor laws in Mexico preclude substantial upward pressure on wage rates for many years. As a result, NAFTA might lower wages in the United States without raising them in Mexico, which would be especially alarming because

AT A MAQUILADORA

Wage bargaining at a maquiladora. Danziger © *The Christian Science Monitor*

wages for unskilled labor are already declining in the United States. For example, during the 1980s the real wages of those without a high school diploma fell 10 percent, and a similar effect seems to be spreading to high school graduates.

Second, capital mobility, which makes the relocation of labor-intensive production to Mexico easy, sharpens the competition between U.S. and Mexican labor, especially by eroding productivity differences between them. The factor price equalization theorem holds that wage rates will fully equalize only if the productivity of workers in the two countries is identical. Thus, the current gap in wage rates should persist so long as U.S. workers remain so much more productive than Mexican workers, but the modernization of the Mexican economy fueled by the foreign direct investment (FDI) of U.S. firms could erode that difference for unskilled labor. By the end of 1991, foreign direct investment in Mexico totaled about $33 billion, with nearly two-thirds of it originating in U. S. corporations. In anticipation of NAFTA, capital inflows to Mexico were estimated at $18 billion in 1992, including $5 billion in foreign direct investment.

The *maquiladora* program can be seen as a kind of pilot project for NAFTA, demonstrating the power of combining U.S. capital with Mexican labor. Since 1965, firms on the Mexican side of the U.S. border, known as maquiladoras, have been permitted to import parts duty-free from the United States and to export the assembled product back into the country, also duty-free. By 1992, nearly 2,000 factories operating under this program employed nearly 500,000 workers, about 20 percent of the total manufacturing labor force in Mexico. Meanwhile, employment and wages for U.S. unskilled labor had stagnated.

Third, unlike the EU, NAFTA contains very little provision for dealing with dislocations, and, unlike in Europe, the social welfare system in the United States provides less protection from structural unemployment. In Canada, where the welfare state is more advanced than in the United States, the left feared that dislocations would overwhelm its capacity and force the abandonment of prized programs of social insurance. Indeed, from 1990 to 1997, the proportion of the unemployed eligible to collect unemployment insurance dropped from 89 percent to 43 percent.[24]

Partisan alignments reflect the Stolper-Samuelson expectation that free trade will benefit the abundant factor of production (capital, in the United States) and harm the scarce one (unskilled labor is scarce in the United States relative to the huge surplus of cheap labor in Mexico). These distributional implications of free trade explain why more than 75 percent of Republicans voted for final passage of NAFTA in the U.S. House of Representatives and why more than 60 percent of Democrats voted no even after heavy lobbying by Democratic president Bill Clinton.

THE IMPACT OF NAFTA AND THE MEXICAN COLLAPSE

More than five years after its inception, NAFTA's effects continue to be disputed, not because the three economies remain unaltered but because the dramatic changes that have taken place cannot be definitively associated with NAFTA. Trade among the three countries has increased even more than expected—by 1999, it was more than twice its 1990 level—but the effect of NAFTA cannot be isolated from the broader liberalization strategy that was well under way in all three nations before NAFTA took effect. Moreover, trade levels were not the only source of the strikingly divergent paths taken by the three nations in this period. Both Canada and the United States entered recessions shortly after CUSTA took effect in 1989, but the downturn was far longer and deeper in Canada than in the United States. The period from 1989 to 1996 was the longest period of below-potential growth for Canada since the Great Depression in the 1930s, with unemployment rates exceeding 11 percent. Nearly 20 percent of all Canadian manufacturing establishments closed during this period, as many as half in response to the increasing competition under first CUSTA and then NAFTA. This trade competition encouraged fiscal and monetary policy designed to keep production costs low, but the competitiveness strategy also stifled growth in output, wages, and employment, while weakening government programs that provided social protection. Thus, rising levels of trade and even a growing trade surplus with the United States have not prevented a substantial increase in inequality in Canada. However, advocates of liberalization argue that these dislocations were temporary. Furthermore, they contend that the trade competition produced by CUSTA/NAFTA did not *cause* the painful policy changes but only demonstrated that they were necessary to correct preexisting conditions in Canada.

By contrast, in the United States the recovery that began in 1992 produced the longest expansion of the post–World-War-II period, and unemployment rates fell to around 4 percent, the lowest in more than 30 years. NAFTA does not appear to have played any substantial role in this growth, which has, however, easily absorbed whatever modest job loss may have been associated with NAFTA. Fewer than 200,000 workers—under 4 percent of the total number of U.S. workers dislocated during this period—have been certified as qualified for NAFTA-related Trade Adjustment Assistance. There is also little evidence that NAFTA has had much effect on U.S. wage rates; although real hourly compensation certainly has grown much less slowly than corporate profits, executive compensation, or productivity gains, such inequality in allocating the benefits of prosperity has been a growing trend since at least the late 1970's. In short, though NAFTA has surely benefitted some and harmed others, its aggregate effect on the U.S. economy appears to have justified neither the most optimistic nor the most pessimistic predictions.

In Mexico too the effect of NAFTA is disputed because of its entanglement with other dramatic economic events, but here it is far easier to see the case made by critics. It is certainly impossible to evaluate NAFTA without considering the dramatic collapse of the Mexican economy barely a year after its initiation. The meltdown began with a currency crisis, which was marked by a 43 percent decline in the value of the peso that not only disrupted regional trade and precipitated a deep depression in Mexico but also triggered concern about Mexico's ability to meet its foreign-debt obligation. In response, the Clinton administration, fearful of the political and economic consequences of a collapse in the Mexican economy, provided a $20 billion line of credit as part of a $50 billion international effort to rescue Mexico from imminent default.

It is instructive to note that NAFTA both contributed to Mexico's economic problems and helped export them to the United States. The key role was played by the Mexican peso, which despite a temporary boost from NAFTA could not maintain its value under the pressure imposed by Mexico's trade liberalization. As trade barriers fell throughout the liberalization of the late 1980s and early 1990s, Mexican imports soared, producing a trade deficit that finally reached 8 percent of GDP in 1994. Ordinarily this deficit would have caused the peso to decline steadily until its equilibrium value was reached, but instead it was offset for a while by a huge—but temporary—inflow of capital from abroad, more than $60 billion in portfolio investment alone from 1990 to 1993. Much of this inflow originated from foreign investors, especially in the United States, who were persuaded by enthusiastic supporters of liberalization that post-NAFTA Mexico represented the next great investment opportunity. Inevitably, this capital inflow began to decline, putting downward pressure on the value of the peso. The Salinas government recognized that a falling peso would produce domestic inflation, erode the confidence of foreign investors, and undermine the reputation of the PRI for financial management, all of which it wanted to avoid during the 1994 presidential election. Thus, it expended treasury funds to artificially support the peso (and pressured the central bank to expand the money supply by over 20 percent). With foreign reserves nearly exhausted—falling below $7 billion—the new president, Ernesto Zedillo, was forced to announce a 13 percent devaluation of the peso less than three weeks after his inauguration in December 1994.

This devaluation became the last in a string of incidents—among them the Chiapas revolt, a contested election result, and a political assassination—that had alarmed foreign investors over the previous year. The devaluation effectively acknowledged an economic crisis, which drove frightened investors to react in panic. Nearly $30 billion fled the country in a few weeks. During 1995, the peso declined by 43 percent, the Mexican stock market sank by 38 percent, inflation soared to 60 percent, and unemployment nearly doubled. With U.S. economic interests now tied to the stability of the Mexican economy and NAFTA's prestige bound up with the success of the Mexican liberalization program, the Clinton administration arranged an emergency bailout with help from the IMF and other institutions. When default on foreign debt loomed, both the Zedillo administration and its supporters (primarily in the Clinton administration and the IMF) were seen to give priority to bailing out investors—especially those abroad—while ignoring the plight of the Mexican masses.

The changes in Mexican macroeconomic policy required by the crisis itself and those imposed as part of the bailout agreement guaranteed a sharp recession that, among other effects, would reduce the trade between Mexico and the United States that NAFTA was designed to boost. More significantly, real GDP per capita, already 10 percent below the level it had reached at the beginning of the 1980s, declined another 7 percent in 1995. As the economy hit bottom in 1995, Mexico registered a 13 percent decline in private consumption, a 50 percent inflation rate, interest rates at 40 percent, a 20 percent decline in real wages, and a 70 percent increase in official unemployment (to 6.3 percent, but another 20 percent were reduced to part-time work). Since then Mexico has experienced a recovery, once again led by foreign investment.

At the turn of the century, the dislocations associated with Mexico's trade liberalization and the NAFTA agreement meant to signify its permanence are more apparent than the benefits that remain projected for the future. The dilemmas of trade have been expressed in a variety of ways. Inequality has grown substantially throughout the liberalization process. The percentage of GDP going to labor declined from 38 percent in 1980 to under 25 percent in 1990 and has likely fallen further since then. The wage gap has widened between white-collar and blue-collar workers, skilled and unskilled labor, export-oriented and domestic manufacturing, and between border and nonborder areas. The security of workers is increasingly precarious, with fewer covered by Social Security and more employed in the informal sector, while the minimum wage has fallen to half its 1987 value. Foreign dependence has grown and self-sufficiency has declined. Not only has trade expanded, but it is increasingly integrated into the productive capacity of the economy. In 1994, 58 percent of the value of exports was composed of the imported inputs required to produce them (up from 12 percent in 1983). Foreign debt exceeds $170 billion, two and a half times its level during the debt crisis of 1982. As Teresa Gutierrez Haces put it, "Mexico has converted itself into a country that is very attractive to international investors but not for millions of Mexicans who daily face conditions of extreme poverty."[25]

CONCLUSION: LESSONS FROM NAFTA

Trade ties together the fate of nations. Prosperity in one country can be "exported" to another through trade, but dependence on others can also transmit less pleasing conditions. Trade is not equally desirable under all circumstances or with all possible partners, especially because its effect on value trade-offs, distributional patterns, and state concerns can vary dramatically. In this light, regional integration offers a cautious compromise between self-sufficiency and global free trade by allowing a nation to selectively choose its partners in destiny. Despite difficulties in the past and uncertainties about the future, the EU exemplifies the virtues of such an approach, taking advantage of the economic, political, and social compatibility of its members to forge an organization that can address common problems and achieve shared goals.

The early experience with NAFTA is less clear, and the decision to bind together the fate of all three North American nations cannot yet be definitively assessed. However, a major currency crisis that began less than a year after NAFTA's implementation in January 1994 has cast doubt on whether Mexico is yet stable enough to be a reliable member of a regional trade organization.

Nonetheless, enthusiasm for liberalizing regional agreements remains strong, especially in the western hemisphere, where MERCOSUR, the Central American Common Market, CARICOM, and the Andean Community are all in operation. In fact, less than a year after NAFTA's inauguration, thirty-four democratically elected leaders in the region met to initiate negotiations over a Free Trade Area of the Americas (FTAA), which would reach from Alaska to Argentina and encompass a market of nearly 800 million people. Nine different negotiating groups are now considering various facets of this proposal, with negotiations scheduled to conclude by 2005. On a separate track, the United States is a leading member of the Asia Pacific Economic Cooperation (APEC) forum, a group of twenty-one nations on both sides of the Pacific committed to greater liberalization of trade and investment. This is a far larger group—its members account for more than half of global trade—but it is much more loosely integrated and at an earlier stage in its development.

Trade generates dilemmas that can overwhelm its advantages unless nations and organizations are prepared to respond to them. The regional option is one strategy that appeals to some nations, but others, such as the Asian newly industrializing countries (NICs) considered in the next chapter, are not located in a region where such an approach is feasible. For them, trade-led growth must occur in a context of globalization.

SEVEN

□　□　□

Globalization and
Outward-Oriented Development

In today's globalized economy, goods and capital flow easily across national borders, offering unprecedented trade opportunities. Newly industrializing countries (NICs), especially in Asia, have exploited this
globalization to introduce a new model of **outward-oriented** national development that relies upon export expansion financed through global
capital markets. (This strategy is sometimes called "export-oriented", but
that term fails to recognize the key role played by imports. Thus, "trade-
led" is better, but it ignores the dominant influence of international investment and lending.) Outward-oriented development was pioneered
by a group of rapidly growing nations, dubbed the Asian Tigers, whose
spectacular success from the mid-1970s to the mid-1990s forced analysts
to reassess the trade strategies available to less developed nations. Japan's
rapid growth in the 1950s and 1960s paved the way for the first tier of
Tigers—South Korea, Hong Kong, Singapore, and Taiwan—who were
soon emulated by a second tier of Malaysia, Indonesia, and Thailand.
Each group, in sequence, emerged as the fastest growing group of
economies in the world.

In 1997, however, the spectacular collapse of Thailand, Malaysia, Indonesia, Korea, and the Philippines sent shock waves through newly
industrializing countries around the world, threatened the powerful
economies of Europe and North America, and exposed the vulnerability
of both the global financial architecture and the trade system built upon
it. Within a few months, these countries saw their currencies decline by
more than 50 percent and their stock market valuations fall by 80 percent.
Massive declines in GDP, employment, and political stability followed.
The rest of the world was caught in the downdraft, as global economic
growth rates fell below population increases for the first time in decades
and the chief institutions of the global economic system, the World Bank

and the International Monetary Fund, came under critical attack. Once again, the Asian NICs have forced a fundamental reevaluation of trade policy. This time the questions concern the durability of trade financed from abroad, the dangers inherent in trade deficits, and the institutional architecture required to prevent national-level failure from detonating a system-level crisis.

This chapter begins with a brief sketch of globalization—an unprecedented interaction among open and efficient market conditions, the dominance of liberal theories and values, and the hegemony of transnational actors and institutions. The strategy of outward-oriented development made possible by globalization is then described, together with the dilemmas it must confront. Finally, the Asian meltdown in 1997 illustrates the dangers of such extreme external dependence, whose worst effects are triggered by trade deficits, which make the economy especially vulnerable to adverse capital flows.

GLOBALIZATION

Outward-oriented strategies could not have arisen in the absence of massive changes in the global political economy, especially the increasing efficiency of global markets, the growing influence of internationally oriented economic actors in banking, brokerage, and corporation management, and the newly dominant **neoliberal** ideology; it is this combination of forces that is collectively referred to as globalization. The most visible aspect of this globalization has been the seventeenfold expansion of trade since World War II, which accounted for nearly a quarter of global production by the end of the 1990s.[1] Of course, globalization means much more than higher trade levels. The conception of "international" trade— literally, between nations—accords prominence to the role of distinct sovereign units. The term "globalization" suggests that *all* transactions occur as if these sovereign units were largely irrelevant, since states have reduced the policy barriers that demarcate national borders and restrict economic flows.

Several factors have been responsible for the increasing importance of trade over this period.[2] Just as major advances in transportation technology during the mid-nineteenth century enabled trade to expand, similar reductions in transport costs over the last two decades have presented new possibilities.[3] Because freight and insurance costs now average less than 5 percent of the value of trade, firms with quite small cost advantages can profitably export.[4] The rise of cheap, efficient, instantaneous computer-based communication is an even more important technological development because it has transformed the nature of trade while expanding its volume. It has spurred corporations to plan globally by organizing geographically dispersed operational units into a single production and trade network. Each stage of production is shifted to the region where it can be performed most cheaply, with trade in raw materials, parts, and intermediate products linking the stages into an integrated commodity chain. The result is a finely calibrated and very efficient division of labor.

"Buyer-driven" commodity chains are centered around large commercial retailers, like Nike or Wal-Mart, that operate in textiles, consumer electronics, and other labor-intensive consumer goods industries.[5] The design, specification, and marketing of goods is performed by a retailer located in the large, developed markets of the United States, Europe, or Japan. Actual production, however, occurs in privately owned subcontracting firms located in developing countries where manufacturing costs are lower. Huge, far-flung, multinational corporations (MNCs) also organize "producer-driven" commodity chains. The largest of these multinationals now rival nation-states in economic size and influence. For example, General Motors' 1996 sales of $158 billion exceeds the GDP of all but 26 nations. Exxon's foreign sales of $102 billion eclipses the export revenues of all but 15 countries.[6] Usually headquartered in a developed country, multinational corporations use **foreign direct investment** (FDI) to purchase existing firms or build production facilities from scratch in poorer nations where costs are lower. The parent corporation can centrally control the resultant network of branches and affiliates because it retains ownership of the peripheral operating units.[7] This is the preferred form of business organization in industries such as automobiles, computers, and consumer durables, which require more capital and greater technology than is usually available to a local firm. These products also contain many components that can be produced and assembled in a complex chain of branches and affiliates located all over the world. One of the earliest forms of production sharing involved the assembly in Hong Kong, Malaysia, Singapore, and Thailand of electronic components made elsewhere. One World Bank study estimates that such production sharing now accounts for at least 30 percent of total global trade in manufactures.[8] Global exports by foreign affiliates approach $2 trillion, over 7 percent of global GDP.

This production sharing enlarges considerably upon the gains from trade envisioned by Ricardo, who defined comparative advantage in terms of the production costs of final goods rather than their various components. In one sense, the global production chain of the multinational corporation represents the logical extension of comparative advantage, but in other senses it completely recasts its basic logic. Ricardo—and later Heckscher-Ohlin—conceived of trade as a means to take advantage of the different factor endowments inherent in the basic geographic, economic, technological, and human attributes of national units. By contrast, this new pattern of global production requires extensive cross-national movements of the factor endowments themselves, especially capital and technology. These flows transform fundamental aspects of national economies in order to *create* the comparative advantages that under Ricardian assumptions were preexisting and only *discovered* through trade. The factor-based trade envisioned by Ricardo restructures production patterns and alters the economy relatively slowly, allowing time for the nation to adjust socially and politically. By contrast, since capital flows respond to fleeting conditions, the globalized economy of an outward-oriented nation dominated by production sharing is constantly in flux, and the social and political aspects of national life cannot keep up with economic changes. Moreover, under production sharing, factors of production and intermediate goods are increasingly exchanged among operating units within a single multinational firm, bypassing the market, which lies at the heart of classical liberal theory.

The key to production sharing lies not only in new technology and a new form of business organization, but also in a favorable policy environment. Most obviously, efficient commodity chains require highly reliable and barrier-free trade networks, because even small tariffs add up to prohibitive levels when components and intermediate products cross several national borders before final sale. Thus, production units are located in countries with liberal trade policies as well as low costs. But because the strategy of multinational corporations depends as much on the effective movement of capital across national borders as on the flow of goods, they also locate in countries with a policy environment that ensures the safety and profitability of investment. That environment includes a stable system of currency exchange, not only to finance the initial investment and subsequent trade, but also to easily convert profits into another currency for **repatriation** to the home country. The risk of relying upon intensive cross-border movements is also reduced where the regulation of investment and capital transactions is minimized.

The Bretton Woods institutions have been critical in facilitating a favorable environment for the business strategy that underlies outward-oriented development. In particular, the GATT liberalized trade, the IMF stabilized currency exchange and liberalized capital regulations, and the World Bank prodded countries toward market-based domestic economic policies. Each expanded the scope of its operations throughout the post–World War II era as they drifted toward a more extreme form of liberalism. This neoliberalism affirmed a sweeping faith in markets and a wholesale rejection of state interference not seen since the Golden Age of English free trade a century earlier. Indeed, it went well beyond classical liberalism by advocating noninterference with huge capital movements that would have been unthinkable in an earlier age.

The neoliberal swing in global sentiment reached its zenith in the late 1980s with the so-called **Washington Consensus** of the IMF and World Bank. That doctrine embraced the competitiveness strategy, but went beyond it by emphasizing market-based solutions to development problems, including privatization of state-owned enterprises, diminished state regulation of the economy, lower tax rates, cuts in government spending, and, above all, greater integration with a world economy advancing rapidly toward globalization. This movement reflected the resurgence of neoliberal theorists such as Milton Friedman, who denounced the welfare state that had emerged after World War II in Western Europe and, to a lesser extent, in North America. Ironically, the welfare state itself was, in part, a reaction to the values and distributional dilemmas arising from the higher trade levels engendered by the liberalism of Bretton Woods.

By the late 1970s, however, Friedman's critique of this expanding state role was lent credence by persistent unemployment and slow growth in Western Europe, the increasingly evident weaknesses of the state socialist systems of Eastern Europe, and the continuing stagnation of Latin American economies pursuing protectionist policies of import substitution.[9] Championed especially by Margaret Thatcher in Britain and Ronald Reagan in the United States, this theoretical perspective fit well with the business interests of multinational corporations, internationally oriented banks, Wall Street brokers, and the expanding external sectors that benefitted from globalization.

As more and more developing nations encountered debt problems that required financial assistance from the IMF and World Bank, especially in the early 1980s, these institutions used their enhanced leverage to push national policies in a liberal direction. As a condition for granting loans, they required that the recipients liberalize the domestic economy, free international trade, and dismantle barriers to investment flows. In part because of the success of the Asian Tigers in exploiting the opportunities offered by globalization, many nations did not greatly resist this pressure, and others embraced the advice with enthusiasm. Thus, restrictions on foreign direct investment declined globally, especially in the early 1990s.

Nations that had previously restrained foreign investment through capital controls, currency restrictions, and other regulations instead sought to *attract* foreign investors by offering incentives, including tax holidays, government subsidies, access to cheap credit, and freedom from regulation. In 1994, for example, 49 nations introduced a total of 110 changes in regulations governing foreign direct investment; 108 of them reduced restrictions on FDI or increased the incentives offered to MNCs. From 1991 to 1994, 368 of the 373 changes were favorable to FDI. From 1995 to 1997, the pattern became less unidirectional, but still only 38 of the 377 policy changes made the regulatory environment less favorable to FDI.[10]

As a result, foreign direct investment exploded. In 1996, the WTO reported that annual flows of new foreign direct investment had increased fivefold in the previous decade and seventeenfold (from $21.5 billion to almost $350 billion, an annual growth rate of over 12 percent) from 1973 to 1996. The accumulated value of previous foreign direct investments grew from $165 billion in 1973 to $3205 billion in 1996.[11] A year later, the United Nations Conference on Trade and Development (UNCTAD) estimated that new flows had reached $424 billion in 1997 and existing asset values had grown to $3541 billion.

Furthermore, the same constellation of economic interests, political forces, technological developments and theoretical ideas that encouraged FDI also boosted other forms of capital flows. Nearly three-quarters of IMF members (140 countries) subscribe to the IMF's Article 8, which stipulates free current account transactions. Over 1,500 bilateral investment treaties and 1,800 double-taxation treaties, all designed to encourage foreign investment, were in place at the end of 1997.[12] As a result, all forms of capital movements flourished under relaxed regulation. The World Bank reported that gross private capital flows amounted to nearly 13 percent of global GDP in 1997 (up from 7 percent in 1987), of which less than 2.5 percent was FDI.[13] The remainder consisted of bank loans and portfolio investment in both equities and financial assets like corporate and government bonds.[14]

These huge capital movements, together with the even larger volumes of international trade, require highly liquid foreign exchange markets, because most cross-border transactions involve parallel exchanges of the currencies used by the respective parties. Since the values of currencies fluctuate much more than the value of goods and financial assets they are used to purchase, these exchange markets are the weak link in the chain of transactions required for globalization. Fluctuations in currency values discourage cross-border activity because adverse changes can overwhelm the narrow profit margins that often motivate trade and investment decisions. Suppose, for example, that an American investor had purchased shares in a Mexican company for 2,000 pesos in October of 1994, when the peso was trading for about $.30. To acquire that 2,000 pesos, he would have had to exchange $600. Even if he had sold that stock for 3,000 pesos by March of 1995—a handsome 50 percent increase in only five months— he still would have lost money in dollar terms, because by then the peso was worth only about $.15. At prevailing exchange rates, that 3,000 pesos would have been worth only $450.

National governments and international institutions have long sought to control this kind of volatility, usually with very limited success.[15] However, investors can respond to the risk that a currency devaluation will render an investment unprofitable with a variety of complex financial transactions—called "hedging"—that amount to paying a small premium for a kind of insurance policy against adverse currency movements. This hedging in turn provides a large niche for the speculative activities of financial firms and currency brokers, who bet very large sums of money that they can correctly guess whether a currency is about to increase or decrease in value. Most currency trade involves a "round trip," in which a speculator or hedger buys a currency, not to finance trade or long-term investment, but in order to sell it again as soon as its value rises. About 80 percent of all transactions involve a round trip of a week or less and 40 percent occur in less than two days.

These activities can destabilize currency markets if at any moment there should be a large imbalance between the number of speculators who want to buy the currency (because they guess it will go up in value) and those who want to sell it (because they guess it will go down). Such guesses sometimes become self-fulfilling prophecies, but whether they do or not, they always add enormously to the volume of currency transactions. By 1995 the value of currency trading on global foreign exchange markets reached $1.3 trillion *daily* (it had been about $200 billion in the mid-1980s). It is hardly surprising that this market cannot be reined in by governments, because its daily volume is nearly equivalent to the entire foreign exchange reserves of all national treasuries and central banks combined. In comparison, global trade amounts to only $4.3 trillion *annually* (about 3.5 days of trading on foreign exchange markets), and capital movements require still less foreign exchange.[16]

The instability inherent in the foreign exchange market has triggered many of the historical disasters involving international trade that we have previously documented. Competitive exchange rate devaluations and monetary chaos doomed the trade economy of the 1930s. Irresistible downward pressure on the value of the dollar forced the abandonment of the Bretton Woods fixed exchange rate regime in the early 1970s. The challenge of the Mundell-Fleming constraint blew apart the European Monetary System's Exchange Rate Mechanism in 1992. The post-NAFTA collapse of Mexico was instigated by a free fall of the peso. As we shall see, these same foreign exchange markets that are the weak link of globalization also lie at the heart of the 1997 Asian crisis.

TRADE OPTIONS FOR POOR COUNTRIES

The trade policy options of all modern nations are shaped by the combination of market conditions, theoretical currents, and power relations that constitute globalization. But their choices are also conditioned by their own domestic circumstances. Poor countries are especially susceptible to globalization's lure, because their poverty both increases the priority they attach to growth and decreases their capacity to achieve it without trade. Nearly a quarter of humanity survives on an income of less than $1 per day, including over 20 percent of the population in Latin America and nearly 40 percent in Africa and Asia.[17] In 1997, the fifth of the world's people who lived in the richest countries had incomes seventy-four times greater than the fifth who live in the poorest.[18] Naturally, this difference affects judgments concerning the dilemmas of trade.

Such poverty is an extreme challenge to economic policy, because the historical record shows that income growth can seldom exceed 2–3 percent per year, barely enough to keep ahead of population increases, and much too slow to make substantial progress in living standards within a human lifetime.[19] From 1965 to 1997, average annual world growth in GDP reached 3.2 percent, but since population growth ate up 1.8 percent of that, the per capita increase was only 1.4 percent per year. In 1998, the United Nations Development Programme (UNDP) reported that "in 70 countries with nearly a billion people consumption today is lower than it was 25 years ago.[20] Only 33 countries managed to sustain 3 percent annual growth in GNP per capita during 1980–1996.[21]

Proponents of globalization such as the IMF and World Bank have presented evidence that nations unable to expand trade find it especially difficult to accelerate national growth. In sub-Saharan Africa, where trade grew more slowly than any other region, per capita growth from 1965 to 1997 was actually *negative*, –0.2 percent annually, and the Middle East and North Africa did only slightly better, +0.1 percent.[22] The modern era is replete with the failures of countries that have consciously eschewed trade expansion. Most of Latin America achieved some initial successes with protectionist policies of import substitution from the 1940s to the 1960s, but by the 1970s their stagnating economies had become a symbol of the limitations of inward-oriented development, especially in contrast to the vibrant outward-oriented economies then emerging in Asia. The liberal explanation for trade's contribution to prosperity is especially compelling in poor countries, where the growth dynamic of the domestic economy is so weak. It is hard for them to establish powerful industries, because the capital available from domestic savings is low, the level of technology is limited, and the workforce is poorly trained and educated. Even if industry could be established, the domestic market alone is too small to sustain production at efficient volumes, so trade becomes a critical complement to any development planning.

The trade and development choices made by Asian nations are understandable in this context. For a poor country like Thailand, the first to fall in the meltdown of 1997, a projected pace of growth of 2–3 percent per year would seem agonizingly slow. Beginning from a per capita GDP of only $210 in 1970, this would have left average income still below $1 per day by the turn of the century. With more than 12 percent of its children dying before age five and only 17 percent of its population with access to safe water in 1970, it is hardly surprising that economic growth would take precedence over state goals like autonomy or alternative values like stability or equality. Offered an opportunity to exploit trade for more rapid national growth, many poor countries have been willing to compromise alternative values, to accept the risk of substantial distributional effects, and to tolerate the loss of national self-determination and state sovereignty.

Like most poor nations, Thailand's capacity to initiate substantial change was limited by its modest assets. In 1970, fully 80 percent of the labor force was employed in a stagnant agricultural sector and 87 percent of the population of 35 million lived in rural areas.[23] The manufacturing sector was tiny and the low savings rate of such poor people—average income was under $.60 per day—could not generate the investment funds to expand. Even if production could be increased, who would buy it? Thus, limited internal prospects made trade appear absolutely essential.

Yet Thailand, like most poor countries, struggled to find a comparative advantage that would allow them to earn Ricardian gains by participating in international trade. The comparative advantage of some nations rests on climate or natural resource endowments that allow so-called "primary products" to be culled directly from the land by mining or agricultural operations. The oil producing countries are the clearest example, but several other nations export ores and metals, and many sell such tropical agricultural commodities as sugar, coffee, and bananas that cannot be grown elsewhere. Indeed, in 1970 75 percent of Thailand's exports were in such food and agricultural raw materials, another 15 percent in metal ores, and less than 5 percent in manufactures. But for several reasons export specialization in such primary commodities offers very poor prospects for long-term development. First, the prices of primary products do not increase as rapidly as those of industrial products. For example, *all* primary commodity categories had lower prices in 1998 than in 1980, with an average decline of 45 percent. Meanwhile, the prices of manufactured goods had *increased* by 44 percent. Second, global demand for primary products grows much more slowly as well. Since 1950, agricultural products have fallen from 47 percent of global merchandise trade to 12 percent, while manufactures, which comprised 38 percent of the total in 1950, had grown to 77 percent by 1996.[24] With such adverse trends in both price and volume, nations specializing in primary products invariably find that their export revenues cannot keep up with their import costs. Third, natural variations in the weather induce dramatic volatility in agricultural prices and harvests, so that even these limited export earnings fluctuate so much from year to year that planning becomes extremely difficult. Finally, although these sectors do earn profits, they do not generate much innovation or induce growth elsewhere in the economy.

Thus, most developing countries try to expand exports in manufactures. But Thailand's minuscule manufacturing sector was not globally competitive. To provide the investment funds and technical expertise necessary to develop industry required a strategy to attract an influx of foreign capital.[25] Loans, foreign direct investment, and portfolio investment would come only in response to profit-making opportunities, and Thailand had only one real source of comparative advantage to exploit—cheap labor. In the early 1980s, its labor cost per worker in manufacturing was just $2,305 per year, compared to $19,103 in the United States, $12,306 in Japan, and between $11,000 and $22,000 in Europe. Thailand's labor costs were lower even than in Central America and far lower than in Mexico, which at $3,772 was itself lower than anywhere in South America. Of course, as Thailand was to painfully discover within the next two decades, China was waiting in the wings with labor costs of only $472 per worker.[26] But, at the time, the most urgent need for Thailand was to build globally competitive industries by attracting the foreign capital and technology needed to combine with its cheap labor. Of course, that also required the strategic vision and marketing expertise of more advanced firms as well.

Thailand used the experience of previous Asian economies as a guide to its own outward-oriented development. The movement of Asia to the forefront of the global trading system has been likened to the V-shaped pattern of flying geese, with Japan in the 1950s and later the first-tier Asian Tigers leading the way for those that followed. A similar "product cycle" has been repeated countless times, most visibly in textiles, which has been the first industry to appear in the manufacturing sector of most nations since it sparked the Industrial Revolution and the global dominance of mercantilist England long ago. The heart of the textile industry subsequently migrated from Western Europe and North America to lower-cost Japan, and during its meteoric ascent in the 1950s, clothing represented a third of Japanese exports and nearly a quarter of its manufacturing employment. The growth in wages necessary to improve living standards soon eroded Japan's comparative advantage in labor-intensive exports, however. In the 1960s and 1970s Japanese firms reacted by investing in Korea, Taiwan, and Hong Kong in order to create networks of affiliates and contractors that would perform the most labor-intensive parts of the production process. The more technologically advanced and more profitable functions in these commodity chains remained in Japan.

Still, this investment enabled the first tier of East Asian Tigers to achieve greater skills, technological expertise, and capital concentrations, but along with productivity gains came the inevitable escalation of wage rates. Thus, two decades later, they followed the Japanese model by shifting to more sophisticated production that relied more on their emerging strengths and less on cheap wages, thus clearing the way for the next tier of nations to assume their prior location at the bottom of the division of labor. The share of global textile exports from these East Asian Tigers was cut in half during the 1980s and early 1990s, with much of that gap filled by their firms' affiliates in Thailand, Malaysia, and Indonesia, which experienced a nearly sixfold expansion of exports.

Similar patterns emerged in other sectors. For example, Korea initially entered the electronics industry by assembling components made elsewhere, especially in Japan, but has since moved up the commodity chain. First its firms expanded into making the components themselves, later they produced finished products for established firms in Japan, and now Korean firms such as Hyundai and Samsung are established name brands on their own, though much of the production actually takes place in their affiliates, located in the second-tier NICs of Southeast Asia. Given the absence of alternatives, Thailand, along with the other Southeast Asian economies, followed this "flying geese" model by seeking a position at the bottom of these commodity chains.

OUTWARD-ORIENTED DEVELOPMENT

Thailand adopted a strategy of outward-oriented development that emphasized integration with the global economy, not only through trade, but also through the capital flows that were necessary to make it work. To do so, the Thai government adopted aspects of the Japanese strategy of export promotion and industrial policy, but added to them the deliberate integration with both production networks and global capital markets that has become possible only with the recent ascendancy of globalization.

This outward-oriented approach did not fall neatly into either the mercantilist or liberal category. It resembled an extreme form of liberalization strategy in relying upon unimpeded access to foreign markets for the export of final goods, the import of intermediate goods, and the acquisition of capital, technology, and business services. It also adopted America's unregulated labor markets and low tax rates, both associated with the liberal drive for competitiveness. However, to attract foreign capital also required the heavy involvement of the state reminiscent of mercantilist strategies, especially in adopting industrial policies that guaranteed success for the export sector. Commercial policy also remained quite protectionist:

Thailand's weighted mean tariff on all products, for example, was 38.7 percent in 1989 and 41.5 percent in 1993, among the highest in the world.[27]

The unusual mix of liberal and mercantilist policy elements, together with the variations among these nations, made their strategies controversial and difficult to evaluate.[28] A heated scholarly debate flared over the appropriate diagnosis of the success attained by the first tier of Asian NICs. Liberals, who extolled the virtues of relying upon international markets, credited the NICs' success to the openness of their economies. They frequently cited the Tigers as proof that free trade was superior to the import substitution practiced in Latin America.[29] Much to their later embarrassment, they failed to anticipate the Asian collapse, even on its very eve, even though they had expressed disquiet about the elements of this approach that resembled Japan's "network capitalism" more than America's "market capitalism."[30] Ethnic Chinese minorities, especially in Malaysia, maintain cross-national trade and investment networks via extended family connections. In Korea, huge *chaebols* emulate Japan's *keiretsu*. Critics decried these arrangements as "crony capitalism," emphasizing the corruption bred by close connections among key business leaders and political elites. In Indonesia, for example, the family and friends of President Suharto controlled a disproportionate share of heavy industry and the banking sector. Liberals observed that conducting business through personal relationships rather than free markets violated liberal principles just as deeply as did government interference in markets. However, foreign interests did not object to Asia's outward-oriented development as they had to Latin America's import substitution, because it offered opportunities for foreign investors, banks, brokers, multinational corporations, and foreign exporters.

Critics of liberalism also found support for *their* views in these successes. They insisted that Asian strategies were heretical to the neoliberal faith in self-regulating markets—and located the source of their success in that very deviance. Some theorists emphasized the clever interventions of the state reminiscent of Japan's industrial policy, especially in Korea, whereas others suggested that unique "Asian values"—hard work, willingness to sacrifice for the future, and emphasis on society and family rather than the individual—were responsible.[31] Still others questioned whether any miracle at all had occurred, observing that growth was to be expected, given the large inflows of capital and technology, the growing labor force, and such favorable external conditions.[32]

The defining characteristic of the Southeast Asian strategy of outward-oriented development was its total commitment to deep integration with the global economy. Reliance on trade is hardly a new approach in itself, but the extent of that dependence in Southeast Asia was certainly un-

Why Southeast Asia Adopted Outward-Oriented Development

1. State of theory

Neoliberal economic theory encouraged integration with the global economy, and the industrial policy ideas inherited from Japan and the "flying geese" model illustrated how to use commodity chains to bring it about. In ethical theory, "Asian values" dominated.

2. State of markets

Globalization made trade and capital flows easy, and the absence of a self-sustaining development dynamic in the domestic economy made them essential to produce growth.

3. Political power balances

The absence of democratic representation allowed externally oriented commercial elites to ignore other interests. Foreign actors (investors, MNCs, consumers, international financial institutions, and states) dominated domestic ones.

usual. In Thailand, for example, exports constituted 42 percent of GDP in 1996, about twice the global average.[33] In previous eras, during which today's developed countries grew to dominance, global trade played a smaller role and, more importantly, required a less radical reorientation. Large developed countries had substantial pre-existing production capacity and relatively sophisticated economic structures, so they could export goods previously produced for domestic consumption. Even Japan, whose trade provided an indispensable impetus to national development and constituted a core component of its economic strategy, remained more or less self-sustaining. Its trade amounted to only 10 percent of GDP and capital inflows were insignificant. In these cases, trade was used to *augment* a development dynamic that remained primarily domestic; no major transformation of the economy was required and external dependence remained relatively modest. Even among the smaller developed countries of Europe, where dependence was more extensive, it grew more slowly from an established base of technical capabilities and business expertise.[34]

The deep integration of the manufacturing sector in Southeast Asia with the global system was very different. Its location within the division of labor created by globalization was initially orchestrated by external actors, who retained control over the entire process and reserved the most profitable activities for their own countries. Business strategy was dictated by Japanese industrial firms and banks, American retailers, multinational corporations, and mutual funds, and investors from the first-tier Tigers as well as developed nations. Final products were targeted almost exclusively to markets abroad, but the design and marketing functions were not performed in Thailand. Operations could be sustained only with continuing inflows of foreign capital, technology, management functions, and intermediate goods. The distinctiveness of outward-oriented development's foreign reliance lies less in export volumes than in the depth of the transformation required to achieve an entirely new mix of products. Given the unsophisticated economic structure from which Thailand's export drive began, the composition of its trade is truly remarkable—71 percent of its 1996 exports were manufactures, up from 5 percent in 1970.[35]

Building export capacity from foreign inputs has one often overlooked and potentially fatal consequence: It requires very large import levels, both to initiate the production process and to sustain it subsequently. Malaysia, for example, has become the world's largest exporter of semiconductors and air conditioners, yet both are high technology products that require sophisticated machinery and equipment that cannot be produced by Malaysia's modest industrial sector. Thus, so-called capital goods, equipment needed to produce other products, had to be imported before these industries could even be established. Because such capital goods also require constant replacement as they wear out and frequent upgrading as technology develops, substantial imports are an inherent and ongoing feature of outward-oriented development strategy. Furthermore, many of Southeast Asia's labor-intensive exports come from the simple assembly of intermediate products that are imported. Much of the labor is performed by a largely female workforce in specially designated export-processing zones, akin to the maquiladora of Mexico. This intensive import dependence certainly distinguishes the Southeast Asian experience from the "early industrializers" of Europe and North America. As the first nations to industrialize, they had no predecessors from whom to acquire manufacturing capacity, which thus was built much more slowly from indigenous resources. Even the model economies of Japan and Korea began their export drive from a much stronger industrial base that could provide many of these capital goods without recourse to imports.

As a result, import levels of these economies are not only unusually high—almost half of GDP in Thailand— they are composed of indispensable products. Thailand's import pattern in 1996, on the eve of its financial crisis, exemplifies the difficulty: 46 percent of its merchandise imports were capital goods and another 26 percent were intermediate goods. Adding in the 15 percent made up of oil and motor vehicles, also essential products that could not be produced locally, these necessary imports totaled $63 billion. Meanwhile, *exports* amounted to less than $55 billion, guaranteeing a trade deficit of more than 5 percent of GDP even if all other consumer good imports could be halted entirely. In fact, its actual deficit was about 9 percent of GDP in 1996, and Thailand also ran a trade deficit every year but two between 1970 and 1997, about 4 percent of GDP per year, on average.

Long-term trade deficits require a nation either to find a way to acquire the capital flows that can balance them or to permit a currency devaluation. The latter option was effectively closed to Thailand because it would undermine its attractiveness as a locale for commodity chain production and as a destination for foreign investment. After all, the exchange rate between the Thai baht and the U.S. dollar had been fixed at about 25:1 since the mid-1980s, precisely so that no investor need fear losing money through a devaluation. It was this policy that gave Thailand its special appeal to foreign investors: Many other nations could match Thailand's cheap labor but few had a comparably credible commitment to currency stability.

Thus, Thailand encouraged capital inflows in a variety of ways, each appealing to foreign investors' desires for high rates of return with minimal risk. Foreign direct investment was lured with special incentives, including tax holidays and rebates; subsidized credit, rent, and infrastructure; direct and indirect export subsidies; and freedom from import duties, exchange controls, or limits on profit repatriation. Domestic interest rates were kept high to attract portfolio investment seeking lofty returns. These high interest rates also encouraged Thai businesses, often in partnership with foreign interests, to borrow abroad, and many of those foreign loans were guaranteed by a government commitment to repay them if the firms themselves could not. Above all, capital flows were largely unregulated, so that investors would be able to remove their money whenever they wished, and the exchange rate of the baht was fixed so that repatriation entailed no loss due to currency devaluation.

For similar reasons, all the other Southeast Asian NICs also ran substantial trade deficits, and all relied very heavily upon external finance to balance them. The source, as well as the extent, of these capital inflows varied from country to country, however. Malaysia relied most heavily on multinational corporations, with foreign direct investment averaging over 5 percent of GDP annually since 1970 and 9 percent of GDP from 1991 to 1995.[36] Thailand's inflows amounted to 10.4 percent of GDP in the 1990s, but barely a tenth of that was direct investment; instead, loans averaged nearly 6 percent of GDP from 1989 to 1996.[37] These massive acquisitions of capital, together with unusually high domestic savings rates, produced rates of investment around twice the global average.[38] Of course, they also laid the groundwork for an eventual reversal of the capital inflows, because loans eventually must be repaid and investment profits are invariably repatriated.

Nevertheless, outward-oriented development undeniably spawned explosive GDP growth. Indonesia, Malaysia, and Thailand all grew by more than 8 percent per year from 1990 to 1996, making them the fastest growing economies in the world. Thailand's GDP had increased at more than 7 percent per year in real terms since 1970, a rate far in excess of that promised by any other development policy option. By 1996 Thailand had achieved GDP per capita of over $3100, a level of wealth unimaginable two and a half decades earlier. Moreover, the risks inherent in the trade-offs required to generate this result remained latent for several years, as the dilemmas of trade frequently do.

THE DILEMMAS OF OUTWARD-ORIENTED DEVELOPMENT

Outward-oriented development's unusually heavy reliance on the global economy intensifies the trade dilemmas faced to a lesser extent by all nations. The loss of autonomy implicit in extensive external dependence and the risks inherent in incurring massive future liabilities are especially prominent, but value trade-offs involving the sacrifice of stability for growth, and distributional patterns featuring high levels of inequality are also inherent in this approach.

The distributional impact of outward-oriented development in Thailand was especially severe, because the growth it induced was heavily concentrated in a few sectors. In 1997, 39 percent of Thai exports to the United States were in apparel and footwear, and another 37 percent were in the semiconductor sector. The concentration of 76 percent of exports in just these two sectors was actually less extreme than in Malaysia (89 percent), Singapore (88 percent), China (88 percent), Philippines (86 percent), and Taiwan (84 percent), and only marginally greater than in Korea (73 percent) and Indonesia (63 percent).[39] Of course, *some* narrowing of the productive capacity of an economy is implicit in all trade strategies; after all, Ricardo's comparative advantage is predicated upon investors abandoning relatively inefficient sectors and concentrating resources on those which are globally competitive. But such an extreme distributional pattern is proportionately risky: The entire economy could collapse should a key sector encounter problems. However, the state accepted this risk, in exchange for unusually rapid growth, by actively steering the economy to a more rapid and more complete specialization than the free market would have achieved on its own.

Furthermore, though these industries dominated the export profile, they actually affected a small minority of citizens. Thailand's development effort was focused on manufactured exports, yet even in the mid-1990s employment in manufacturing remained under 4 million in a population of nearly 60 million. The trade and investment boom created a wealthy new class, especially in Bangkok, but large parts of the mostly rural nation remained unaffected. Agriculture still employed more than 60 percent of the labor force but produced only about 12 percent of GDP, not much more than the tiny financial sector. Such distributional patterns may not be conducive to long-term and broad-scale development, even in the absence of catastrophic failure.

The concern about narrow development is reminiscent of the critique applied to strategies relying upon mineral exports—they create an export enclave largely insulated from the rest of the economy and unlikely to fuel broader development. Oil drilling in Saudi Arabia, for example, generates tremendous wealth for a few, but it does not employ many workers nor encourage the growth of other sectors.[40] The production enclaves of Southeast Asia appear somewhat less insulated, because the light-assembly sector combines substantial domestic labor with foreign inputs, foreign capital, and foreign management.[41] However, production at the bottom of the commodity chain does not produce many spill-over effects in growth of technology or skills. The Southeast Asian nations hope to follow the flying geese, but progress up the commodity chain will be harder for them than for their predecessors, not least because those predecessors remain in place. Unlike Taiwan and Korea, Southeast Asia had no established base of industrialization prior to their full-scale immersion in global trade networks. Furthermore, key links in the commodity chains these nations have entered have remained foreign. Since many Thai firms have played almost no role in overall design, management, marketing, or finance—those functions retained by the United States, Japan, or the first-tier Tigers—they have not acquired the experience, skills, technology, or contacts required to step out on their own.[42]

Furthermore, a comparative advantage predicated on cheap unskilled labor may be quite impermanent and even self-limiting. If wages rise—and they must if standards of living are to improve—cost competitiveness will immediately disappear. Even if they do not, there are other nations with even lower wage rates—China, Bangladesh, and India, for example—scrambling to gain a foothold on the lowest rung of the buyer-driven commodity ladder. Defending this position is difficult, because Thai firms that possess narrow expertise, exhibit a thin competitive advantage, and sell to a single buyer, have very limited bargaining power. They can disappear overnight if they should lose a single contract, which makes the nation exceedingly dependent upon inherently volatile business relationships. These pressures make the lowest rung an inherently precarious perch, but the way ahead is also blocked.

In Thailand, outward-oriented development benefitted urban dwellers over rural ones, and financial, commercial, and manufacturing interests over agricultural and more traditional sectors. As a result of these distributional effects, income gains were highly skewed. Once among the most egalitarian nations in the world, by 1992 Thailand saw the incomes of the richest 10 percent increase to twenty-eight times the income of the poorest 10 percent.[43] Furthermore, the crisis that eventually ensued hit the poor harder than other elements of society, so inequality grew even more rapidly during the collapse of this strategy in the 1990s than it had during its successful era. Some distributional effects were inevitable and even necessary to align incentives with the priority on innovation and growth, but when patterns of income, wealth, and living standards reach such extremes of inequality, social cohesion is endangered and fundamental value questions arise.

Although the distributional effects of this strategy across sectors, classes, and regions are easy to recognize, any assessment of the distributional effects across time is more speculative. At issue is whether the growth experienced by Thailand has come at the expense of its own future. The possibility of intergenerational transfers can never be discounted when current prosperity is built upon the accumulation of future liabilities, especially foreign debt. The World Bank estimated that Thais owed foreigners the equivalent of 61 percent of GDP in 1997. Since nearly all of that is denominated in dollars, repayment will have to come largely from dollar-denominated revenues, the vast bulk of which are in the form of future export earnings. (Thailand's small foreign currency reserves could provide some assistance, and, like a consumer that pays off one credit card by borrowing from another, future capital inflows could defer the problem for a while.) The World Bank estimates that more than 15 percent of annual export receipts will be needed to service that debt—that is, to pay the annual interest plus retire a portion of the outstanding principal. Thus, 15 percent of export revenue must be diverted away from its principal use—to purchase imports—and instead used to service debt. Such a diversion would require a sizable trade surplus (nearly 8 percent of GDP) for a sustained period, yet Thailand has run a trade surplus only twice in the last thirty years—never more than 2 percent of GDP—while averaging an annual trade deficit of 5 percent of GDP over that same period. Repaying the debt will certainly require a major adjustment, and it may entail a substantial sacrifice that embodies the dilemma of intergenerational distributional patterns. The next generation may have to pay for the prosperity of the current one.

However, even that daunting scenario rests on an optimistic estimate of the debt burden, because it assumes that the repayment of principal can be stretched out over time. In fact, much of Thailand's debt—72 percent of its total in 1995—was short-term, meaning it would come due within one year. Most short-term debt can usually be "rolled-over": Either the original lender will extend its maturity date or the borrower can repay old debt by borrowing anew from another investor. As debts accumulate, however, potential lenders become reluctant to assume the added risk, and it becomes difficult to anticipate just how much of the short-term debt will have to be repaid as it comes due rather than rolled-over. If short-term debt is added to the above estimated debt service, the total in 1996 far exceeded the total foreign exchange reserves of Thailand, a dangerous mismatch between assets and liabilities.[44] Furthermore, other future liabilities were also accumulating, especially portfolio investment that was bound to depart eventually and was likely to flee quite quickly if credit-worthiness was called into question by accelerating debt.

Though intertemporal distributional effects are likely in such a situation, even an alarming volume of liabilities does not make it inevitable that current prosperity will require painful sacrifice in the future. This uncertainty helps explain why different observers offer alternative assessments of outward-oriented development. If foreign capital is invested wisely, some argue, it could earn enough profit to repay investors and lenders, and it could generate export earnings large enough to create future trade surpluses. If so, the risk could pay off. Others point out, however, that wise investment is not enough, because the success or failure of outward-oriented development rests at least as much on events and conditions abroad as on any decisions made inside the country itself. The fate of a highly dependent nation passes out of its own control, and this loss of self-determination reflects a fundamental trade dilemma involving both state goals and citizen values.

In fact, the most difficult dilemma posed by this strategy is that its promise of prosperity requires the acceptance of unusually extreme dependence upon external forces. Dependent states usually find that they must adopt a passive foreign policy, subordinating other state goals to the need to maintain good relations with the foreign actors that control the nation's destiny. Dependence also limits the ability of the state to attend to domestic goals if they compete with the interests of foreign investors or lenders. For example, the demand of multinational corporations that the state guarantee export competitiveness makes it difficult to adopt the tax and social welfare policies that mitigate inequality. Critics of globalization contend that such constraints on government policies amount to an erosion in national sovereignty so severe that the very principles of

Trade Dilemmas Inherent in Outward-Oriented Development

1. Distributional outcomes

Industrial policy that favors trade in manufactured goods shifts opportunities to the efficient export sector and income to its various domestic and international constituencies, at the expense of others. Financing trade deficits through foreign investment and borrowing may shift income to the present generation at the expense of the future.

2. Effects on the state

External dependence diminishes national autonomy and state sovereignty.

3. Value trade-offs

Trade generates growth, but also instability and inequality that undermines social justice.

democracy are threatened, because government officials find that they must respond more to foreign actors than to their own citizens.

Moreover, such high levels of dependence make a poor country like Thailand vulnerable to changes in impersonal market forces it cannot forestall, even if it were willing to sacrifice all other values and state goals. This vulnerability is best revealed by revisiting the precarious state of Thailand's balance of trade and the consequent pressure on the value of its currency, the baht. Although all nations must concern themselves with trade deficits, for heavily dependent Thailand the margin for error was infinitesimal and the penalty for failure huge.

THE COMING STORM: DILEMMAS REVEALED

Given the large volume of imports required by outward-oriented strategies, the key to Thailand's delicate trade balance lies in the external forces that determine its export competitiveness. Given its perennial trade deficit, Thailand's economic stability also rests on the external forces that shape its ability to attract foreign capital to finance that deficit. The imbalances which marked Thailand's trade and investment patterns for most of three decades were barely sustainable so long as external events were favorable. Eventually, however, Thailand was pushed from the tightrope, less by its own mistakes than by external events it could not control. In the 1990s, Thailand's export competitiveness was declining just as that of its competitors was increasing. And just as the need to finance its trade deficit was growing, the available pool of foreign capital was shrinking.

Thailand's persistent trade deficits sharply escalated in the mid-1990s, the result of ordinary events magnified by extraordinary reliance on visibly unreliable external markets. Much of Thailand's remarkably high investment had gone to increase productive capacity in a few export industries, but similar investment had also been occurring in other poor countries as well. In clothing, for example, Southeast Asia moved to fill the supply gap left by the declining competitiveness of the first-tier Asian Tigers. Korea, Taiwan, and Hong Kong were forced into speciality niches in which their wage rates (four to six times higher than Thailand's by the 1990s) were not such a large handicap. Thailand's exports in apparel and footwear consequently expanded, constituting about 60 percent of its labor-intensive manufactures by 1995. During the 1990s, however, the export capacity in these industries was growing even more rapidly in India, Pakistan, Bangladesh, Sri Lanka, Indonesia, and, most importantly, China, in each of which labor costs were only about $.25 per hour, one third of Thailand's wage rate.[45] As a result, the global supply of textiles and footwear outstripped demand as nation after nation competed for the same U.S. market, especially after China's aggressive export expansion and currency devaluation produced a Chinese trade surplus in the range of $50 billion per year.

The global crisis of overproduction was accentuated for the Southeast Asian countries that pegged their currency to the U.S. dollar, including Thailand. By pegging the baht to the dollar, Thailand automatically inherited all of the dollar's fluctuations against other currencies and consequently experienced major swings in trade competitiveness from events that were totally out of its control. From the mid-1980s to the mid-1990s, the dollar's movement had been highly favorable for Thai export competitiveness. From 1985 to 1995, the U.S. dollar had been declining in value against the major currencies, falling from 260 yen to about 80 yen (and from 3.30 Deutsche marks to DM 1.40), largely as a response to continuing U.S. trade deficits. As a result of the baht-dollar peg, the Thai baht was also declining, from almost 11 yen to under 3.5 yen. That made Thai products cheap for Japanese consumers and Thai assets cheap for Japanese investors, both of which induced Japanese firms to move even more of their production abroad by investing in Southeast Asia. Thailand experienced double-digit increases in exports during this period, fueling a growth boom and a rising reputation as an economic powerhouse that attracted additional international investors, especially from American mutual funds.

Despite these favorable developments, Thai trade deficits averaged nearly 6 percent of GDP from 1990 to 1994, in part because the outward-oriented strategy entailed substantial growth in imports that could not be avoided. Of course, the same baht depreciation that made Thai exports cheap also made these imports more expensive. Ordinarily, a trade imbalance of this magnitude, which creates a parallel imbalance in the supply and demand for the currency, would be expected to place irresistible downward pressure on the baht. Indeed, even the more modest trade deficits of the previous decades would ordinarily have produced the same effect. However, thanks to massive capital inflows that offset the trade deficit, each of the Southeast Asian currencies was able to maintain its value against the dollar.

Meanwhile, the dollar depreciation that was improving U.S. (and Thai) trade competitiveness was encountering an increasingly hostile response from U.S. trade competitors in Europe and Japan. In April 1995, the seven large developed nations that make up the so-called Group of Seven, or G-7, convened in Washington to address the corrosive effect of the dollar's value on European and Japanese competitiveness. With the health of their own economies paramount in their minds, the G-7 deliberations gave no weight to the consequences of their actions for Southeast Asia. After the meeting, coordinated action including higher U.S. interest rates, helped drive the value of the dollar from 80 yen to about 125 yen two years later. Of course, this movement also affected the Asian currencies pegged to the dollar, with the baht increasing from about 3.40 yen to about 4.80 yen. Now, the same Southeast Asian products which had been such a bargain in Japan and Europe suddenly became much less competitive.[46] As the supply of goods from other labor-abundant countries increased and the competitiveness of Thai firms declined, their exports fell and trade deficits mounted—to over 7 percent of GDP in both 1995 and 1996.

Capital flows still filled the gap, however, so during the mid-1990s all of the Southeast Asian currencies were actually appreciating in real terms, in the face of trade deficits that would otherwise have been driving them downward toward a more realistic value. But the same increase in U.S. interest rates that affected exchange rates and trade deficits also began to shrink capital flows to Asia. Higher returns in the United States not only made American investors more content to keep their money at home, they also began to attract Japanese and European investors who had previously been flocking to Asia. At first, Thailand was able to retain capital by borrowing it abroad at increasing rates, but eventually capital flows to Asia began to decline. Throughout 1995 and 1996, rising trade deficits and falling capital inflows exerted strong downward pressure on the baht. However, a voluntary currency devaluation was unthinkable, because Thailand's fixed exchange rate had been the linchpin of its entire development strategy for years. The absence of currency risk gave Thailand its special appeal for foreign investors, constituting its "comparative advantage" against other low-wage-rate countries in luring the international capital upon which Thailand's export growth and remarkable prosperity had been built.[47] Furthermore, a devaluation would set off a panic among investors. In addition, Thai firms had borrowed heavily from foreign banks, and most of those loans were denominated in dollars, so a devaluation of the baht would have left them unable to meet the higher payments that would result. By this point, reliance on external capital was so great that any interruption of it could collapse the entire system. Thus, the commitment to a fixed rate for the baht was repeatedly reiterated in the strongest possible terms throughout early 1997, even as financial troubles loomed.

However, the massive trade deficit was seen by investors and currency speculators as a virtual guarantee that the exchange rate could not be sustained much longer, because an excess of imports over exports created a proportionally massive imbalance in the supply of and demand for the baht itself. That is, there were many more Thais who wanted to sell baht for the dollars needed for imports than there were foreigners who wanted to buy baht to purchase Thai exports. Such an imbalance had been sustainable only so long as foreign investors had been willing to absorb the excess baht, purchasing them in order acquire financial assets in Thailand. However, in the face of mounting trade deficits and alternative opportunities, investor sentiment turned against the baht and capital inflows dried up, removing the chief source of support for the baht's increasingly unrealistic value.

None of this should have come as a surprise, because Thailand was experiencing the classic roller coaster pattern of a dependent economy: Reliance upon markets abroad produces superior results when external forces are favorable, but cataclysmic results when they are not. The inevitable cyclical movements in foreign market conditions induces accentuated swings in economies dependent upon them. Rapid growth in the 1980s and early 1990s had encouraged the conviction of Thai officials that their policies were sound, but this was a self-serving misunderstanding of the source of their initial successes. After all, the capital inflows that fueled Thailand's ascent were caused as much by "push" factors from the developed countries—for example, low U.S. and Japanese interest rates encouraged capital to flee—as by "pull" factors associated with Thailand's unique attractions. Evidence for the preponderance of push factors is that capital flows to all developing countries grew from $46 billion in 1990 to $236 billion in 1996. These movements suggest that it was not the special appeal of Thailand that led to their capital inflows at all; instead,

Thailand simply garnered a share of the excess capital sloshing around the world during this period. The logical corollary to the observation that Thailand was not fully responsible for its successes is the caution that it would not have to do anything terribly wrong to suffer a failure either. Indeed, since much of the portfolio investment in Thailand resulted from low interest rates in the United States, foreign investors left Thailand as quickly as they arrived when those rates rose again. As one commentator elegantly put it, "After all, one cannot expect more birds to fly into rather than out of an open birdcage indefinitely, since the basic premise of financial liberalization is 'easy come, easy go'."[48]

In short, Thailand's early success should have been seen in the context of the distributional dilemmas of trade, that is, with the knowledge that the prosperity associated with trade deficits and capital inflows are not permanent. Instead, that prosperity represented the positive phase of a shift of income from future to the present. By the middle 1990s Thailand had seen only the benefits of capital inflows, but by the end of the 1990s it had also experienced the inevitable fallout. Loans increase wealth today, but they must be repaid tomorrow—and with interest. Investment spurs the economy, but it is not a gift: Foreign investors fully expect to repatriate both the initial investment and the profits it earns. In both cases, of course, more money eventually will be removed from the economy than was initially put in. If capital inflows are invested wisely, of course, the net result even over the long term can be quite favorable, but that is a big "if," especially because the magnitude of the initial inflow tends to diminish the care with which these decisions are made. Just as lottery winners are known to spend money "like a drunken sailor," economies absorbing large capital inflows are prone to major errors in allocating funds.

The usual danger of capital inflows in trade deficit countries is that they will be used to fund current consumption rather than investment, when it is investment that generates the growth necessary to repay loans and repatriate profits. This was not the problem in Thailand, however, where investment exceeded 41 percent of GDP in the early 1990s, twice the rate in the United States and Western Europe. Initially, this investment fueled rapid construction of factories destined to produce exports, especially in textiles and electronics. However, capital availability so far outstripped labor supplies that over a million foreign workers eventually entered the country, mostly from neighboring Myanmar. This outcome, of course, negates the reason for such a development strategy in the first place—to acquire enough capital to employ excess supplies of labor.

Further, though high investment rates are ordinarily considered an indicator of a healthy and fast growing economy, such massive volumes of funds could not hope to find productive investment opportunities in such a small and poor economy as Thailand. Increasingly, investments were diverted into areas that would not produce the export revenues on which the entire strategy was based. For example, from 1993 to 1997 more foreign direct investment went into real estate than all sectors of industry combined. Indeed, from 1993 to 1995, industry absorbed less than a quarter of FDI. This speculative investment produced liabilities in the form of eventual repatriation, but no future revenue stream to meet those obligations. Worse yet, the initial successes of early investors goaded later investors to continue to pour money into the economy. These massive flows succeeded only in bidding up the prices of the relatively few productive assets in the economy, adding still more to the widely publicized profits of the early investors who now owned those assets. With capital flows too large to be absorbed efficiently, the excess simply fueled asset inflation, especially a speculative bubble in real estate prices. For several years in the early 1990s, property prices in Bangkok rose more than 40 percent per year.[49] These prices were, of course, wildly out of line with the underlying economic value. When they inevitably declined to a more realistic level, Thai banks—25 percent of whose loans were for real estate—and finance companies (40 percent of whose assets were in real estate) became insolvent.

It can certainly be argued that Thai officials should have exerted greater control, but the underdeveloped financial markets and regulatory structure of an emerging market like Thailand left them hopelessly overmatched by the combined expertise of the financiers of Wall Street, the City of London, and Tokyo. After all, even the sophisticated regulatory apparatus in the United States—the Security and Exchange Commission, the Federal Reserve, and so on—could not prevent the massive collapse of the U.S. savings and loan industry in the 1980s, and Japan's vaunted economic ministries could not prevent widespread insolvency in its banking sector, which persisted throughout the 1990s.

Besides, Thai officials were hemmed in on all sides by the operative logic of their outward-oriented development strategy. Inherent in it were specific commitments not to exercise sovereignty—to alter the exchange rate, to impede capital, or to control markets. By the time it became apparent that trade deficits and capital flows were dangerously large, it was far too late to do anything about it. Any policy designed to deal with the problems would not only alienate investors, but signal how serious the problems really were. Both would trigger capital flight that would bring down the whole house of cards. Thailand was an accident waiting to happen.

THE ASIAN MELTDOWN

Much to the anger of Thai officials, in early 1997 shrewd investors began to speculate that a devaluation was imminent. They sold as many baht as they could get their hands on, increasingly confident that in a matter of days the baht would decline in value and allow them to repurchase the baht at a markedly lower price and to earn huge windfall profits in the process. Now the only substantial support for the baht came from the Thai treasury, which used its dollar reserves to buy the baht being sold by speculators. As these reserves were nearly expended, officials had no choice but to acknowledge that they could no longer support the baht. Instead, they were forced to allow it to float, with its value determined solely by supply and demand on foreign currency markets.

The Asian financial crisis exploded on July 2, 1997, when the Bank of Thailand announced an abandonment of the fixed exchange rate of the baht, which had remained between 24.5 and 26 to the U.S. dollar since the mid-1980s. This abandonment allowed the baht to devalue, and when it reached a record low of 29 to the dollar on July 2, foreign investors found that the value of their Thai investments, when converted to dollars, had declined by more than 15 percent in a single day. Not surprisingly, many immediately sold their Thai assets, converted the proceeds to dollars, found safer homes for their investment in the U.S. and elsewhere—and breathed a sigh of relief that their losses had not been greater. They had won the game of "Musical Chairs." The first investors to act escaped with relatively minor damage, but their actions spooked everyone else. The panic that followed drove the baht down to 56 to the dollar by the end of the year—a decline of nearly 60 percent from its high a few months earlier. In response to panic selling by investors and the massive outflow of capital, similar declines occurred in all financial markets, especially real estate and company stocks.

The lesson was not lost on those with investments in nations experiencing similar pressures. After all, the other Southeast Asian nations had adopted similar strategies and were experiencing similar problems. Furthermore, the Thai panic had important contagion effects, especially for casual foreign investors who knew little about the region except that it had been a highly profitable investment. Fearing imminent losses, they began to sell assets in other countries as well, triggering a cascade of currency pressures. On July 2 and 3, the Philippines central bank was forced to intervene heavily to defend its peso. It also raised the overnight lending rate from 15 percent to 24 percent, hopeful that investors nervous about a potential devaluation would be assuaged by much higher returns. On July 8, Malaysia's central bank had to intervene aggressively to defend its ringgit, but within a week it was forced to abandon the effort. On July 11, Indonesian officials were forced to allow its rupiah to devalue. On July 17, the Singapore monetary authority allowed the Singapore dollar to fall to its lowest level since February 1995. On July 24, the ringgit hit a 38-month low of 2.6530 to the dollar, and

Currency Collapses

FIGURE 7.1   *Currency Collapses*
SOURCE: Pacific Exchange Rate Service, http://pacific.commerce.abc.co/xr/

Malaysian Prime Minister Mahathir Mohamad launched a bitter attack on "rogue speculators."

By the end of 1997, Thailand, Malaysia, Indonesia, and the Philippines had suffered declines of more than 35 percent in the value of their currencies. (Indeed, as the figures show, by the summer of 1998, the Indonesian rupee had lost more than 80 percent of its value.) Even apparently more mature economies suffered, with the currencies of Singapore and Taiwan down by 15 percent and, most shockingly, South Korea by 50 percent (40 percent in one week in December 1997). The Hong Kong dollar remained steady, but officials expended US $1 billion during one two-hour period to keep it so.

The immediate effects were in financial markets, but currency valuation was so integral to the entire system that contagion quickly occurred in several senses—from financial markets to the real economy, from the economy to the polity and society, and from Thailand to other Southeast Asian nations and soon to the rest of the world. The devaluation quickly reached the real economy via the financial sector. Foreign debts became unserviceable after the decline of the baht. Faced with dollar-denominated debts and baht-denominated assets, many companies went bankrupt, and banks failed in large numbers as well. Furthermore, domestic debts secured by collateral in real estate and stocks devastated bank balance sheets, particularly since so many borrowers were unable to make payments. Indeed, in June 1999, two years after the crash, nearly half of all bank loans in Thailand were still nonperforming. The devalued baht doubled the cost of necessary imports, and firms were unable to obtain credit, so production lines shut down.

Recession followed. Company failures led to unemployment that reduced consumer spending. Investment spending fell even faster as capital fled the country. Unemployment doubled and underemployment tripled. Meanwhile, inflation raged, since the devaluation made foreign products more expensive in baht terms. Thus real wages, adjusted for inflation, declined by 6–8 percent among those still employed, but the effects varied greatly by sector. Real wages in manufacturing declined by 13 percent and in construction by 15 percent. Consumption declined, and at least 1 million Thais fell below the poverty line in the first six months of 1998 alone. In baht terms, GDP declined by 8 percent in 1998. Of course, converted at the new (lower) market rate of exchange, in per capita dollar terms that GDP was about what it had been at the beginning of the decade. Such economic effects were bound to have severe social consequences. Sharp increases were reported in crime, drug use, and school dropouts (and only 35 percent of secondary school-aged children were enrolled even before the crisis). Suicides doubled. To add to the chaos, the decline in economic activity reduced government revenues dramatically, requiring cuts in government spending, including social programs (a 9 percent cut for education and a 15 percent decline for public health). Political protests and antiforeign activity increased.

Soon the problems spread to other Southeast Asian nations, which were suffering from similar forces in their own economies as well as the contagion from Thailand. The declining baht made Thai exports cheaper, which further stressed their trade competitors. Nervous foreign investors fled all the Asian economies and even emerging markets in Latin America. The capital movements were staggering in scope and speed. Between 1996 and 1998, capital outflows from Thailand alone reached 20 percent of GDP, after inflows of more than 10 percent of GDP per year in the 1990s. "Net financial inflows to Indonesia, Korea, Malaysia, the Philippines and Thailand totaled $93 billion in 1996. In 1997, as turmoil hit financial markets, these flows reversed in just weeks to a net *outflow* of $12 billion, a swing of $105 billion, or 11 percent of the pre-crisis GDPs of the five countries"[50] In 1998, net outflows from the five most affected economies reached $46 billion, another 7 percent of GDP. Net private capital flows to all emerging markets plunged in 1998 to $152 billion, down from $260 billion in 1997 and $327 billion in 1996.

Political instability and anti-Chinese protests grew, especially in Indonesia, where in 1998 alone GDP declined by more than 16 percent, unemployment increased sevenfold to over 17 percent, inflation reached 60 percent, and real wages dove by an estimated 25 to 35 percent. Takeovers of insolvent banks left the Indonesian government owning more than 80 percent of the assets of its banking system. In Korea, unemployment rose by 1.5 million and average real wages fell by 10 percent in the first year of the crisis, triggering a 36 percent increase in secondary school dropout rates, a 50 percent increase in suicides, and a 700 percent increase in calls to a hotline reporting domestic violence against women.[51] A 1999 survey in Korea revealed that more than a third of those who had thought they belonged to the middle class a year before no longer thought so, and the number who consider themselves to be in the low-income bracket more than doubled. Only 1 percent of those surveyed, down from the precrisis level of 5.9 percent, answered that they belong to the upper class. In addition, 44.3 percent of those polled said their income had declined by more than 30 percent since January 1998. Nearly 92 percent of respondents replied that the income gap between haves and have-nots had widened further, with the majority saying income inequality had reached a serious level.[52] The damage in Korea was especially shocking because it was about to be proclaimed a developed country, with an economy that was the eleventh largest in the world. Yet it had to seek an IMF bailout in December 1997, when its short-term debt became fourteen times greater than its foreign reserves.

Soon the contagion reached outside the region. Financial-market contagion affected first currency values and stock markets and then quickly the so-called "real economy" with massive unemployment and bankruptcies in Brazil, Russia, and many other countries around the globe. The trading system also transmitted shocks abroad, because the recession and currency troubles caused Asian consumption of imports to decline. Not only did the nations that exported extensively to Asia suffer from these volume declines, the global price of many commodities, most notably oil, plummeted from lack of demand. Export earnings declined by about a quarter in oil-exporters Angola, Gabon, Kuwait, Nigeria, and Venezuela, with GDP declines of over 13 percent in the first three of these and about 5 percent in the others. Copper prices fell by over 30 percent and Zambia, Chile, and Mongolia experienced GDP declines between 3 and 9 percent in response.[53] In a globalized economy, a collapse in any part of the system is felt throughout the world. The IMF reduced its estimate of global growth by 2.3 percent between October 1997 and October 1998. Overall, global growth rates declined by 1–2 percent due to the Asian crisis, which explains why the international financial institutions took such an interest in their problems and why the choice of development strategy and trade policy cannot be a matter of indifference to governments, institutions, and citizens even half a planet away.

All of this occurred despite the intervention of international financial institutions, which poured money into the most affected countries. The initial $17 billion bailout package of Thailand in August 1997 was inadequate, constrained in part by restrictions imposed by the U.S. Congress after the massive Mexican bailout in 1994. The bailout of Indonesia in November 1997 amounted to $42 billion. The IMF organized a $58 billion bailout of Korea to avoid widespread default by Korean firms of debts to U.S., Japanese, and European banks. Since nearly all of these packages were in the form of loans, they increased the indebtedness of these countries, even though they were designed to ease their short-term misery: In 1998 foreign debt reached 80 percent of GDP in Thailand and the Philippines (up from 50 percent in 1996), 48 percent in Korea (from 15 percent in 1994), 60 percent in Malaysia, and over 100 percent in Indonesia.

These bailouts were themselves highly controversial. The IMF granted loans only after the affected countries agreed to its standard austerity terms, which included a cut in government spending of 3 percent of GDP, about 20 percent of the budget in Thailand. These cuts certainly deepened the economic and social chaos, but judgments differ as to whether they were necessary or not. IMF supporters stressed the danger of contagion, citing the massive damage done to the global system and the need to contain the chaos before it engulfed all emerging markets and derailed the developed economies as well. Many liberals who have interpreted this collapse as "the death throes of Asian state capitalism" have supported the IMF and lauded their efforts at reform, arguing that the excessive role of Asian governments in steering the economy was responsible for the crisis.

Others dissent. As Joseph Stiglitz put it, "Inadequate oversight, not over-regulation, caused these problems."[54] Jeffrey Sachs, the influential head of the Harvard Institute for International Development, also questioned the IMF interpretation, especially because it represented a complete turnaround in their view of the Asian economies. He noted that "just three months ago in its 1997 annual report '[IMF] Directors welcomed Korea's continued impressive macroeconomic performance [and] praised the authorities for their enviable fiscal record.' . . . In the same report, 'Directors strongly praised Thailand's remarkable economic performance and the authorities' consistent record of sound macroeconomic policies.' . . . With a straight face, Michel Camdessus, the IMF managing director, now blames Asian governments for the deep failures of macroeconomic and financial policies that the IMF has discovered."[55]

The sharply different evaluation of the IMF's actions expressed by Stiglitz and Sachs rests on an alternative diagnosis of the crisis. Many commentators emphasize the role of currency speculators and unreasoning panic—in effect blaming markets, not states. Such views are especially popular in Southeast Asia, where they have been championed by Malaysian prime minister Mahathir Mohamad. This is a self-serving portrayal in that it absolves his government of blame, while shifting it to a conspiracy by international financiers like George Soros. However, no conspiracy is required to explain massive flows of volatile, short-term capital in an unregulated system. Financial markets witness a constant battle between greed and fear—and profit-seeking investors occasionally panic. Sachs argued that the IMF's misinterpretation of the cause of the crisis led them to exacerbate it, forcing policy changes that made a bad situation worse. Failing to see that the fundamental problems were modest and that the real culprit was unwarranted panic, "instead of dousing the fire the IMF in effect screamed 'fire' in the theater."[56] Sachs is not surprised. "It defies logic to believe that the small group of 1,000 economists on 19th Street in Washington should dictate the economic conditions of life to 75 developing countries with around 1.4 billion people. . . . That is an average of about seven economists per country."[57]

In Korea, the IMF not only required an austerity program similar to Thailand's, but also demanded a complete overhaul of the financial system. This overhaul included a commitment by the government to cease intervention in banking decisions and credit allocation—the heart of Korean industrial policy—and to break up *chaebols*, the dominant form of business organization in Korea. It also demanded the liberalization of labor markets, trade policy, and capital flows. Critics noted that none of these policies had much to do with the actual crisis. Instead, they claimed that liberals such as U.S. Federal Reserve Chairman Alan Greenspan and IMF deputy managing director Stanley Fisher have used this episode to trumpet what Robert Wade referred to as "American triumphalism," forcing nations to move away from the Asian model that emulates Japan's industrial policy and toward American style laissez faire.[58]

Some have suggested that this advice has less to do with solving problems in Asia than with advancing the agenda of a formidable collection of international institutions and private interests. For example, Wade referred to a "Wall Street-U.S. Treasury-U.S. Congress-City of London-UK Treasury-IMF complex" that has led a concerted drive to liberalize capital movements.[59] Embodied in the WTO's financial services agreement, the IMF's extension of its jurisdiction to **capital accounts** as well as current accounts, and the effort of the OECD to negotiate a Multilateral Agreement on Investment, this approach offers unprecedented profit-making opportunities for financial firms in developed countries, especially the United States. As we have seen before, hegemons always prefer open economies, not only because they are most likely to benefit, but also because they have the greatest capacity to resist or compensate for the dilemmas that result.

So many disparate diagnoses of the Asian crisis have been advanced that it is tempting to regard the Asian crisis as an ink-blot test that says more about the conceptual lenses of the various observers than about the objective situation.[60] However, all of these diagnoses point back to the fundamental dilemmas of trade, which are exposed in their most acute form whenever trade policies reach either extreme on the continuum from liberalism's reliance upon markets to mercantilism's reliance upon states.

Of course, everyone acknowledges that Asian authorities made mistakes, particularly in failing to adequately regulate domestic banking systems.[61] On the other hand, the commonality of these errors—they occurred in Malaysia, Indonesia, and Korea as well as Thailand—suggest that such mistakes are exceptionally likely when countries are placed in the precarious situation required by outward-oriented development. Even Singapore, Taiwan, and Hong Kong suffered similar problems— albeit less severe—and they were thought to be far more sophisticated. Officials in the United States may well have been capable of managing the complex regulation required, but of course they would not have chosen for their own country the strategy of outward-oriented development that required this level of dependence upon external forces.

Furthermore, these mistakes—whether by national officials, international institutions, or private actors—go to the heart of outward-oriented development. The decision to seek rapid growth and base it upon high levels of trade inevitably commits an economy at low levels of preexisting development to much broader patterns of deep integration. For Southeast Asia, trading successfully required the large inflows of foreign investment and loans made possible by globalization. In turn, such inflows required open capital markets and fixed exchange rates. This policy choice has been as frequently indicted for the crisis as the absence of regulation, but trade-led growth could not have succeeded without it, because this kind of openness represented the comparative advantage of these otherwise unremarkable nations.

Without free capital accounts and underregulated financial markets, Thailand could not have attracted huge amounts of capital. Without such capital, they could not have expanded export capacity. And without the expansion of export capacity, the whole edifice of liberalization would not have been available. Thus diminished national autonomy, volatility, and the risk of intertemporal distributional effects are inherent in outward-oriented development, just as slow growth in material standard of living is inherent in strategies of closing the economy to trade and investment. No other approach held out the hope of accomplishing such an ambitious goal as Mahathir's Vision 2020, for example, that Malaysia would join the ranks of the industrialized countries by 2020.

In short, outward-oriented development is not without its benefits, but neither is it without its drawbacks. Even when the formula works, its inherent byproduct is the intensification of dilemmas, especially extreme inequality, heavy dependence, diminished national sovereignty, and, often unrecognized until too late, massive insecurity. More troubling yet, national problems become global ones, because globalization connects the system together. A more sober assessment recognizes the wisdom of nations that have gone before: Some compromise must be fashioned between the extremes of reliance on external markets advocated by liberals and the disabling of market operations advocated by protectionists. If that compromise does not occur at the national level, greater care must be taken to build an international financial architecture capable of coping with the inevitable collapses, a theme discussed in the concluding chapter.

At the time of this writing it is impossible to tell how long recovery from this collapse will take, and until then no final evaluation of the strategy of outward-oriented development can be definitive. UNDP reports, "Past crises show that while economies regain output growth and macroeconomic balances—inflation, exchange rates, balance of payments—fairly quickly, it takes longer for employment and wages to recover. An analysis of more than 300 economic crises in more than 80 countries since 1973 shows that output growth recovered to pre-crisis levels in one year on average. But real wage growth took about four years to recover, and employment growth five years. Income distribution worsened on average for three years, improving over pre-crisis levels by the fifth year."[62] Of course, none of those crises was as severe or as widespread as the 1997 crash. Nor can we be sure that the next crisis will not be more severe yet.

THE DANGERS OF DEFICITS: WHO'S NEXT?

For all the drama of the final plunge and the breathtaking scope of the eventual consequences, the background causes of the Asian crisis could hardly have been more ordinary. It is hard to argue that they were unprecedented or unforeseeable. After all, ample historical precedent demonstrates that export-led growth fueled by foreign investment is always highly contingent on impermanent external conditions. The Mexican trade liberalization of the early 1990s that culminated with NAFTA produced huge trade deficits, but also massive capital inflows that for a time balanced them. When the commitment to the stable exchange rate was overwhelmed by trade and capital deficits, the bottom dropped out of currency markets and stock markets. Not only did the "tequila crisis" foreshadow Asian troubles, they also contributed to them through "moral hazard." Seeing that imprudent foreign investments had generated quick fortunes, whereas the bailout negated any losses, investors judged the risk in Asia to be small, so caution was thrown to the wind even as the crisis could be seen building. What better way to cope with a dilemma than to gain all the benefits for oneself and pass off all the costs to someone else?

Although trade deficits signify one of the most dangerous risks associated with liberalization, they are not the exclusive province of outward-oriented development. The final collapse of import substitution in Latin America—the very antithesis of liberalism—was also centered on trade deficits. Initially they were easily financed by huge foreign loans, but eventually these economies were choked by the resulting foreign debt. We have learned that trade deficits loom as a danger to all trade policy approaches. There is also evidence that currency collapses associated with them are becoming more common and more damaging: Mexico and much of Latin America in the 1980s, Mexico again in 1994–1995, Southeast Asia, Russia, and Brazil in 1997.

Largest Current Account Imbalances, 1995–1997, in billions of U.S. dollars

Surpluses	Current Account	Merchandise Trade	Deficits	Current Account	Merchandise Trade
Japan	54.6	105.6	United States	77.1	185.8
Italy	19.8	50.8	Brazil	21.4	5.7
Netherlands	14.0	20.5	Korea	11.5	7.5
Switzerland	13.4	1.7	Germany	10.8	69.4
Singapore	13.1	1.5	Australia	10.4	1.0
China	11.9	27.9	Thailand	8.5	5.3
France	9.1	18.0	Indonesia	6.0	7.5
Belgium	8.5	8.9	India	5.3	14.2
Russia	5.7	20.6	Argentina	5.0	0.2
Venezuela	4.9	10.5	Colombia	4.2	2.5
Norway	4.5	10.9	Mexico	3.5	4.7
Sweden	3.2	17.5	Peru	3.4	2.0

SOURCE: *World Development Indicators 1999* CD-ROM

Since we have also discovered that persistent trade deficits eventually reach a point of no return, it seems wise to attempt to identify potential problems before they reach that stage. So we ask, where can such potential problems be found? For Americans, the answer lies much too close to home. As commentator Doug Henwood observed in September of 1999, "Accounts of the U.S. economic 'miracle' of the 1990s typically omit one embarrassing detail: its dependence on massive amounts of foreign money. In 1982—the year that Wall Street's great bull market began—the U.S. international debt account dipped solidly into the red. . . . The U.S. debt position . . . reached 22.6% of GDP in 1999, or just over $2 trillion." He quoted Alan Greenspan: "A more distant concern, but one that cannot be readily dismissed, is the very condition that has enabled the surge in American household and business demands to help sustain global stability: our rising trade deficits. There is a limit to how long and how far deficits can be sustained, since they add to net foreign claims on the United States. It is very difficult to judge at what point debt service costs become unduly burdensome and can no longer be sustained."[63] Since Greenspan's comments, the U.S. trade deficit—and the associated debt—has exploded, approaching $350 billion in 1999.

The danger is that foreign creditors will abandon the United States, just as they did Mexico in 1994 and Thailand in 1997. Doug Henwood pondered, "What happens to a colossus when it gets cut off is very hard to predict. Maybe it will luck out . . . and . . . export its way out of debt by selling 747s, Windows 2000, and Shania Twain CDs. Or maybe the U.S. in the early 2000s could be like Japan in the 1990s—stuck with a massive hangover from a burst bubble. Hard to say."[64]

EIGHT

□ □ □

Looking Ahead

This book has had two missions. First, I have attempted to explain the issues and problems that surround international trade, especially the dilemmas that arise from the opportunities it presents. Second, I have traced how perceptions of these dilemmas have shaped trade policy choices in several different nations, institutions, and time periods, and discussed the consequences of those choices.

MISSIONS REVIEWED

Few would deny the contention of liberal theory that trade permits a higher level of aggregate consumption than would be possible if consumers were prevented from purchasing foreign products. It is hard to imagine modern life without the benefits of trade. However, this aggregate economic effect tells only part of the story; trade also carries with it important social and political implications. Trade shapes the distribution of income and wealth among individuals, affects the power of states and the relations among them, and constrains or enhances the ability of both individuals and nations to achieve goals built on other values. These other effects of trade are more equivocal and sometimes less tangible than the aggregate economic effects. Empirically, they are more difficult to predict because they vary with circumstances; normatively, they are more difficult to assess because they touch values that are far from universal. They present dilemmas, because no trade policy choice can avoid all negative consequences, since some negative consequences are inherent in each alternative.

National governments select trade policies according to how these dilemmas have been understood and assessed. They have been viewed differently depending upon the efficiency of markets and the competitive positioning of firms from different countries within them. An important

Life without international trade. Danziger © *The Christian Science Monitor*

role is also played by empirical theories that describe and predict the effects of trade and normative theories that elucidate the principles appropriate for judging the desirability of these outcomes and choosing among them. In the final analysis, the balance of political power among those with alternative views shapes the policy choices of governments.

It is striking how recurrently these themes appear in different contexts. Across several centuries, trade policy choices have been debated in the language of liberalism and mercantilism. The strengths and weaknesses of these intellectual traditions remain very much as they were when they were founded. The explanations for the choice between them exhibit similar continuity over time.

MERCANTILISM AND LIBERALISM: A SUMMARY PERSPECTIVE

Classical mercantile trade policy represented a distinctive response to the dilemmas posed by trade. Mercantilists advocated government control of markets, especially in international trade, in order to generate specific distributional outcomes, especially the protection of consumers and grain producers. They also pursued the values of social justice, national development, and self-sufficiency with greater zeal than the values of greater consumption and efficiency, which have been associated with liberalism. They saw unregulated trade more as a threat to state power and national defense than as a guarantor of international peace.

Mercantilism evolved in response to existing conditions in the economy and foreign affairs, in tune with prevailing currents of social and economic theory, and in recognition of the realities of the distribution of power. Inevitably, these foundations eventually crumbled: By the middle of the nineteenth century, the theories and values that sustained mercantilism, the conditions of markets that limited its alternatives, and the political power of its supporters and opponents had all changed.

In fact, mercantilism can be interpreted as a middle ground—a transition—between the sharp antagonism to the market characteristic of the Middle Ages and the modern era's acceptance of market principles. For most of Western history, social theory had favored the control of markets for the public good (especially by government), but a rapidly evolving economy began to offer material advantages too large to so easily dismiss on ethical grounds. Mercantilism sought to accommodate the material needs and opportunities of this changing economic order yet not fully abandon the commitment to manage economic affairs in accord with other values. Although this economic system was maintained by the predominant powers of the period—the Crown and the church—the growth of political challengers to those powers and the fading of their social views doomed classical mercantilism. By the middle of the nineteenth century, mercantilism was seen as a curious anachronism that was ill suited to meet the modern challenge.

No doctrine can escape the fate of obsolescence. Perhaps theories are mortal: Just as they are born, they must die. They can be "true" but they cannot be universal. Or perhaps theories are more like endangered species: Though born to a habitat whose destruction they rarely survive unchanged, they can evolve and adapt to a new environment. In either case, it is wise to understand the roots of theories and the limits that are imposed by the values they assume and the material conditions to which they apply. But it would be a mistake to underestimate the adaptability of a viewpoint that has arisen in as many different times and places as mercantilism.

Certainly, the classical brand of mercantilism seems foreign today, but we dismiss its lessons at considerable peril. Mercantilism was neither as ignorant nor as ill advised as many contemporary commentators imply. Unfortunately, history is written by the victors. Too often, the wisdom of the losers is thus lost, denied its rightful place in our arsenal of weapons waiting to be applied should new challenges require. Mercantilism's lessons are eclipsed by self-congratulatory hubris, but our abandonment of the issues raised by this vision is as dangerous as our failure to appreciate the inner logic of mercantilism as a whole.

The challenges faced by classical mercantilism reappear in the modern era: trade deficits, reliance upon other nations, the need for government revenues, the difficulty of initiating infant industries, the desire to provide security for all citizens, the use of trade for other foreign policy purposes, and the unfair practices of other nations. These issues are not dead but only recast. The protection of consumers and workers may no longer be seen principally as a Christian imperative, but it is just as surely mandated by democratic political systems erected to fulfill the modern values of justice and citizen welfare. Fear of dependence on others for food may no longer lead nations to policies of self-sufficiency in grain, but the Persian Gulf War reminds us of the alternative when other nations control trade in a vital product. We need no longer fret about the revenues of the Crown or accommodate the privileges of a landed aristocracy, but the government still needs revenue and some groups still command greater attention from the state than others.

So it should not be a surprise that mercantilists survive, fueled by the original logic even if rooted in a different soil or known by a different label. We need not be baffled or enraged by the Japanese system of import protection and export subsidies or the European Union's Common Agricultural Policy, both of which have more in common with the Anglo-American past than we may be prepared to admit. Nor are the mercantilist impulses in our own trade system extinguished; we call them fair trade rather than protection, but the distinction is elusive. Most unfortunately, we deny that trade raises many of the same dilemmas today that were confronted with more candor and vision by those whose names we can no longer recall.

Liberalism, too, represents a distinctive reaction to the dilemmas of trade. Though rooted initially in a particular historic period, liberalism has subsequently been adapted to a wide range of circumstances and remains of contemporary relevance. Liberalism resolved the dilemma over competing values by rejecting mercantilism's early Christian emphasis on communitarianism and social stability while embracing the aggregate consumption and individualism of secular utilitarianism. Liberalism resolved the distributional dilemma by accepting market-based outcomes over state-mandated ones, with clear benefits for industrialists and clear losses for landowners. Finally, liberalism resolved the dilemma over the effect of trade on the state by accepting interdependence and forsaking self-sufficiency.

The key to the acceptance of liberalism was the powerful theory of comparative advantage exemplified by Ricardo's memorable demonstration of the gains from trade: The standard of living of consumers improves under the efficient specialization unleashed by free trade. However, the seed of free trade had to be planted in ground made fertile by the dominance of values and social ideas compatible with liberalism. A theory that appealed to aggregate material interests and trusted the market to bring about acceptable social outcomes had to wait until the middle of the nineteenth century, by which time the liberal ideas of private property, materialism, individualism, and the division of labor had become familiar and ethically acceptable. The commercialization of agriculture, the rapid growth of towns and industry, change in church doctrine, and the growing influence of secular utilitarian social and political ideas doomed the village-based communal ethics of an earlier age.

At the same time, the market and the productive forces that it organized had developed sufficiently to play their appointed role in liberal theory. Britain's industries were the most competitive in the world, foreign agriculture had the capacity to both feed England and earn revenues to purchase British manufactures, and trade was easier and more reliable because of transportation improvements and relative peace among nations. Against this backdrop, optimistic estimates of transition costs and favorable assessments of short-term risks versus long-term gains are understandable.

Finally, the need for a political force capable of tending the crop with skill and enthusiasm was filled by the industrial class, which was growing in political strength and economic importance. The distributional implications of free trade—particularly when grain prices were so vividly apparent to consumers—operated to the advantage of free traders. After British industry's competitive dominance allowed it to forsake protection for itself, free traders were able to present a compelling case in broad national-interest terms.

However, the flowering of free trade that was symbolized by the repeal of the Corn Laws in 1846 was not lasting, but was only one phase of a now familiar cycle in which any approach to trade generates the very forces that eventually bring about its reversal. The more extreme the policy approach, the more visible are the dilemmas it produces. The most radically protectionist of the Corn Laws in the early nineteenth century fueled the free-trade sentiment that dominated by the mid-nineteenth century. The resultant unbridled market—though it generated rapid economic growth and technical progress—produced an ideological backlash and an alteration in social and political structures that together created market-interventionist states. The trade suppression of the 1930s—

though it sought security for workers—produced a depression and war that led to renewed internationalism and restored faith in markets. The extreme reliance on global markets represented by the outward-oriented development of Southeast Asia near the end of the twentieth century seems likely to signal a reaction early in the twenty-first.

FUTURE CHALLENGES

It is hard to predict what form trade controversies will take in the immediate future—an extension of NAFTA, the refinement of the WTO, another round of trade talks, another skirmish in a trade conflict with Europe or Japan, the integration of new powers such as China into the heart of the global political economy, recasting the international financial architecture. It is easier to predict the broad forces that will be at work in these specific instances—the dilemmas of trade—and how they will be resolved in line with prevailing theories and values, the condition of markets, and the balance of political power.

Perhaps the most striking characteristic of the global political economy at the beginning of the twenty-first century is the extraordinary efficiency of its markets. Transportation and communication advances make the conduct of global trade cheaper, easier, and faster than previous generations could have imagined. Indeed, transportation costs are now so low that we have entered an era of global *production*. This development is also fueled by enormous capital flows between nations.

In economic terms, this extraordinary mobility of both productive capacity (capital and technology) and finished goods means that tiny differences in competitive advantage can be exploited without being eaten up by transportation costs. However, at the same time, residents of the new global village are becoming increasingly uneasy with the small margin of error that makes the difference between success and failure in the modern market. Workers, for whom security is a primary value, fear that comparative advantage will shift so quickly that no jobs will be secure. States, for whom power over other domestic actors and sovereignty against foreign ones are primary values, fear that they will lose the ability to control the national economy at the same time that electorates increasingly hold them responsible for it and just as economic power has begun to displace military power in foreign policy.

Inevitably, this mobility for some actors—multinational corporations and other owners of capital and technology—affords them a bargaining advantage over actors with inherently less mobility, especially workers and nation-states. We can expect that both workers and states will respond to the sharpened dilemmas. Indeed, the Battle of Seattle no doubt

Unemployment in the global market. Danziger © *The Christian Science Monitor*

represents the opening salvo of a renewed controversy over how the balance is to be struck between trade policies that benefit corporations and those that benefit workers. Given the public attention trained on the dilemmas of trade by the WTO protests, it seems likely that these decisions will be more fully debated in the coming years, with enhanced likelihood that trade policy will become a choice rooted in national values, prevailing theories, and market conditions, all adjudicated by citizens acting in their multiple roles.

Thus, the chief challenge for the global trading system is to reinvigorate the institutions that govern international trade without eroding the legitimate rights and responsibilities of national governments. Not only must the global system promote peace and prosperity, it must be seen to do so better than regional arrangements. All this must be accomplished in an era lacking the shared interests and values that made such progress easier in the case of Bretton Woods and lacking a hegemonic leader committed to the process and capable of delivering a globally acceptable compromise.

However, given recent events in Seattle and Bangkok, the necessity of global management is more widely acknowledged than at any time since the Great Depression. As Robert Wade put it, "The [Asian] crisis should provoke a Bretton Woods II, a fundamental debate about the character of the international financial regime in the post–Cold War world."[1] The debate will be spirited, because the stakes are high and the positions of advocates are as far apart as their interests, values, and theories. Wade would emphasize a restriction on the capital flows that animate outward-oriented development, not least because the failure of that kind of development has much greater consequences for other states than previous strategies. As Robert Kuttner said,

> We are learning once again the fundamental difference between free commerce in ordinary goods and free commerce in money. The former is broadly efficient—it subjects business to bracing competition and allows products to find markets anywhere in the world. The latter is destabilizing and deflationary—it holds the real economy hostage to the whims of financial speculation, which is vulnerable to herd instincts, manias, and panics. In ordinary commerce, prices adjust and markets equilibrate. In global money markets, erratic and damaging overshooting is the norm.[2]

Calls for systemic reform may involve an altered role for the IMF or an innovation like the Tobin tax, first discussed by Nobel laureate James Tobin in 1972. He proposes a 0.1 percent tax on all foreign currency transactions, too small to affect trade or long-term movements of capital but large enough to discourage disruptive short-term speculation. The proceeds could be used to fund the international financial and trading institutions themselves, thereby strengthening global architecture. Wall Street interests oppose any such regulation of capital flows, citing the liberal conviction that transaction barriers erode efficiency. However, efficiency is not the only value at stake. For example, Malaysia's Mahathir observed, "The fall in our currency's value has made us poorer, exposing us to the possibility of being controlled by foreign powers. If this happens, we will lose the freedom to run our country's economy and with it our political freedom also. In short, we will be recolonized indirectly."[3]

Some would go further. At the height of the last Great Depression, John Maynard Keynes stated,

> I sympathize with those who would minimize, rather than with those who would maximize, economic entanglement among nations. Ideas, knowledge, science, hospitality, travel—these are the things which should of their nature be international. But let goods be homespun whenever it is reasonably and conveniently possible and, above all, let finance be primarily national.

From this standpoint, the absence of an international regulatory mechanism is only one symptom of carrying belief in markets to an extreme.

Another, some say, is outward-oriented development, a strategy that is, at best, self-limiting and, at worst, more threatening to other nations than the beggar-thy-neighbor adjustment policies that Bretton Woods was created to control. The real problem lies in failing to adequately weigh the dilemmas of trade at the systemic level.

To deal with the dilemmas of trade at the systemic level will require that a consensus be achieved among nations that represent greater diversity than ever before. If accommodating Japanese trade policy has generated tensions, the dislocations implicit in dealing with the People's Republic of China (PRC) loom even larger. The PRC is among the fastest-growing economies in the world and has quickly become a major force in global trade. Its vast potential market of 1 billion consumers represents a lure that has led the international community to tread lightly on Chinese violations of international norms even when they are dramatically visible. China, whose bilateral trade surplus with the United States is second only to Japan's, does not permit workers to organize for the purpose of increasing wages or improving working conditions, and even exports many products manufactured by slave labor. Not only does this offend the sensibilities of many foreigners, it creates an impossible competition problem for American workers. Already under threat from poor labor in Mexico, they are now being challenged to produce at lower unit cost than slaves. This issue was about to be the first to test the American commitment to free trade as this book went to press in early 2000, when both Chinese entry into the WTO and a continuation of American membership in the WTO were due to come before Congress. For years, Congress debated the extension of most-favored-nation status for China on a yearly basis and presidential action granted it annually. In 1999, the United States and China negotiated terms under which China would be admitted to the WTO, thus settling the issue more permanently. Although President Clinton is satisfied with the negotiated formula, neither Congress nor other major powers, especially the EU, had yet agreed to it.

Absent systemic action, states have responded to trade dilemmas by increasing the use of NTBs and by creating regional arrangements that give them a geographical range comparable to the actors they are trying to control. Increasing regionalism solves some problems and exacerbates others, of course. In particular, the emerging pattern of regionalism amounts to a discriminatory trading system of superblocs that some fear could endanger international peace. The trade discrimination implicit in regionalism creates foreign policy tensions between blocs at the same time that conflict-dampening global interdependence, which otherwise might help contain it, declines.

For the nation, the greatest challenge will be to cope with the dilemmas of trade that become more binding as trade levels increase. In particular, states must deal adequately with distributional dilemmas without eliminating the beneficial trade that brings them about. In doing so, they must view the value underlying the theory of comparative advantage—the maximization of consumption—as only one policy goal among many components of what Max Corden has called the "conservative social welfare function." According to this function, nations avoid income declines for most groups even if they would be balanced by larger income gains among other groups. The reason is fourfold. First, it is regarded as unfair to diminish incomes via government policy. Second, because most individuals are risk averse, the knowledge that this function is being pursued provides security benefits to all. Third, social peace is endangered by sharp increases in income inequality. Fourth, for all of the previous reasons, governments are likely to fall if incomes decline.[4]

The most successful policies are likely to be those that create institutional structures that ease trade dilemmas rather than relying on either pure liberalism or pure mercantilism. The creation of such structures has been accomplished in very different ways in Europe and in Japan, where the challenges have been felt more acutely and for a longer time than in the United States.

In Europe, regional regulation has sought to structure trade competition so as to minimize value clashes, especially by protecting the ability of the welfare state to ameliorate the distributional effects of trade. Of course, in the process of responding to trade dilemmas, regional organizations must cope with the competing priorities that cut across nations and political parties. The European right sees the slow growth of output and employment in recent years as evidence that a regional welfare state is not economically sustainable. The left counters with the observation that trade expansion without social protection to cope with the dislocations it produces is not politically sustainable.

In Japan, the effects of markets are muted by a variety of societal and governmental arrangements, including employment practices and private network structures, that purchase security at the expense of consumer benefits. Furthermore, aggressive foreign marketing shifts some of the dilemmas to foreign nations. Evidence increasingly suggests that resistance from both domestic consumers and foreign governments makes this solution only temporary.

These experiences should help to shape attitudes in the United States, where efforts to resolve these dilemmas are somewhat more recent in origin. The central lesson does not promote optimism: Trade dilemmas cannot be fully resolved because they inevitably require choices. High levels of trade promote distributional effects that are beneficial to some but harmful to others. Regulations designed to protect the environment and to meet other societal goals often constrain the benefits to be earned from free trade. When the role of markets is strengthened, the role of the state must decline. Nations must choose.

CONCLUSION: INDIVIDUAL CHOICES

For the individual, the challenge is to recognize the central role that issues of international political economy—especially trade—will play in determining the kind of society, polity, and economy in which one will live. Individuals must demand that advocates of different policies respond to the entire range of considerations that lurk beneath the dull surface of trade policy. They must insist upon comprehensive policy packages that address all the trade dilemmas rather than rely only upon narrow considerations. They must require that the universal and eternal truths of Smith and Ricardo be balanced with the messy reality of specific cases. They must weigh the dilemmas posed by trade for the individual in his or her various roles—as consumer, as worker, and as citizen. Choose wisely.

□ □ □

Discussion Questions

CHAPTER ONE

1. Should a consumer consider the social and political effects of trade when deciding whether to buy a domestic or foreign product?

2. Some imports produce social costs, such as unemployment of domestic autoworkers or the need to maintain military forces to protect oil routes around the Persian Gulf. Should governments apply a tax on foreign products equal to these social costs?

3. Why are some nations so much more reliant on foreign trade than others?

4. Should Americans be concerned about the U.S. trade deficit?

CHAPTER TWO

1. What foreign policy conditions made reliance on trade unattractive to Britain during the mercantile period? Have similar conditions existed for developed countries in the last half of the twentieth century?

2. What changes in ethical outlook fueled the rise of liberal economic ideas? Have there been any changes in values or philosophy since Bretton Woods that might have a comparable influence on economic policy? (Environmentalism, perhaps?)

3. What changes in political power balances led to the repeal of the Corn Laws? Have similar changes occurred in the twentieth-century United States?

CHAPTER THREE

1. Can you identify any recent changes in the operation of markets that would be comparable to the improvements in transportation systems in early England? What effect would you expect these changes to have on trade policy preferences?

2. What change would you expect in U.S. trade policy from an election that left either the Democrats or the Republicans fully in control? Why?

3. Why do you think U.S. consumers did not exert more political pressure to eliminate restrictions on imports of Japanese autos, which increased prices on all autos significantly?

4. It is an interesting exercise to attempt to explain why liberalism or mercantilism emerged as the policy choice of particular individuals, groups, and nations in particular periods. Choose your own position. Why is U.S. organized labor more protectionist now than in the 1950s? Are Canadian farmers free traders or protectionists? French farmers?

CHAPTER FOUR

1. On balance, did Bretton Woods favor the United States at the expense of other nations?
2. Why didn't the United States assume leadership of the global political economy after World War I instead of delaying until after World War II?
3. On balance, is Bretton Woods primarily a liberal or a mercantilist system?

CHAPTER FIVE

1. Why hasn't the United States adopted an explicit industrial policy comparable to those in Japan and Europe?
2. Why hasn't the United States taken a harder line with Japan, threatening dramatic trade sanctions if the bilateral trade deficit doesn't diminish?
3. Why has U.S. trade policy taken a protectionist turn in recent years?
4. Does Japan's export of goods to other countries create a moral obligation for it to purchase foreign imports? If individuals choose not to do so, does the government have a moral obligation to force them?

CHAPTER SIX

1. What factors explain why the EU and NAFTA have a different balance between the economic and social dimensions of regional integration?
2. Why did President Bill Clinton so enthusiastically support NAFTA when Democratic candidate Bill Clinton did not?
3. On balance, is Mexico better off after NAFTA than before it?

CHAPTER SEVEN

1. Why did the Korean economy decline after Thailand's collapse?
2. What are the similarities and differences between the Mexican peso crisis and the southeast Asian meltdown?
3. On balance, is Thailand better off today than before it adopted outward-oriented development?

CHAPTER EIGHT

1. What courses of action are available for individuals to register their attitudes toward the dilemmas of trade?

2. Should a consumer consider the social and political effects of trade when deciding whether to buy a domestic or foreign product?

3. Should the United States support WTO membership for China?

4. Should a Tobin tax be adopted to restrain capital movements?

□ □ □

Notes

CHAPTER ONE

1. If economists are uncertain about some of the negative effects of these developments, the public is not. For example, in 1988 (during the Cold War), Americans were asked, "Which poses the greatest threat to our national security, a military adversary like the Soviet Union or economic competitors like Japan?" Almost twice as many Americans answered the latter. John Marttila, "American Public Opinion: Evolving Definitions of National Security" in Edward K. Hamilton, ed., *America's Global Interests: A New Agenda* (New York: W. W. Norton, 1989), pp. 261–315.

2. Richard Lamm, "The Uncompetitive Society," in Martin K. Starr, ed., *Global Competitiveness: Getting the U.S. Back on Track* (New York: W. W. Norton, 1988), pp. 12–42.

3. Laura D'Andrea Tyson, "Competitiveness: An Analysis of the Problem and a Perspective on Future Policy," in Starr, *Global Competitiveness.* Emphasis added.

4. These are among the American institutions that Richard Lamm suggests that we must reform and revitalize. See his essay "The Uncompetitive Society," in Starr, *Global Competitiveness.*

5. The original agreement restricted imports to 1.68 million cars, then to 1.85 million in 1984. Since then Japan has voluntarily remained under that target. However, Japanese auto companies evaded these restrictions by producing cars in the United States. Further, they increased revenues with the same number of imports by shifting from cheap cars to luxury models.

6. See Rene Schwok, *U.S.–EC Relations in the Post-Cold War Era: Conflict or Partnership?* (Boulder: Westview Press, 1991), chapter 6.

CHAPTER TWO

1. The phrase actually originates in physiocracy, an eighteenth-century economic theory propounded by François Quesnay, an adviser to Louis XV of France. Although they advanced a very different conception of the economy than liberals—emphasizing agriculture to the near exclusion of industry—physiocrats were, like liberals, free traders. When asked how best the state might foster the creation of wealth in the economy, Vincent de Gournay, an associate of Quesnay, responded, "Laissez faire, laissez passer," literally, "Allow it to be made, allow it to be traded."

2. The term "corn" is synonymous with "grain" and includes wheat, oats, rye, barley, malt, peas, and beans, as well as maize (which Americans call corn).

3. There are also major differences among these strategies. Latin America de-emphasized eventual export success, whereas Japan encouraged cartels among multiple firms instead of granting monopolies.

4. See E. Lipson, *The Growth of English Society: A Short Economic History* (New York: Henry Holt, 1950), p. 54.

5. Import taxes account for about 1.5 percent of U.S. federal government rev-enues, about average among developed countries. Among less developed coun-tries the percentage is typically much higher.

6. See W. Cunningham, *The Growth of English Industry and Commerce in Modern Times, Volume 2: The Mercantile System* (Cambridge: Cambridge University Press, 1938), p. 503.

7. See N. S. B. Gras, *The Evolution of the English Corn Market* (Cambridge: Har-vard University Press, 1915).

8. See Donald Grove Barnes, *A History of the English Corn Laws from 1660–1846* (London: George Routledge, 1930), pp. 5–6.

9. Adam Smith, *An Inquiry into the Nature and Causes of the Wealth of Nations* (London: J. M. Dutton, 1910), p. 408.

10. J. Russell Major, *The Western World: Renaissance to the Present* (Philadelphia: J. B. Lippincott, 1966), p. 235.

11. Quoted in Cunningham, *The Growth of English Industry*, p. 387.

12. Similar arrangements were common in Europe at various times. In Russia, for example, they survived virtually intact until the agricultural reforms of 1904.

13. It is tempting to glorify such an ethical stance, but it must be remembered that what was regarded as "suitable for his station" reflected contemporary stan-dards that tolerated massive inequalities in economic standards of living and vast differences in political rights between those of one station and another.

14. See Barnes, *A History of the English Corn Laws from 1660–1846*, p. 34.

15. R. H. Tawney, *Religion and the Rise of Capitalism* (New York: New American Library, 1954), p. 43.

16. See Lipson, *The Growth of English Society*, p. 145.

17. Of course, government was not the only source of interference with mar-kets. As early as the thirteenth century, skilled artisans formed craft **guilds** that developed standards of workmanship to protect the public from shoddy goods, but an elaborate system of apprenticeships also protected established artisans from the competition of newcomers and outsiders. Only members of a craft guild—masters and journeymen—were permitted to be employed in the industry or to sell their goods. Membership in the guild could be attained only after a lengthy period of apprenticeship with a master who would train the newcomer. Modern economists would call these arrangements **oligopolies**, meaning markets dominated by a small number of suppliers who may collude to keep prices high.

18. In the middle of the eighteenth century, a coach took fourteen days to make the trip from Edinburgh in Scotland to London in the south of England, a journey now accomplished in six hours by train and under two hours by plane.

19. By the middle of the nineteenth century about a quarter of the land was owned by 1,200 individuals, with about 6,200 owning another quarter. Only about an eighth of the land was worked directly by its owners; the remainder was farmed by rent-paying tenants.

20. R. H. Tawney, *The Agrarian Problem in the Sixteenth Century* (London: Longmans, Green, 1912), p. 409.

21. Although the church now plays a more passive role in most countries, the modern state, especially in its democratic form, has filled the role of a check on the distributional and value allocation propensities of markets. The capitalist market and the democratic state, two institutions that represent distinctive ethical theories, battle for primacy in directing the organization of modern society. Both are necessary, but nations vary in the extent to which each is dominant. See Karl Polanyi, *The Great Transformation*, (Boston: Beacon Press, 1944).

22. Lipson, *The Growth of English Society*, p. 48.

23. Ibid., p. 182.

24. Smith, *Wealth of Nations*, p. 401.

25. Ibid., p. 400.

26. Ironically, the trade in Portuguese wine resulted more from political restrictions than market forces. French wine was preferred by English consumers, but for foreign policy reasons differential English tariffs were negotiated under the Methuen Treaty of 1703 to encourage the importation of port wine from Portugal. See Lipson, *The Growth of English Society*, p. 155.

27. Though effective early in the Corn Law debates, this argument had less power by the 1840s, because by this time an industrial sector had already emerged in most of Europe.

28. Even if employment declines somewhat, later liberals have shown that protectionism is less efficient than combining free trade with unemployment compensation. Indeed, this is the approach widely used in Europe today. In this period, however, the state did not maintain such a social safety net.

29. Dani Rodrik, *Has Globalization Gone Too Far?* (Washington, DC: Institute for International Economics, 1997).

30. Quoted in Lipson, *The Growth of English Society*, p. 315.

31. Ibid., p. 320.

32. Even after the Reform Bill of 1832, about 80 percent of the members of Parliament were landowners. See W. O. Aydelotte, "The Country Gentlemen and the Repeal of the Corn Laws," *English Historical Review* 82, 322 (1967):51. However, the landed gentry were becoming less reliant on the agricultural sector because they were rapidly investing in industry and transportation. See Cheryl Schonhardt-Bailey, "Specific Factors, Capital Markets, Portfolio Diversification, and Free Trade: Domestic Determinants of the Repeal of the Corn Laws," *World Politics* 43 (July 1991):545–569.

33. Quoted in Barnes, *A History of the English Corn Laws*, p. 119.

34. Smith, *Wealth of Nations*, pp. 411–412.

35. Ibid.

36. Quoted in Barnes, *A History of the English Corn Laws*, p. 119.

CHAPTER THREE

1. The average import duty tumbled from more than 50 percent in 1820 to 30 percent in 1846 and finally to under 10 percent by the 1870s.

2. See Charles Kindleberger, "The Rise of Free Trade in Western Europe," *Journal of Economic History* 35, 1 (1975).

3. Increasing demand for food was a greater factor, however, as the population grew from 9 million to 33 million during the nineteenth century.

4. Two-thirds of those imports came from the United States because of the advent of steam-powered shipping. In 1846, English farmers were largely insulated from American competition by transatlantic transport costs that added more than a third to the price of American grain in Britain, but by the 1890s, transport costs had fallen by 75 percent.

5. *Das Kapital*, published in 1867, was his classic statement on capitalism.

6. Given the conditions of the time, Marx himself was a free trader, but most subsequent Marxists have disagreed with him on this point.

7. E. Lipson, *The Growth of English Society: A Short Economic History* (New York: Henry Holt, 1950)

8. The regulation of industrial labor—especially the Ten Hours Act of 1847—was passed by a parliament still dominated by landed interests, partially out of revenge against industrial interests for their leading role in the demise of the Corn Laws.

9. Quoted in Lipson, *The Growth of English Society*, p. 285.

10. Middle-class suffrage is not to be confused with working-class suffrage. Even after the Reform Act of 1832 increased the number of eligible voters by half, only about a seventh of the adult male population met the stringent requirements.

11. In the modern era, parties of the right include British Conservatives, American Republicans, and European Christian Democrats; parties of the left include British Labour, American Democrats, and European Socialists and Social Democrats.

12. For example, Labour was the party of free trade in Britain throughout the 1920s; it was the Conservatives who enacted the protectionist policies associated with the collapse of the trading system. Similarly, in the United States, Democrats were free traders and Republicans were protectionist during this key period.

13. The famous Leontief paradox shows that the United States after World War II did not fit the predicted pattern because American imports were more capital intensive than American exports. This paradox is hotly debated; most economists deny that the Leontief paradox constitutes a disconfirmation of Heckscher-Ohlin theory, arguing instead for a reformulation that encompasses other factors of production.

14. Geographic cleavages also occur, but these are largely the product of sectoral considerations.

15. See Gary C. Hufbauer, Diane T. Berliner, and Kimberly A. Elliot, *Trade Protection in the United States: Thirty-one Case Studies* (Washington, D.C.: Institute for International Economics, 1986).

16. Friedrich List, *The National System of Political Economy* (Philadelphia: J. B. Lippincott, 1956), p. 440.

17. Forrest Capie, *Depression and Protectionism: Britain Between the Wars* (London: George Allen and Unwin, 1983), chapter 4.

18. Armed with very steep tariffs enacted in 1931 and 1932, Britain did negotiate **bilateral** agreements with sixteen nations between 1932 and 1935 to improve British access to those markets. In the United States, the high Smoot-Hawley tariff of 1930 provided the leverage for eighteen bilateral treaties between 1934 and 1938.

19. John A. C. Conybeare, *Trade Wars: The Theory and Practice of International Commercial Rivalry* (New York: Columbia University Press, 1987), p. 241.

20. Michael Kitson and Solomos Solomou, *Protectionism and Economic Revival: the British Inter-War Economy* (Cambridge: Cambridge University Press, 1990), p. 4.

21. See Conybeare, *Trade Wars*, p. 242.

22. This result was not unforeseen. The unsuccessful Labour campaign to retain free trade had cautioned, in vain, regarding the global consequences of rising British protectionism, asking, "Will the British people take the responsibility for the setting up of a fascist despotism in a Germany, driven to despair?" See Gerhard Kumleden, *The Workers' Case for Free Trade* (London: International, 1932)

23. Barry Eichengreen and T. J. Hatton, eds., *Interwar Unemployment in International Perspective* (Dordrecht, Netherlands: Kluwer Academic, 1988), chapter 1.

24. For a survey, see Charles Kindleberger, *The World in Depression, 1929–1939* (Berkeley: University of California Press, 1973).

25. Recent scholarship suggests that protectionism played a smaller role in the economic collapse than was generally assumed at the time. For example, it has been estimated that Smoot-Hawley and the resulting retaliation from other countries cost the United States only 0.44 percent of GNP. See Lawrence Brunner, "The Effect of Trade Restrictions on the U.S. Economy in the Great Depression," paper presented to the American Economic Association, New York, December 1985 (cited in Conybeare, *Trade Wars*). Moreover, Kitson and Solomou, *Protectionism and Economic Revival*, contend that the British tariff of 1932 was actually beneficial to the British economy.

26. Recall that the explosion of protectionist and anti-Japanese sentiment of the early 1990s and President Bush's defeat in his 1992 bid for reelection were triggered by an American unemployment rate that never reached 8 percent.

CHAPTER FOUR

1. See Charles Kindleberger, *The World in Depression 1929–1939* (Berkeley: University of California Press, 1973); and Robert Gilpin, *U.S. Power and the Multinational Corporation: The Political Economy of Foreign Direct Investment* (New York: Basic Books, 1975).

2. American leadership was long overdue. Britain's ascendance peaked around 1880 and its relative decline had been unmistakable since World War I. The United States surpassed Britain in total income by the middle of the nineteenth century, in per capita income by the beginning of the twentieth, and in volume of global trade and investment shortly after World War I.

3. This standard component of liberal theory appeared as early as 1808 in the work of Robert Torrens, who also developed the theory of comparative advantage a decade before Ricardo. See Fritz Machlup, *A History of Thought on Economic Integration* (New York: Columbia University Press, 1977).

4. American isolationism before World War II was manifested in rejection of the League of Nations, insistence on the repayment of World War I loans, refusal to cooperate during the London Economic Conference of 1933, and very high tariff rates even prior to Smoot-Hawley. For the contention that the United States adopted a free-rider posture more often than any other nation, see John A. C. Conybeare, *Trade Wars: The Theory and Practice of International Commercial Rivalry* (New York: Columbia University Press, 1987).

5. Quoted in John H. Jackson, *The World Trading System: Law and Policy of International Economic Relations* (Cambridge: MIT Press, 1989), p. 10.

6. The ITO proposed commodity agreements to ensure prices that were fair to consumers and provided a reasonable return to producers. It also provided for governmental cooperation in a variety of areas only tangentially related to trade.

7. For a brief overview, see Robert Baldwin, *Trade Policy in a Changing World Economy* (Chicago: University of Chicago Press, 1988), chapter 11.

8. There are many exceptions, which I will discuss shortly. Even the MFN clause cannot eliminate discrimination if a tariff schedule contains categories that apply only to the products of one country. For example, the 1902 German tariff law charged a lower duty on "brown cattle reared at least 300 metres above sea level and having at least one month's grazing at least 800 metres above sea level." The practical effect was to give preference to Swiss cattle. See Richard Pomfret, *Unequal Trade* (Oxford: Basil Blackwell, 1988), chapter 1.

9. For similar reasons, the United States had been able to achieve a decrease in tariffs of about one-third in bilateral treaties with thirty-one nations between 1934 and 1945 under the U.S. Reciprocal Trade Agreements Act, which contained a similar MFN provision.

10. Quantitative restrictions such as quotas are prohibited because, unlike tariffs, they require government administration that can easily disguise discrimination.

11. Developed nations less frequently invoke the escape clause today, preferring to offer "trade adjustment assistance" to industries and enhanced welfare benefits to workers.

12. Richard N. Gardner, *Sterling-Dollar Diplomacy: Anglo-American Collaboration in the Reconstruction of Multilateral Trade* (Oxford: Clarendon Press, 1956), p. 376.

13. Because this book focuses upon trade issues, I can mention only in passing those monetary problems not linked directly to trade.

14. While the highly protectionist Multi-Fiber Agreement is being phased out, the United States will lower its textile tariffs by an average of only 12 percent, phased in over ten years—not the 50 percent cut demanded by the EU. Even so, U.S. Senate ratification was delayed by Senator Ernest "Fritz" Hollings of South Carolina, a powerful committee chairman who claimed that 40,000 jobs in his home state would be endangered by even these modest reductions.

15. "Free Trade's Fading Champion," *Economist*, April 11, 1992, p. 65.

16. Jeffrey J. Schott, ed., *Completing the Uruguay Round* (Washington, D.C.: Institute for International Economics, 1990).

17. Donald B. Keesing, *Improving Trade Policy Reviews in the World Trade Organi-zation* (Washington D.C.: Institute for International Economics), 1998, p. 1.

18. Quoted in Robert Dodge, "Grappling with GATT," *Dallas Morning News*, August 8, 1994, p. 1D.

CHAPTER FIVE

1. Lydia Saad, "Americans Support Active Role for U.S. in World Affairs," Gallup News Service, April 1, 1999.

2. Gallup poll, May 1999. http://www.gallup.com/poll/releases/pr990504c.asp

3. "Japan Gives Its Answer," *Economist*, May 13, 1995, p. 36.

4. Because of the larger U.S. market, American dependence, in percentage terms, is smaller: In 1997, less than 10 percent of U.S. exports went to Japan, and about 15 percent of U.S. imports were from Japan. See *Annual Report 1998* (Geneva: World Trade Organization), p. 18.

5. Quoted in Steven Schlossstein, *Trade War: Greed, Power, and Industrial Policy on Opposite Sides of the Pacific* (New York: Congdon and Weed, 1984), p. 4

6. Quoted in Jon Woronoff, *World Trade War* (New York: Praeger, 1984), pp. 144–145.

7. Some argue that these unusual bilateral imbalances simply reflect the com-parative advantage in manufacturing inherent in Japan's unique factor endow-ment of abundant capital but few natural resources. Critics suggest that protec-tionism is responsible for the unusually small penetration of the Japanese manufacturing market by foreign firms (about 1 percent in the early 1990s).

8. Charlie Turner, *Japan's Dynamic Efficiency in the Global Market: Trade, Invest-ment, and Economic Growth* (New York: Quorum Books, 1991), p. 104.

9. Although global production of automobiles nearly tripled between 1960 and 1990, American production was almost unchanged. Thus, the American share of global production fell from over 51 percent in 1960 to 19 percent in 1990. For greater details, see Peter Dicken, *Global Shift: The Internationalization of Economic Activity*, 2nd ed. (New York: Guilford Press, 1992).

10. List also noted that a trailing nation typically feels bitterness toward the dominant nation, especially in response to its exhortation for more liberal policies. Given the reaction of the United States, it appears that a declining power accepts the loss of its preeminent position with even less grace than a trailing nation ac-cepts its long-standing status as a second-rate power.

11. Adam Smith, *An Inquiry into the Nature and Causes of the Wealth of Nations* (London: J. M. Dutton, 1910), p. 439.

12. Ibid., p. 437.

13. Stephen D. Cohen, *An Ocean Apart: Explaining Three Decades of U.S.–Japanese Trade Frictions* (Westport, Conn.: Praeger, 1998), p. 5.

14. Quoted in Woronoff, *World Trade War*, p. 230.

15. In 1955, Japanese output per worker was one-tenth of the U.S. level, but it reached 65 percent by 1985. See Turner, *Japan's Dynamic Efficiency*, p. xi.

16. However, in the early 1990s the U.S. government funded more than twice as large a share of R&D as the Japanese government, 44 percent to 20 percent. Of course, the priorities were different: Sixty-six percent of that was for defense in the United States but only 5 percent in Japan.

17. Takatoshi Ito, *The Japanese Economy* (Cambridge: MIT Press, 1992), p. 203.

18. C. Fred Bergsten and Marcus Noland, *Reconcilable Differences? United States–Japan Economic Conflict* (Washington, D.C.: Institute for International Economics, 1993), p. 7.

19. David B. Audretsch, *The Market and the State: Government Policy Toward Business in Europe, Japan, and the United States* (New York: New York University Press, 1989), chapter 4.

20. Ito, *The Japanese Economy*, chapter 7.

21. Ibid., p. 190.

22. Statement by U.S. Trade Representative Charlene Barshefsky and Commerce Secretary William M. Daley, June 9, 1999. See http://www.ustr.gov/releases/1999/06/99–49.html.

23. Another result is that unemployment is very low in Japan, which may partially explain why fiscal and monetary policy tends to be less expansionary than in the United States, where slack demand causes businesses to lay off workers. Because unemployment depresses the entire economy, it generates strong political pressure for stimulative macroeconomic policy, including budget deficits.

24. Identification of these technical barriers involves a subjective component, however. For example, defenders argue that demanding safety standards are not deliberate protectionist devices but rather an appropriate adaptation to a Japanese legal system that makes product-liability lawsuits extremely rare.

25. Economies of scale are especially significant in small markets and where substantial learning occurs during production. For example, in the large commercial aircraft industry, production costs per plane decline by about 20 percent with every doubling of volume. But only one or two firms can benefit from these economies of scale because the total global market is less than 500 planes per year. See Gernot Klepper, "Industrial Policy in the Transport Aircraft Industry," in Paul Krugman and Alasdair Smith, eds., *Empirical Studies of Strategic Trade Policy* (Chicago: University of Chicago Press, 1994), pp. 101–129.

26. Of course, the United States also has an industrial policy, though it is less sophisticated, extensive, and coordinated than Japan's. Its elements include foreign aid tied to purchase of U.S. products, military sales abroad, subsidized power and water, government R&D, and government procurement policies.

27. Governments can impose restraints on imports whenever domestic industries are threatened, but the standard of injury and the method of remedy they can use varies. If the increase in imports results from market forces, "serious" injury has to be proven and the nation increasing protection is required to compensate with reduced protection in other sectors. If trade results from subsidies offered by foreign governments, the injury must be only "material," and nations need not offer compensation for tariffs that balance the subsidies.

28. The USTR reported that from 1986 to 1998 524 anti-dumping investigations were initiated and 277 antidumping orders were imposed. Over the same period 132 countervailing duty investigations were initiated and 70 orders imposed.

29. Exporters usually prefer voluntary export restraints administered by the exporting government rather than quotas administered by the importing government. Both usually involve charging firms a fee for the privilege of exporting, but in the former case the revenue goes to the exporting rather than the importing government.

30. Cited in Bergsten and Noland, *Reconcilable Differences?* p. 71.

31. See Julio Nogues, Andrzej Olechowski, and L. Alan Winters, "The Extent of Non-tariff Barriers to Industrial Countries' Imports," in J. Michael Finger and Andrzej Olechowski, eds., *The Uruguay Round: A Handbook for the Multilateral Trade Negotiations* (Washington, D.C.: World Bank, 1987).

32. Turner, *Japan's Dynamic Efficiency*, p. 68.

33. See ibid.

34. Advisory Committee on Trade Policy and Negotiations, "Major Findings and Policy Recommendations on U.S.–Japan Trade Policy," 1993, Washington, D.C. Quoted in ibid., p. 19.

35. See Leon Hollerman, *Japan, Disincorporated: The Economic Liberalization Process* (Stanford: Hoover Institution Press, 1988).

CHAPTER SIX

1. Regional integration can take a variety of forms. In a preferential trade area, a group of countries establishes lower barriers to the import of goods from member countries than from outside countries. The free-trade area is a special case of a preferential trade area in which trade barriers between members are reduced to zero. A customs union is a preferential trade area in which the members adopt a common external tariff. A common market allows the free movement of factors of production such as capital and labor as well as free trade in goods. Finally, an economic union or community occurs when the economic policies of common market nations are coordinated and harmonized under supranational control and a single currency.

2. Between 1990 and 1994, twenty-six preferential trade agreements were signed in the Western Hemisphere alone. Twenty-two new regional trade agreements were reported to the WTO between mid-1997 and mid-1998.

3. Quoted in Timothy M. Devinney and William C. Hightower, *European Markets After 1992* (Lexington, Mass.: Lexington Books, 1991), p. 21.

4. The Benelux customs union among Belgium, Luxembourg, and the Netherlands had been formed in 1948.

5. For convenience, I will use the label EU to refer to both the current European Union and its predecessor organizations.

6. The twelve whose applications have been accepted, in rough order of their likely acceptance dates, are Hungary, Poland, Cyprus, Estonia, Malta, Czech Republic, Latvia, Slovenia, Lithuania, Slovakia, Bulgaria, and Romania. Turkey has applied but has not yet been recognized as a candidate.

7. The EU remains slightly smaller than NAFTA in GDP, but its trade is more than twice as large.

8. The United States has never fully accepted the EU's conformity with Article 24 because the EU has not eliminated tariffs on "substantially all" goods (failing, most notably, with respect to agriculture). Nonetheless, the United States has not opposed the EU, but it has been active in pushing the WTO to examine the conformity of all regional agreements with GATT.

9. Quoted in Devinney and Hightower, *European Markets*, p. 16.

10. Quoted in Richard Pomfret, *Unequal Trade* (Oxford: Basil Blackwood, 1988), p. 25.

11. "The Slippery Slope," *Economist*, July 30, 1994.

12. Commission of the European Communities, *Everything You Wanted to Know About Europe Without Frontiers*, vol. 6 (Brussels: CEC, January 1992), p. 117.

13. Margaret Thatcher, "Britain and Europe," Speech delivered to the College of Europe, Bruges, Belgium, Sept. 20, 1988.

14. "Gambling on the Euro," *Economist*, January 2, 1999.

15. Congress had nearly blocked the initial negotiations for the less controversial CUSTA but failed to do so when the Senate Finance Committee deadlocked at 10 to 10.

16. Cited in John Cavanagh, John Gershman, Karen Baker, and Gretchen Helmke, eds. *Trading Freedom: How Free Trade Affects Our Lives, Work, and Environment* (San Francisco: Institute for Food and Development Policy, 1992), p. 35.

17. Cited in Paul Wonnecott, *The United States and Canada: The Quest for Free Trade* (Washington, D.C.: Institute for International Economics, 1967), p. 3.

18. Rick Salutin, "Keep Canadian Culture off the Table—Who's Kidding Who?" in Laurier LaPierre, ed. *If You Love This Country* (Toronto: McClelland and Stewart, 1987), pp. 205–206.

19. Ibid.

20. Cavanagh, et al., pp. 68–70.

21. Ibid., p. 74.

22. James Stamford, "Continental Economic Integration: Modeling the Impact on Labor," in Sidney Weintraub, ed. *Free Trade in the Western Hemisphere*, special volume of *Annals of the American Academy of Political and Social Science* (March, 1993), pp. 92–110.

23. Bruce Campbell, Andrew Jackson, Mehrene Larudess, and Teresa Gutierrez Haces, "Labour Market Effects under CUFTA/NAFTA," (Geneva: International Labour Office,1999), p. 8.

24. Ibid., p. 9.

25. Ibid., p. 118.

CHAPTER SEVEN

1. During this period, GDP increased only sixfold. Merchandise exports grew 6 percent annually in real terms while output grew only 3.7 percent annually. *Annual Report 1998* (Geneva: World Trade Organization, 1998), pp. 33–34. Since trade

had fallen considerably after 1929, some of the increase only recouped those earlier losses. See Angus Maddison, *Monitoring the World Economy 1820–1992* (Paris: Organization for Economic Cooperation and Development, 1995).

2. Regional variations provide a clue to the forces which have expanded trade. In Latin America, where most nations adopted protectionist policies of import substitution, trade was a smaller percentage of GDP in the early 1990s than it had been a century earlier and far below comparable levels elsewhere. See introduction to Dean Baker, Gerald Epstein, and Robert Pollin, eds., *Globalization and Progressive Economic Policy* (Cambridge: Cambridge University Press, 1998), pp. 5–8. Trade has declined as a proportion of GDP where manufactures constitute a minor share of exports. Falling oil prices drove the exports of the Middle East and North Africa from 43 percent of GDP in 1980 to 33 percent in 1997. Due to declining prices for its primary commodities, African exports remain below their level of two decades ago. *World Development Indicators 1999* (Washington, D.C.: World Bank, 1999), p. 222.

3. The golden era of English free trade became feasible only when declining transatlantic transportation costs opened the American grain market.

4. Between 1940 and 1980, the cost of sea freight declined by 62 percent, air transport by 78 percent, and overseas phone calls by 97 percent. *Annual Report 1998* (Geneva: World Trade Organization, 1998), p. 35.

5. See Gary Gereffi, "Commodity Chains and Regional Division of Labor in East Asia," *Journal of Asian Business* 12, 1 (1996):75–112.

6. *World Investment Report 1998* (Geneva: United Nations Conference on Trade and Development, 1999), p. 5; *World Development Indicators 1999* (Washington, D.C.: World Bank, 1999), pp. 12–15.

7. This operational control is what distinguishes foreign direct investment from portfolio investment. The portfolio investor may purchase a foreign bond or even a stock that represents as much as a 10 percent ownership stake in a business, but this does not control its operations.

8. Alexander Yeats, "Just How Big Is Global Production Sharing?," World Bank Policy Research Working Paper No. 1871 (Washington, D.C.: January, 1998).

9. For a discussion of the cycle of ebb and flow in liberal and mercantilist sentiments, see John Rapley, *Understanding Development: Theory and Practice in the Third World* (Boulder: Lynne Rienner Publishers, 1996).

10. *World Investment Report 1998* (Geneva: United Nations Conference on Trade and Development, 1999), p. 1.

11. *Annual Report 1998* (Geneva: World Trade Organization, 1998), pp. 32–33.

12. *World Investment Report 1998*, p. 11.

13. At least 14 countries had gross private capital flows amounting to more than 20 percent of GDP, led by Ireland (129.9 percent, up from 10.8 percent in 1987) and Singapore (109.3 percent in 1997 and 24.1 percent in 1987). *World Development Indicators 1999*, p. 326.

14. These private capital movements exclude about $80 billion annually in official flows, about evenly divided between national foreign aid programs and multilateral institutions (the World Bank, IMF, regional development banks, and agencies of the United Nations).

15. The best example at the global level is the fixed exchange rate system of Bretton Woods. The ERM and euro were regional efforts, and the currency pegs of many Southeast Asian nations are examples at the national level.

16. The flow of foreign direct investment is only about $400 billion per year, and the turnover in global stock markets, the vast majority of which does not cross a national border or require a currency transaction, is only about $21 trillion annually. These estimates come from Mahbub ul Haq, Inge Paul, and Isabelle Grunberg, eds. *The Tobin Tax: Coping with Financial Volatility* (New York: Oxford University Press, 1996), pp. 2–4. By July 1998 the WTO estimated the daily volume of foreign exchange transactions at $1.5 trillion.

17. *World Development Indicators 1999.*

18. Furthermore, this gap has grown from a 3:1 ratio in 1820 to 7:1 in 1870, 11:1 in 1913, 30:1 in 1960, and 60:1 in 1990. The assets of the richest 200 people now exceed the incomes of 41 percent of the world's population. The assets of the *three* richest people in the world exceed the combined GNP of the world's 48 least developed nations, with a population of 600 million people. See United Nations Development Programme, *Human Development Report 1999* (Oxford: Oxford University Press, 1999), p. 3. If Bill Gates's assets were compared to the GDP of nations, he would rank forty-eighth, between New Zealand (with a population of four million people) and the Czech Republic (with 10 million).The 400 richest Americans for the first time have collectively amassed $1 trillion, a figure greater than the gross domestic product of China. *Forbes*, "400 Richest People in America," http://www.forbes.com.

19. Over the last three centuries global growth has exceeded the 2–3 percent range only during the brief recovery period following World War II, during which trade grew at nearly 10 percent annually. By contrast, global GDP grew less than 2 percent per year from 1720 to 1950 and under 3 percent from 1973 to 1996, even with trade growing considerably faster than total output. *Annual Report 1998* (Geneva: World Trade Organization, 1998), p. 34.

20. United Nations Development Programme, *Human Development Report 1998*, http://www.undp.org/hdro/e98over.htm.

21. United Nations Development Programme, *Human Development Report 1999*, p. 31.

22. *World Development Indicators 1999* CD-ROM.

23. Agricultural growth was limited by weak capitalization and sparse mechanization. Even after a decade of substantial change, there was only one tractor per thousand agricultural workers and eleven per hundred hectares in 1980, about 6 percent of the global average. *World Development Indicators 1999* CD-ROM.

24. Merchandise trade excludes the 25 percent of total trade made up of services. *World Development Indicators 1999* CD-ROM.

25. Foreign aid was, of course, one source, and Thailand's geopolitical location during a time of superpower conflict did enable it to attract aid amounting to a little over 1 percent of GDP per year for much of the 1970s and 1980s.

26. However, productivity in China was far lower than in Thailand, where value added per manufacturing worker was $11,072 in the early 1980s. Thus, Thai labor costs were only 21 percent of output, contrasted with 22 percent in Mexico,

36 percent in Japan, 40 percent in the US, and 60 percent in France. *World Development Indicators 1999*, p. 62.

27. Tariff rates in the other Tigers have been reduced to markedly lower levels than in Thailand, but they remain high by global standards. Indonesia's declined from 23.6 percent in 1989 to 13.8 percent in 1996, Korea's from 17.1 percent in 1988 to 9.5 percent in 1996, Malaysia's from 12.6 percent in 1988 to 9.4 percent in 1997, and the Philippines' from 27.2 percent in 1988 to 9.3 percent in 1998. See *World Development Indicators 1999*, p. 340.

28. Hong Kong and Singapore were more city-states than national economies, which virtually forced them to concentrate on commerce and maintain more open markets. Both Korea and Taiwan had more diversified economies, each including a sizable agricultural sector. This structure tempted the state to protect the most vulnerable areas and invited greater use of industrial policy to steer the economy in a desirable direction. The second-tier economies also differed from one another in both circumstance and policy. For example, Indonesia's size—its population is fourth among the world's nations, trailing only China, India, and the United States—would seem to give it a more realistic chance for self-sufficiency than Malaysia or Thailand, but it was also far poorer than any of the others.

29. For a review of this perspective, see Werner Baer, William R. Myles, and Allen B. Moran, "The End of the Asian Myth: Why Were the Experts Fooled?," *World Development* 27, 10 (October 1999):1735–1747.

30. See, for example, World Bank, *The East Asian Miracle: Economic Growth and Public Policy* (New York: Oxford University Press, 1993).

31. Most prominent among these theorists was Alice Amsden, in *Asia's Next Giant: South Korea and Late Industrialization* (New York: Oxford University Press, 1989).

32. Paul Krugman, "The Myth of Asia's Miracle," *Foreign Affairs* November/December 1994, pp. 62–78.

33. Malaysia's exports were equal to 94 percent of its GDP, but much of their value was contained in components manufactured elsewhere and imported into Malaysia for assembly. Exports made up 38 percent of GDP in South Korea, 49 percent in the Philippines, and 28 percent in Indonesia. *World Development Indicators 1999* CD-ROM.

34. The negative impact of the dependence was also attenuated by internal structures such as democratic representation and welfare states that balanced the internal and external pressures and by external political structures such as the EU that managed the resulting interdependence.

35. With tourism accounting for another 12 percent, this means that Thailand's traditional exports have become nearly inconsequential. *World Development Indicators 1999*, p. 206. Similarly, Malaysia's manufacturing exports grew from 19 percent of total exports to 84 percent between 1980 and 1994, while Indonesia's expanded from 2 percent to over 52 percent in the same period. Peter Dicken, *Global Shift: Transforming the World Economy*, 3rd ed. (New York: Guilford Press, 1998), p. 36.

36. Malaysia was also the most dependent of these countries on total capital inflows, 11.5 percent of GDP in the 1990s. Its FDI inflow represented 12 percent of its

total investment since 1970, a figure more than double that for any other country in the world except Singapore. This figure reached a staggering 25 percent by 1993. See Ha-joon Chang, "Globalization, Transnational Corporations, and Economic Development: Can the Developing Countries Pursue Strategic Industrial Policy in a Globalizing World Economy?" in Baker, et al., *Globalization and Progressive Economic Policy*, p. 102.

37. Thailand's reliance on FDI was relatively brief: FDI inflows were under 1 percent of GDP per year until 1988, peaked at 2.7 percent in 1990, and declined to under 1 percent again by 1994. Portfolio investment has had peaks and valleys—inflows exceeded 2 percent of GDP in Thailand during 1985, 1989, and from 1993 to 1996 (4.5 percent in 1993). FDI made up one-third of Indonesia's capital inflows (which amounted to 4.0 percent of GDP) and half of the Philippines (3.8 percent of GDP).

38. Savings between 1991 and 1995 averaged 28.6 percent of GDP in Indonesia, 32.3 percent in Malaysia, and 34.8 percent in Thailand. Investment rates were 31.0 percent in Indonesia, 38.7 in Malaysia, and 41.5 percent in Thailand.

39. Giancarlo Corsetti, Paolo Pesenti, and Nouriel Roubini, "What Caused the Asian Currency and Financial Crisis?" *Japan and the World Economy* 11, 3 (October, 1999):353.

40. These export enclaves may also distort development by draining resources needed elsewhere. Infrastructure, for example, is usually tailored to export needs rather than the needs of the broader economy, with roads and rails linking ports to the main centers of export production, while large areas have primitive communication and transportation systems. Political systems in such economies tend toward authoritarianism, so as to suppress dissent and to provide the conditions for profitable export operations (such as labor and tax law favorable to producers).

41. It is also true that that sector generated a service and financial sector enclave to support it (e.g., travel, construction, and real estate). It is testimony to the sophistication of some sectors and the backwardness of others that Malaysia's capital, Kuala Lumpur, boasts three of the ten tallest buildings in the world, but 11 percent of its citizens do not have access to safe drinking water.

42. Indeed, even Korea has found that its position is more precarious than it appeared.

43. "Thailand Social Monitor," World Bank, January 1999. http://www.worldbank.org/poverty/eacrisis/library/socialnote1.pdf.

44. All the figures in this paragraph come from Corsetti, et al., "What Caused the Asian Currency and Financial Crisis?" pp. 305–373.

45. Gary Gereffi, "Commodity Chains and Regional Division of Labor in East Asia," *Journal of Asian Business* 12, 1 (1996):92–93.

46. For estimates of the relative overevaluation of Southeast Asian currencies, see Menzie Chinn, "Measuring Misalignment: Purchasing Power Parity and East Asian Currencies in the 1990s," International Monetary Fund Working Paper 99/120 (Washington, D.C., September 1999).

47. The fixed exchange rate assured profitability and predictability for producers in commodity chains, where risk reduction is a key attraction. Production sharing is especially vulnerable to disruption because interference with any stage can stop an entire production process.

48. Jomo K. S., ed., *Tigers in Trouble* (Hong Kong: Hong Kong University Press, 1998), p. 6.

49. Robert W. Wade, "The Asian Debt-and-Development Crisis of 1997–?: Causes and Consequences" *World Development* 26, 8 (1998):1541.

50. United Nations Development Programme, *Human Development Report 1999*, p. 40.

51. Ibid.

52. Kwak Young-sup, "Korea's Economic Crisis Leading to Collapse of Middle-Income Class," *Korea Herald*, June 15, 1999.

53. United Nations Development Programme, *Human Development Report 1999*, pp. 41–42.

54. "World Bank Questions IMF Plan: Austerity in Asia May Worsen Crisis," *Wall Street Journal*, January 8, 1998.

55. Jeffrey Sachs, "IMF Is a Power unto Itself," *Financial Times*, December 11, 1997.

56. Jeffrey Sachs, "The IMF and the Asian Flu," *The American Prospect*, March-April 1998, p. 17.

57. Jeffrey Sachs, "IMF Is a Power unto Itself," *Financial Times*, December 11, 1997.

58. Wade, "The Asian Debt-and-Development Crisis of 1997–?" *World Development* 26, 8 (1998): 1535–1553, passim.

59. Ibid.

60. Indeed, it is striking that almost all observers portray this event as an historical watershed after which we can no longer see issues of trade policy and international finance as we have before, yet their interpretations reinforce their own previously expressed views. That is, everyone feels that their views have been vindicated and that others have been discredited.

61. For a detailed analysis, see Corsetti, et al., "What Caused the Asian Currency and Financial Crisis?" 305–373.

62. United Nations Development Programme, *Human Development Report 1999*, p. 40.

63. *The Left Business Observer.* September 27, 1999. http://www.panix.com/~dhenwood/USForDebt.html.

64. Ibid.

CHAPTER EIGHT

1. Robert W. Wade, "The Asian Debt-and-Development Crisis of 1997–?: Causes and Consequences" *World Development* 26, 8 (1998):1550.

2. "What Sank Asia? Money Sloshing Around the World," *Business Week*, July 27, 1998.

3. Quoted in James Ridding and James Kynge, "Complacency Gives Way to Contagion," from "Special Report: Asia in Crisis," *Financial Times*, January 13, 1998, p. 6.

4. W. Max Corden, *Trade Policy and Economic Welfare* (Oxford: Clarendon Press, 1974), p. 107.

□ □ □

Suggested Readings

Audretsch, David B. 1989. *The Market and the State: Government Policy Toward Business in Europe, Japan, and the United States*. New York: New York University Press.

Baker, Dean, Gerald Epstein, and Robert Pollin, eds., *Globalization and Progressive Economic Policy*, Cambridge: Cambridge University Press, 1998.

Barnes, Donald Grove. 1930. *A History of the English Corn Laws from 1660–1846*. London: George Routledge.

Bergsten, C. Fred, and Marcus Noland. 1993. *Reconcilable Differences? United States-Japan Economic Conflict*. Washington, D.C.: Institute for International Economics.

Capie, Forrest. 1983. *Depression and Protectionism: Britain Between the Wars*. London: George Allen and Unwin.

Cavanagh, John, John Gershman, Karen Baker, and Gretchen Helmke, eds. 1992. *Trading Freedom: How Free Trade Affects Our Lives, Work, and Environment*. San Francisco: Institute for Food and Development Policy.

Conybeare, John A. C. 1987. *Trade Wars: The Theory and Practice of International Commercial Rivalry*. New York: Columbia University Press.

Corden, W. Max. 1974. *Trade Policy and Economic Welfare*. Oxford: Clarendon Press.

Cunningham, W. 1938. *The Growth of English Industry and Commerce in Modern Times*. Cambridge: Cambridge University Press.

Devinney, Timothy M., and William C. Hightower. 1991. *European Markets After 1992*. Lexington, Mass: Lexington Books.

Dicken, Peter. 1998. *Global Shift: Transforming the World Economy*, 3rd ed. New York: Guilford Press.

Finger, J. Michael, and Andrzej Olechowski. 1987. *The Uruguay Round: A Handbook for the Multilateral Trade Negotiations*. Washington, D.C.: World Bank.

Gardner, Richard N. 1956. *Sterling-Dollar Diplomacy: Anglo-American Collaboration in the Reconstruction of Multilateral Trade*. Oxford: Clarendon Press.

Gilpin, Robert. 1975. *U.S. Power and the Multinational Corporation: The Political Economy of Foreign Direct Investment*. New York: Basic Books.

_____.1987. *The Political Economy of International Relations*. Princeton: Princeton University Press.

Gras, N. S. B. 1915. *The Evolution of the English Corn Market*. Cambridge: Harvard University Press.

Grinspun, Ricardo, and Maxwell Cameron. 1993. *The Political Economy of North American Free Trade*. New York: St. Martin's Press.

Haggard, Stephen, and Chung-in Moon. 1989. *Pacific Dynamics*. Boulder: Westview Press.

Hocking, Brian, and Steven McGuire, eds. 1999. *Trade Politics: International, Domestic and Regional Perspectives.* London: Routledge.

Hufbauer, Gary C., and Jeffrey J. Schott. 1993. *NAFTA: An Assessment.* Washington, D.C.: Institute for International Economics.

Hufbauer, Gary C., Diane T. Berliner, and Kimberly A. Elliot. 1986. *Trade Protection in the United States: Thirty-one Case Studies.* Washington, D.C.: Institute for International Economics.

Ito, Takatoshi. 1992. *The Japanese Economy.* Cambridge: MIT Press.

Jackson, John H. 1989. *The World Trading System: Law and Policy of International Economic Relations.* Cambridge: MIT Press.

Kindleberger, Charles. 1973. *The World in Depression, 1929–1939.* Berkeley: University of California Press.

_____.1975. "The Rise of Free Trade in Western Europe." *Journal of Economic History* 35: 20–55.

Krasner, Stephen. 1976. "State Power and the Structure of International Trade." *World Politics* 28, 3 (April):317–347.

Lipson, E. 1950. *The Growth of English Society: A Short Economic History.* New York: Henry Holt.

List, Friedrich. 1956. *The National System of Political Economy.* Philadelphia: J. B. Lippincott.

Lustig, Nora, Barry P. Bosworth, and Robert Z. Lawrence. 1992. *North American Free Trade: Assessing the Impact.* Washington D.C.: Brookings Institution.

Polanyi, Karl. 1944. *The Great Transformation.* New York: Farrar & Rinehart.

Pomfret, Richard. 1988. *Unequal Trade.* Oxford: Basil Blackwell.

Schott, Jeffrey J. 1990. *Completing the Uruguay Round.* Washington, D.C.: Institute for International Economics.

Smith, Adam. 1910. *An Inquiry into the Nature and Causes of the Wealth of Nations.* London: J. M. Dutton.

Springer, Beverly. 1992. *The Social Dimension of 1992: Europe Faces a New EC.* New York: Greenwood Press.

Starr, Martin K. 1988. *Global Competitiveness: Getting the U.S. Back on Track.* New York: W. W. Norton.

Stubbs, Richard, and Geoffrey R. D. Underhill. 2000. *Political Economy and the Changing Global Order,* 2nd ed. Oxford: Oxford University Press.

Stopford, John, and Susan Strange. 1991. *Rival States, Rival Firms: Competition for World Market Share.* Cambridge: Cambridge University Press.

Tawney, R. H. 1912. *The Agrarian Problem in the Sixteenth Century.* London: Longmans, Green.

_____. 1954. *Religion and the Rise of Capitalism.* New York: New American Library.

Tyson, Laura D'Andrea. 1992. *Who's Bashing Whom? Trade Conflict in High-Technology Industries.* Washington, D.C.: Institute for International Economics.

Viner, Jacob. 1950. *The Customs Union Issue.* New York: Carnegie Endowment for International Peace.

Wolfe, Robert. 1998. *Farm Wars: The Political Economy of Agriculture and the International Trade Regime.* New York: St. Martin's Press.

Wonnacott, Paul. 1987. *The United States and Canada: The Quest for Free Trade.* Washington, D.C.: Institute for International Economics.

□   □   □

Glossary

Absolute advantage refers to the ability of a nation to produce more of a given commodity than another nation with the same quantity of resources (e.g., labor hours).

Balance of payments is the summary statement of a nation's financial transactions with the rest of the world, often divided into the **current account**, the **capital account**, and the **reserve account**.

Balance of trade is the value of a nation's exports minus the value of its imports. When imports exceed exports, it is said that the balance of trade is negative, unfavorable, or in deficit. When exports exceed imports, the trade balance is positive, favorable, or in surplus.

Beggar-thy-neighbor is a term used to describe policies designed to benefit one nation (or individual) at the expense of another, especially trade barriers and capital restrictions.

Bilateral actions are those that involve two states acting together.

Bretton Woods was the site of the 1944 conference that established the World Bank (IBRD) and the International Monetary Fund (IMF) and laid the groundwork for the General Agreement on Tariffs and Trade (GATT). The name is usually applied to these institutions and the international economic system that they govern.

Budget deficit describes the situation in which the expenditures of a nation's government exceed its revenues.

Buy America is a term applied both to various legislative acts mandating that governments (federal, state, or local) give preference to American products in their purchasing decisions and to public relations campaigns designed to convince citizens to give a similar preference in their own purchases.

Capital is a factor of production often divided into physical capital (plant and equipment, etc.) and human capital (e.g., skills of workers), both of which require the investment of financial capital (i.e., money).

Capital account is the portion of the balance of payments that records the volume of private foreign investment and public grants and loans.

Common Agricultural Policy (CAP) is the set of policies enacted by the EU (and its predecessors) to raise agricultural incomes through various subsidies and tariffs.

Comparative advantage refers to the ability of a nation to produce a given commodity at lower opportunity cost than another nation. That is, it must forgo less of an alternative commodity. A nation has a comparative advantage in that commodity in which its absolute advantage is greatest (or its absolute disadvantage smallest).

Competitiveness is a term used to describe the ability of a nation's firms to produce goods at a price and quality enabling it to meet foreign competition.

The **Corn Laws**, which existed in England for centuries before their repeal in 1846, were a complex series of parliamentary acts designed to control the price of grains and the volume available to consumers. They consisted of barriers and subsidies to both imports and exports.

Countervailing duties are tariffs imposed on imports to offset subsidies by an exporting nation.

Currency markets are the sites where brokers buy the currency of one nation by selling that of another at exchange rates determined by supply and demand.

Current account is the portion of the balance of payments that records trade in goods and services as well as flows of income from investment.

Distributional dilemma refers to the inevitable choice implicit in trade policy between the pattern of income produced by trade and the pattern of income that would exist without trade. Whichever pattern is chosen, some individuals and groups will gain and others will lose.

Division of labor refers to the allocation of tasks among economic units (e.g., individual workers or national economies) in which each specializes in the task it performs most efficiently.

Dumping refers to the practice of placing goods on the market in large quantities and at a low price.

Economic liberalism is a doctrine that affirms a commitment to individualism, to the free market, and to private property; it opposes the intervention of government in markets. It advocates free trade and rejects mercantilism.

Economies of scale refers to the efficiency gains achieved by producing goods at the (large) volume that minimizes the production cost of each unit.

Efficient allocation of resources (or **factors of production**) refers to a situation in which production inputs (like land, labor, and capital) are employed in those sectors where they will produce the maximum output.

Embargo refers to a government order prohibiting the export of certain goods to certain nations.

Enclosure movement refers to the dissolution of agricultural commons and the communitarian economic and social patterns associated with them during the medieval era in Europe. It involved the conversion of commonly used land to private ownership, usually increasing the size and efficiency of plots but dispossessing peasants.

Entrepreneur is an investor who takes risks for economic gain.

The **euro** is the currency unit created by the European Union in 1999 to replace national currencies.

European Community (EC) is a term used to refer to the various organizations that have facilitated regional integration in Europe, especially the European Economic Community (EEC), founded by the Treaty of Rome in 1957, and the European Communities, founded by the 1967 treaty that merged the EEC with EURATOM and the European Coal and Steel Community. All were forerunners of the European Union.

European Union (EU) is the organization created in 1993 to succeed the EC in furthering regional integration in Europe.

Export promotion is a government policy that encourages exports through direct and indirect subsidies.

Factors of production are the resources or inputs required to produce a good, especially land, labor, and capital.

Foreign direct investment occurs when a firm acquires ownership and operational control of a new or existing business enterprise in another country.

Foreign exchange refers both to the currencies of nations and to the process of converting one to another through purchase.

Free rider refers to a nation (or individual) that benefits from a collective good without contributing to its provision, such as a nation that enjoys access to another nation's market but does not permit access to its own.

Free trade refers to a situation in which goods can be bought and sold on international markets without interference from barriers to trade enacted by governments, such as tariffs and quotas.

General Agreement on Tariffs and Trade (GATT) is an international treaty of 1947 that has facilitated trade by convening a series of negotiations to lower trade barriers, most recently the Uruguay Round.

Globalization is an umbrella term that refers to the recent and unprecedented increase in flows of goods, capital, information, and ideas across national borders, together with its causes and consequences. These changes were brought about by a combination of communication technologies, open and efficient markets, and the dominance of actors and institutions (such as multinational corporations) committed to neoliberal theories. Their repercussions include the diminishing relevance of national units for a variety of processes, including business strategies, and declining autonomy for nation-states.

Gold standard refers to the international monetary system in which gold was used as the reference point in valuing national currencies and as the ultimate medium for settling transactions, especially during the period from the 1870s to World War I.

The Great Depression was the catastrophic downturn of the global economy in the 1920s and 1930s, marked by high unemployment, falling production, curtailed trade, and the social and political instability that followed.

Gross domestic product (GDP) is the total final output of goods and services produced by a nation's economy.

Gross national product (GNP) is the total output claimed by residents of a country. It consists of GDP plus net factor income from abroad.

Group of Seven is a consultative group consisting of the economic ministers of the seven largest industrialized democracies: the United States, Canada, Japan, Great Britain, Germany, France, and Italy.

Guilds were oligopolistic organizations of craftspeople (craft guilds) or merchants (trade guilds) that adopted common rules to govern their activities and protect their economic interests. Craft guilds, which were the forerunners of trade unions of workers, administered an apprenticeship system and quality standards.

A **hegemonic leader** (or **hegemon**) is a dominant state that provides the leadership required to create and maintain the rules and organizations that manage the global economic system.

Hegemonic stability theory states that an open economic trading system (and most other forms of large-scale international cooperative arrangements) can be created and maintained only under the leadership of a single dominant state, without which trade is likely to decrease in volume and degenerate into discrimination, rivalry, and conflict.

Import-substituting industrialization (ISI) is a development strategy common to many less developed nations in which the state steers the domestic economy to produce industrial goods that were formerly imported, using trade barriers and sometimes subsidies of various kinds.

Industrial policy refers to any coordinated set of government policies designed to shape the composition of a nation's economy by targeting particular sectors or industries for growth. Usually, subsidies are provided to infant industries with the potential for growth, export success, or achievement of other important economic and political goals.

Infant industry refers to newly established firms that are targeted for import protection or export promotion, usually to enable them to better compete with established firms in other nations.

Interdependence refers to the situation in which various economic linkages between nations, especially trade and capital flows, make the welfare of citizens and the effectiveness of government policy in one nation contingent upon events, conditions, and policies in another nation.

International Bank for Reconstruction and Development (IBRD) is the largest of the international financial institutions that make up the World Bank group. Headquartered in Washington, D.C., it was originally created at Bretton Woods to provide capital for Europe after World War II.

International Monetary Fund (IMF) is the institution created at Bretton Woods to supervise exchange-rate policies of nations and encourage financial cooperation. It provides loans to nations experiencing balance-of-payments deficits and advice on how to correct them.

International Trade Organization (ITO) was the institution envisioned at Bretton Woods and designed at the 1948 Havana conference to coordinate trade policy and reduce trade barriers. Because it was never created, this role was partially filled by the GATT until the establishment of the World Trade Organization (WTO) after the Uruguay Round.

The iron law of wages states that in an unregulated market wage rates for unskilled labor will settle at the level required to keep workers barely alive.

Japan, Inc., is a term used to describe the close relationship between private business and governmental agencies like MITI, which foster Japanese exports, especially in the three decades after World War II.

Keiretsu is the term for a network of Japanese firms that own shares in one another and cooperate in various ways.

Laissez-faire is the liberal doctrine that governments should refrain from interfering with markets in order to maximize efficiency.

(Economic) **liberal** is a term used to describe policies that feature minimal governmental interference with markets, especially trade policies with few barriers to imports.

Liquidity refers to an internationally accepted asset, for example, gold or the U.S. dollar, that can be used to settle payments between nations when national currencies are unacceptable because banks lack confidence in their future value.

Marshall Plan was the massive U.S. foreign aid program that helped to rebuild Europe after World War II.

Mercantilism refers to an eclectic mix of government policies that regulated trade before the advent of liberalism, especially through import barriers and export promotion, in pursuit of various national interests, including the power of the state. Its more modern versions are sometimes called **neomercantilism**.

Ministry of International Trade and Industry (MITI) is the powerful Japanese governmental organization that plays a central role in the industrial policy that plans and manages the Japanese economy, especially by providing credit, expertise, and regulatory relief for favored sectors of the economy.

Monopoly refers to a sector of the economy so dominated by a single firm that the lack of competition gives it the power to set prices that maximize its profits.

The most-favored-nation (MFN) **provision** is the nondiscrimination promise contained in GATT that each signatory will extend to every other signatory at least as favorable a treatment as it extends to any other nation.

Multilateral actions are those which involve many states acting together.

Multilateralism (multilateral liberalism) refers to a trading system in which nations refrain from negotiating lower trade barriers for some nations than others, relying instead upon a nondiscrimination principle such as the MFN provision of GATT.

National autonomy refers to the freedom of a nation-state from the coercion or constraints imposed by others so that it may actually exercise its right to national sovereignty.

National interest refers to the set of core goals said to motivate the foreign policy actions of nation-states, usually assumed to center around the maintenance of national security, sovereignty, and autonomy.

National safeguards refer to the various GATT escape clauses that permit nations to make exceptions to other GATT rules.

National sovereignty is the principle of international law that no state or supranational organization has legal authority within the boundaries of another nation, thus guaranteeing the right of a national government to adopt whatever laws or policies it wishes.

The Navigation Acts were a series of parliamentary laws that regulated shipping as part of the mercantilist policy of early England. They included a requirement that British ships be used to transport British trade goods so as to strengthen the merchant marine and the navy as elements of national security.

Neoliberalism is the doctrine that revives the neoclassical emphasis on markets and the laissez-faire critique of state intervention, now applied more broadly to include an endorsement of free global markets for capital as well as free international trade and deregulation of the domestic economy.

Neomercantilism refers to the eclectic body of theory and policy advice that emerged after Smith and Ricardo to challenge liberal ideas and advocate government regulation of trade to achieve the national interest.

Nondiscrimination is the principle of equal treatment embodied in GATT's most-favored-nation clause. It prohibits a nation from maintaining different import barriers against the products of different nations (though there are many exceptions).

Nontariff barriers (NTBs) are import restrictions such as quotas and other regulations.

North American Free Trade Agreement (NAFTA) is the international treaty among the United States, Canada, and Mexico that has provided for lower regional trade barriers, beginning in 1994.

Oligopoly is a market structure in which a very small number of firms in a sector can together achieve a monopoly.

Optimum tariff is that rate of import taxation that will increase national welfare at the expense of others by inducing foreign producers to lower their export prices.

Outward-oriented development is a national strategy that relies upon export expansion, import growth, and capital inflows to generate rapid gains in national productive capacity. This strategy is put into effect through a variety of policies that promote exports and encourage investment from abroad.

Par value is the official exchange rate for a nation's currency established by that nation's government, often in conjunction with an international agreement such as the Bretton Woods fixed exchange-rate system.

Political economy refers to the interaction between the economic and political aspects of a national or international system, including the behavior of its actors and the structure of its institutions. This perspective questions the adequacy of studying either economics or politics without explicit recognition of the other.

Protectionism is the governmental practice of erecting barriers to imports for the purpose of allowing domestic firms greater market share.

Quota is a nontariff barrier to trade consisting of a limit a government places on the quantity of any given product that it will permit to be imported.

Reciprocity is the principle that nations must extend to others trade benefits that are equivalent to those extended to them, with equivalence usually determined by negotiation.

Regional integration (or **regionalism**) refers to the practice of creating a regional group of nations, each of which extends trade benefits to the others that are not available to nations outside the group.

Repatriation occurs when the profit from a foreign investment is returned to the nation of the investor.

Reserve account is the portion of the balance of payments recording changes in the level of a nation's reserve assets.

Social clause refers to provisions in trade agreements designed to offset the negative effects of trade-induced competition on the welfare of citizens, especially workers.

State goals dilemma refers to the choice that must be made when trade weakens the ability of the state to achieve some of its other goals.

Strategic trade theory describes how a government can help a firm benefit from economies of scale by adopting an aggressive industrial policy that promotes exports.

Subsidy is a direct payment or other benefit provided by the government to a firm to aid in the production or export of a particular good.

Tariff is a tax on imports.

Trade bloc refers to a group of nations that provide to one another trade benefits not available to outsiders, resulting in a great deal of trade within a bloc but little among blocs.

Trade deficit refers to the situation in a nation's balance of trade in which its imports exceed its exports.

Treasure was a term referring to precious metals, especially gold and silver, in the mercantilist period when they were the usual method of payment for imports.

Treasury bonds are certificates purchased by investors from the U.S. Treasury that entitle them to receive periodic interest payments and the return of their initial investment. The sale of bonds is the method used by the federal government to borrow money from investors to cover budget deficits.

Unilateral actions are those that involve one state acting alone.

Uruguay Round refers to the negotiations held under GATT auspices to lower trade barriers, implement trade rules, and create dispute-resolution mechanisms, negotiations that began in Punta del Este in 1986 and concluded in Marrakech in 1994.

Usury laws place limits on the terms that may legally apply to loan agreements, such as those that place a ceiling on the interest rates that may be charged by credit card companies.

Values dilemma refers to the choices that must be made when trade achieves some goals at the expense of others.

Voluntary export restraint (VER) is a unilateral agreement under which a nation places a limit on the quantity of goods that it will export to another.

Voluntary restraint agreement (VRA) is a VER that has been reached on the basis of bilateral negotiations with the importing nation.

Washington consensus is the neoliberal doctrine that guided the activities of the International Monetary Fund and World Bank in the 1980s and 1990s.

Welfare state is a term used to describe the system in which a government provides basic social protection to its citizens, such as unemployment insurance, income supplements to the poor, and health care, and mandates employer practices such as minimum wage and benefits.

World Bank refers to the group of financial institutions, including the International Bank for Reconstruction and Development (IBRD), the International Finance Corporation, and the International Development Agency. It provides loans for development projects all over the world, which are financed by the contributions of governments in developed nations.

World Trade Organization (WTO) is the international institution created by the Uruguay Round of GATT negotiations in 1994 to govern global trade.

A *zaibatsu* is one of the family-owned holding companies that were the predecessors of the *keiretsu* before World War II in Japan.

□　□　□

About the Book and Author

In the Post–Cold War world, trade is the new arena for competition—between nations, between groups, between ethical and theoretical ideas. Political economist Bruce Moon puts contemporary trade events—controversies over the World Trade Organization, labor standards and environmental protection, NAFTA, the European Union, United States–Japan relations, the Uruguay Round of GATT, China's most-favored-nation status—into historical and theoretical perspective with the British Corn Laws, the Great Depression, the Bretton Woods system, and the origins of European regionalism. Economic theory, terms, and concepts are clearly explained and contextualized with those from international relations.

Throughout the book, three central dilemmas are examined: the unequal distribution of income and wealth created by international trade, the trade-off among competing values that trade requires, and the difficult interrelationship between economic and foreign policy goals within and among trading nations. Though internationally framed, each dilemma has ramifications at a variety of levels all the way down to the individual's role in the global economy—as a consumer, as a citizen, and ultimately as a moral agent.

Bruce E. Moon is professor of international relations at Lehigh University.

Index